GRUBER'S

COMPLETE

SAT *

WRITING
WORKBOOK

2nd Edition

*SAT is a registered trademark of the College Entrance Examination Board. The College Entrance Examination Board is not associated with and does not endorse this book.

GARY R. GRUBER, PhD

 sourcebooks

This publication is designed to provide accurate and authoritative information in regard to the subject matter covered. It is sold with the understanding that the publisher is not engaged in rendering legal, accounting, or other professional service. If legal advice or other expert assistance is required, the services of a competent professional person should be sought.—*From a Declaration of Principles Jointly Adopted by a Committee of the American Bar Association and a Committee of Publishers and Associations*

All brand names and product names used in this book are trademarks, registered trademarks, or trade names of their respective holders. Sourcebooks, Inc., is not associated with any product or vendor in this book.

Published by Sourcebooks, Inc.
P.O. Box 4410, Naperville, Illinois 60567-4410
(630) 961-3900
Fax: (630) 961-2168
www.sourcebooks.com

The Library of Congress has catalogued the first edition as follows:

Gruber, Gary R.
   Gruber's complete SAT writing workbook / Gary R. Gruber.
      p. cm.
   Includes index.
  1. English language—Composition and exercises—Examinations—Study guides.
  2. SAT (Educational test)—Study guides. I. Title.
   LB1631.5.G78 2009
   378.1'662—dc22

                              2009008924

         Printed and bound in the United States of America.
              DR 10 9 8 7 6 5 4 3 2 1

Recent and Forthcoming Study Aids From Dr. Gary Gruber

Gruber's Essential Guide to Test Taking: Grades 3–5

Gruber's Essential Guide to Test Taking: Grades 6–9

Gruber's Complete SAT Guide 2011 (14th Edition)

Gruber's Complete ACT Guide 2011 (2nd Edition)

Gruber's SAT 2400 (2nd Edition)

Gruber's Complete SAT Critical Reading Workbook (2nd Edition)

Gruber's Complete SAT Math Workbook (2nd Edition)

Gruber's SAT Word Master (2nd Edition)

Gruber's Complete SAT Guide 2012 (15th Edition)

Gruber's Complete ACT Guide 2012 (3rd Edition)

Gruber's Complete GRE Guide 2012

www.sourcebooks.com

www.drgarygruber.com

www.mymaxscore.com

Contents

TWO SAT WRITING PRACTICE TESTS

Purpose of This Book

The Writing Part of the SAT consists of writing an essay and answering multiple-choice questions that test grammar and usage. In the multiple-choice questions, you have to either identify errors or improve sentences and paragraphs.

Dr. Gruber has developed powerful time-tested strategies for the writing questions on your SAT. He is the originator of the critical thinking skills used on standardized tests and the leading authority on test preparation.

Note that this book can be used effectively for learning shortcuts and strategies and practice for all writing questions on any test.

How to Use This Book Most Effectively

1. Read through the Introduction to familiarize yourself with the SAT and construction of the Writing Part.
2. Read Parts 1 and 2 to see some important grammar rules necessary for the Writing Part of the SAT.
3. Read through Part 3 to see what the Writing Test is like and how to answer the questions.
4. Take the Two Complete Writing Tests (Part 4) and read through the explanatory answers to see the grammatical rules for answering the questions. When an answer refers to a grammatical rule, make sure that you've learned the rule.
5. You can read through various sections of Part 2, the Grammar and Usage Refresher, to see the grammar rules and examples using them.

Important Note About This Book and Its Author

This book was written by Dr. Gary Gruber, the leading authority on the SAT, who knows more than anyone else in the test-prep market exactly what is being tested for in the SAT. In fact, the procedures to answer the SAT questions rely more heavily on the Gruber Critical Thinking Strategies than ever before, and this is the only book that has the exact thinking strategies you need to use to maximize your SAT score. Gruber's SAT books are used more than any other books by the nation's school districts and are proven to get the highest documented school district SAT scores.

Dr. Gruber has published more than thirty books with major publishers on test-taking and critical thinking methods, with over seven million copies sold. He has also authored over 1,000 articles on his work, both in scholarly journals and nationally syndicated newspapers. He has appeared on numerous television and radio shows, and has been interviewed in hundreds of magazines and newspapers. He has developed major programs for school districts and for city and state educational agencies for improving and restructuring curriculum, increasing learning ability and test scores, increasing motivation and developing a "passion" for learning and problem solving, and decreasing the student dropout rate. For example, PBS (Public Broadcasting System) chose Dr. Gruber to train the nation's teachers on how to prepare students for the SAT through a national satellite teleconference and videotape. His results have been lauded throughout the country by people from all walks of life.

Dr. Gruber is recognized nationally as the leading expert on standardized tests. It is said that no one in the nation is better at assessing the thinking patterns of how a person answers questions and providing the mechanism to improve the faulty thinking approaches. SAT score improvements by students using Dr. Gruber's techniques have been the highest in the nation.

Gruber's unique methods have been and are being used by PBS, the nation's learning centers, international encyclopedias, school districts throughout the country, in homes and workplaces across the nation, and by a host of other entities.

His goal and mission is to get people's potential realized and the nation impassioned with learning and problem solving so that they don't merely try to get a "fast" uncritical answer, but actually enjoy and look forward to solving the problem and learning.

For more information on Gruber courses and additional Gruber products, visit www .drgarygruber.com.

INTRODUCTION

I. Important Facts About the SAT

What Is on the Writing Part of the SAT?

It will include a student-written essay and a multiple-choice writing section testing students' ability to identify sentence errors, improve sentences, and improve paragraphs. Although grammar and usage will be tested, students will not be asked to define or use grammatical terms, and spelling and capitalization will not be tested. This essay section will be the first part of the test.

How Will the Writing Test Be Scored?

There will be a range of scores each from 200 to 800.

How Long Will the Writing Test Be?

The total time of the test will be 60 minutes.

Is Guessing Advisable?

Although there is a small penalty for wrong answers ($\frac{1}{4}$ point for five-choice questions), in the long run, you *break even* if you guess *or* leave the answer blank. So it really will not affect your score in the long run if you guess or leave answers out. And, if you can eliminate an incorrect choice, it is imperative that you not leave the answer blank.

Should I Take an Administered Actual SAT for Practice?

Yes, but only if you will learn from your mistakes by seeing what strategies you should have used on your exam. Taking the SAT merely for its own sake is a waste of time and may in fact reinforce bad methods and habits. Note that the SAT is released to students on its *Question and Answer Service* three times a year, usually in the January, May, and October administrations. It is wise to take exams on these dates if you wish to see your mistakes and correct them.

A Table of What's on the SAT Writing Parts

Writing	
Time	60 min. (25 min. essay, 35 min. multiple-choice in two sections)
Content	Multiple-Choice: Identifying Errors, Improving Sentences and Paragraphs; and Student-Written Essay; Effectively Communicate a Viewpoint, Defining and Supporting a Position
Score	W 200–800 Essay Subscore: 0–12 Multiple-Choice Subscore: 20–80

Note: There is an experimental section that does not count toward your SAT score. This section can contain any of the SAT item types (writing [multiple-choice], critical reading, or math) and can appear in any part of the test. Do not try to outguess the test maker by trying to figure out which of the sections are experimental on the actual test (believe me, you won't be able to)—treat every section as if it counts toward your SAT score.

A Table of What's on the PSAT

Writing	
Time	30 min. (one section)
Content	Multiple-Choice: Identifying Errors, Improving Sentences and Paragraphs Measuring: Grammar, Usage, Word Choice
Score	20–80

Can I Get Back the SAT with My Answers and the Correct Ones After I Take It? How Can I Make Use of This Service?

The SAT is disclosed (sent back to the student on request with an $18.00 payment) three of the seven times it is given through the year. You can also order a copy of your answer sheet for an additional $25 fee. Very few people take advantage of this fact or use the disclosed SAT to see what mistakes they've made and what strategies they could have used on the questions.

Check in your SAT information bulletin or log on to www.collegeboard.com for the dates this Question and Answer Service is available.

Should I Use Scrap Paper to Write On?

Always use your test booklet (not your answer sheet) to write on. Many of my strategies expect you to circle important words and sentences, etc., so feel free to write anything in your booklet. The booklets aren't graded—just the answer sheets.

Should I Be Familiar with the Directions to the Various Items on the Writing Test Before Taking the SAT?

Make sure you are completely familiar with the directions to each of the item types on the writing part of the SAT.

How Should a Student Pace Himself/Herself on the Writing Portion of the Exam? How Much Time Should One Spend on Each Question?

Calculate the time allowed for the particular section. For example, 25 minutes. Divide by the number of questions. For example, 20. That gives you an average of spending 1¼ minutes per question in this example. However, the first set of questions within an item type in a section are easier, so spend less than a minute on the first set of questions and perhaps more than a minute on the last set.

How Is the Exam Scored? Are Some Questions Worth More Points?

Each question is worth the same number of points. After getting a raw score—the number of questions right minus a penalty for wrong answers—this is equated to a "scaled" score from 200 to 800. A scaled score of 500 in each part is considered "average."

It's Three Days Until the SAT; What Can a Student Do to Prepare for the Writing Part of the SAT?

Make sure you are completely familiar with the structure of the test (page xvii), and the basic writing skills. Take practice tests and refresh your understanding of the strategies used to answer the questions.

What Is the Most Challenging Type of Question on the Exam, and How Does One Attack It?

Many questions, especially at the end of a section, on the test can be challenging. You should always attack challenging questions by using a specific strategy or strategies and common sense.

What Should a Student Do to Prepare on Friday Night? Cram? Watch TV? Relax?

On Friday night, I would just refresh my knowledge of the structure of the test, some strategies, and refresh some basic writing skills. You want to do this to keep the thinking going so that it is continual right up to the exam. Don't overdo it, just enough so that it's somewhat continuous—this will also relieve some anxiety, so that you won't feel you are forgetting things before the exam.

The Test Is Given in One Booklet. Can a Student Skip Between Sections?

No—you cannot skip between the sections. You have to work on the section until the time is called. If you get caught skipping sections or going back to earlier sections, then you risk being asked to leave the exam.

Should a Student Answer All Easy Questions First and Save Difficult Ones for Last?

The easy questions usually appear at the beginning of the section, the middle-difficulty ones in the middle, and the hard ones toward the end. So I would answer the questions as they are presented to you, and if you find you are spending more than 30 seconds on a question and not getting anywhere, go to the next question. You may, however, find that the more difficult questions toward the end are actually easy for you because you have learned the strategies in this book.

What Is the Recommended Course of Study for Those Retaking the Exam?

Try to get a copy of the exam that you took if it was a disclosed one—the disclosed ones, which you have to send a payment for, are usually given in October, January, and May. Try to learn from your mistakes by seeing what strategies you could have used to get questions right. Certainly learn the specific strategies for taking your next exam.

What Are the Most Crucial Writing Strategies for Students?

All specific writing strategies are crucial, including guessing, writing in your test booklet, and being familiar with directions for each type of question. Also make sure you know the writing basic skills cold (see pages 11–81 for the grammar rules—*make sure you know them*).

I Know There Is an Experimental Section on the Exam That Is Not Scored. How Do I Know Which Section It Is?

The SAT people have now made it so difficult to tell which is the experimental section, I would not take a chance second-guessing them and leaving it out. It will look like any of the other sections. It is true that if you have, for example, two of the same sections, such as two sections that both deal with grid questions, one of them is experimental—but you won't know which one it is. Also, if you have two sections where there is a long double reading passage, one of those sections is experimental, but again, you won't know which one it is.

Can I Take the Test More Than Once, and If So, How Will the Scores Be Reported to the Schools of My Choice? Will All Scores Be Reported to the Schools, and How Will They Be Used?

Check with the schools you are applying to to see how they use the reported scores—for example, whether they average them, whether they take the highest. Ask the schools whether they see unreported scores; if they do, find out how the individual school deals with single and multiple unreported scores.

How Do Other Exams Compare with the SAT? Can I Use the Strategies and Examples in This Book for Them?

Most other exams are modeled after the SAT, and so the strategies used here are definitely useful when taking them. For example, the GRE (Graduate Records Examination, for entrance into graduate school) has questions that use the identical strategies used on the SAT. The questions are just worded at a slightly higher level. The ACT (American College Testing Program), another college entrance exam, reflects more than ever strategies that are used on the SAT.

How Does the Gruber Preparation Method Differ from Other Programs and SAT Books?

Many other SAT programs try to use "quick fix" methods or subscribe to memorization. So-called "quick fix" methods can be detrimental to effective preparation because the SAT people constantly change questions to prevent "gimmick" approaches. Rote memorization methods do not enable you to answer a variety of questions that appear in the SAT exam. In more than thirty years of experience writing preparation books for the SAT, Dr. Gruber has developed and honed the critical thinking skills and strategies that are based on all standardized tests' construction. So, while his method immediately improves your performance on the SAT, it also provides you with the confidence to tackle problems in all areas of study for the rest of your life. He enables you to be able to look at a problem or question without panic, extract something curious or useful from the problem, and get to the next step and finally to a solution, without rushing into a wrong answer or getting lured into a wrong choice. It has been said that test taking through his methodology becomes enjoyable rather than a pain.

II. Format of the Writing Part of the SAT

Total time for "counted" (not experimental) WRITING (Multiple-Choice): 35 minutes, 49 questions

Total time for WRITING (Essay): 25 minutes, 1 or more prompts

Total time for experimental, pre-test items: 25 minutes; number of questions varies

Note: The following represents a form of the writing sections of the SAT. The SAT has many different forms, so the order of the sections may vary and the experimental section* may not be the third section as we have here. However, the first section will always be the Essay and the last section will be a 10-minute Multiple-Choice Writing section.

*10 Sections of the SAT**	*Number of Questions*	*Number of Minutes*
Section 1: WRITING (Essay)	1	25
		5-Minute break
Section 3: EXPERIMENTAL* Could be Writing, Critical Reading, or Math	varies	25
		1-Minute break
Section 5: WRITING (Multiple-Choice)	35	25
Improving Sentences	11	
Identifying Errors	18	
Improving Paragraphs	6	
		5-Minute break

*10 Sections of the SAT**	*Number of Questions*	*Number of Minutes*
Section 10: WRITING (Multiple-Choice)	14	10
Improving Sentences	14	
	TOTAL MINUTES: 225 (3 ¾ hours)	

*The order of the sections on the actual test varies since the SAT has several different forms.
Note: One of the sections is experimental. An experimental section does not count in your SAT score. You cannot tell which of the sections of the test is experimental.

Part 1
A Brief Review of English Grammar

Frequent Grammatical Problems

Split Infinitive. By the 17th century English had developed a two-word infinitive—*to go*, *to run*, *to talk*, etc. The word *to* was coupled with the verb and stood next to it. Since the Latin infinitive was always treated as one word, scholars decided that the infinitive in English must also be treated as one word. It was considered an error to split these two words by inserting an adverb between them.

But English isn't Latin, so the people went on splitting the infinitive whenever it suited their purpose. And we've been doing it ever since.

It isn't necessary to split the infinitive deliberately, of course, but if it sounds better or seems more natural or will add emphasis, then do so. The following sentence is an example of a permissible split infinitive: "After they had won the baseball trophy, they went to the party *to proudly display* their prize." (*Proudly to display* or *to display proudly* makes the sentence stiff. And *they went proudly to the party to display their prize* changes the original meaning.)

Ending a Sentence with a Preposition. The old "rule" that you should never end a sentence with a preposition was another attempt to force Latin on English, and it also is fading out. Often, to avoid this "error," we have to write a much longer and more awkward sentence. Which sounds better?

> This is a rule up with which I will not put.
> This is a rule I won't put up with.

Distinction between "Shall" and "Will." Formal usage required *shall* in the first person and *will* in the second and third person when forming the simple future. For the emphatic future, these were reversed. Today most of us use *will* in all persons for both simple and emphatic future.

"It Is I." This question of which pronoun to use probably causes more uncertainty than any other problem in grammar. We do not change the form of a noun, whether we use it as a subject or as an object. But we do have different forms for our pronouns.

For example, *I, you, he, they, we, etc.,* are the nominative forms and are used as subjects. *Me, you, him, them, us,* etc., are the objective forms. Normally we use the objective form after a verb, but after the *be* verbs (am, is, are, was, will be, etc.) we have traditionally used the nominative form; thus, *it is I* rather than *it is me*.

Usage, however, is divided on this. In informal conversation we often say, "It's me," just as the French do—"C'est moi." The argument for this usage is pretty sound. The predicate is thought of as object territory, and it feels strange to us to use the nominative form here. Still, the traditional use of this form has come to be regarded as a sign of the well-educated man. So, until "it is me" has become more widely accepted, we should continue to use "it is I."

Examples of the nominative forms for other pronouns may prove helpful:

> It was he (not *it was him*)
> This is she (not *this is her*)
> Had it been they (not *had it been them*)

There should be no question about using the objective case of the pronoun after other verbs. "The chairman appointed *him* and *me*," is considered correct, not "The chairman appointed *he* and *I*." But often in trying to avoid this decision we make an even worse error. Instead of the objective form we use the reflexive—*myself, himself*, etc. "He appointed John and myself" is definitely wrong.

"Who" versus "Whom." The pronoun *who* is used for the subject and *whom* is used for the object.

> Give the letter to *whoever* answers the door. (not to *whomever*...) The pronoun *whoever* is the subject of its clause.
> Tell me *whom* you borrowed the money from. (not *who...from*)
> The pronoun *whomever* is the object of the preposition *from*.

The pronoun *who* used as the subject of a verb is not affected by a parenthetical expression such as *I think, he believes, they say* intervening between the subject and the verb.

He is the person *who* I think is best qualified.
Mr. Jameson is the attorney *who* we suppose will prepare the brief.

Adverbs and Adjectives. We seem to have more trouble with adverbs than with adjectives. A simple guide is this: An *adverb* may modify a verb, another adverb, or an adjective; an *adjective* may modify only a noun or a pronoun.

Our biggest problem comes in confusing adjectives and adverbs. For example, we may use the adjective *good* when we should use the adverb *well:*

Poor: The engines are running *good.*
Proper: The engines are running *well.*

NOTE: Both *good* and *well* may be used after a linking verb as predicate adjectives. For example: "I feel good" indicates a state of well-being; but "I feel well" indicates either that you are not sick or that your ability to use your sense of touch is above average.

Common Errors in Grammar

Most of us do not have too much trouble writing grammatically acceptable sentences. We just habitually follow the basic word order. But sometimes we get careless or we fall into bad habits in our use of this important principle. When we do, we can interfere with the meaning and with the movement of our sentences.

Here are some common grammatical errors which may confuse our reader. They may be so simple that the reader quickly sees the error, revises the sentence in his mind, and gets the proper message. But this is your job, not his. Too often the reader won't catch the error and will get the wrong idea about what you are trying to say.

Misplaced Modifiers

1. Avoid dangling modifiers. When a word or phrase seems to modify another word which it cannot logically modify, we say it has been left dangling. Usually it will be a phrase beginning the sentence. From its position we expect it to modify the subject. But the connection is illogical.

Confusing: Approaching the flight line from the east side, the operations building can be easily seen. (The operations building obviously does not approach the flight line.)
Improved: A person approaching the flight line from the east side can easily see the operations building.
Confusing: To make a climbing turn, the throttle is opened wider.
Improved: To make a climbing turn, open the throttle wider. (The subject *you* is understood.)

2. Keep your modifiers close to the words they modify. Sometimes we widely separate a modifier from its modified word and end up confusing the reader.

Confusing: It was impossible to find the book I had been reading in the dark.
Improved: It was impossible in the dark to find the book I had been reading.
Confusing: He had marked on the map the places where we were to watch for turns in red ink.
Improved: He marked on the map in red ink the places where we were to watch for turns.

3. Avoid using "squinting" modifiers that may refer to either of two parts of a sentence. A squinting modifier is so placed in a sentence that it could logically modify either the words that came before it or the words that follow it; it "squints" both ways. This may confuse the reader. He may not realize the ambiguity and misinterpret the intended meaning.

Confusing:	Personnel who drive their cars to work *only occasionally* can count on finding a parking space.
Improved:	Only *occasionally* can personnel who drive their cars to work count on finding a parking space.
Confusing:	The electrician said Wednesday he would repair the light. (Did he make the statement on Wednesday, or did he say that he would repair the light on Wednesday?)
Improved:	Wednesday the electrician said he would repair the light.

or

The electrician said that he would repair the light on Wednesday.

By misplacing modifiers we make it easy for the reader to misunderstand the meaning of our sentences, sometimes with dire results. We can eliminate such errors by reading and revising our writing before we release it. Don't confuse your reader or make him do your work. Keep your modifiers close to the words they modify.

Confusing Pronouns and Other Reference Words

1. Make sure that a pronoun agrees in number with the noun it refers to.

Confusing:	Though there may be different teacher unions, the policy of *its* delegates should be similar.
Improved:	Though there may be different teacher unions, the policy of *their* delegates should be similar.

2. Make sure a pronoun or other reference word has a definite and clearly understood antecedent. We often use words or pronouns such as *which,* the *latter,* the *former, this it,* etc., to refer to something we have previously mentioned. This reference must be clear to the reader.

Confusing:	A piece of thread dangled over his belt which was at least 8 inches long.
Improved:	A piece of thread which was at least 8 inches long dangled over his belt.
Confusing:	The president told the executive he would handle all personnel assignments.
Improved:	The president told the executive to handle all personnel assignments.

or

The president told the executive that he, the president, would handle all personnel assignments.

Non-Parallel Structure

Express parallel ideas in words with the same grammatical construction. Nothing sounds quite so disorganized in writing as structure that is not parallel.

Not Parallel:	Briefly, the functions of a staff are to advise the general manager, transmit his instructions, and the supervision of the execution of his decisions.
Parallel:	Briefly, the functions of a staff are to advise the general manager, transmit his instructions, and supervise the execution of his decisions.
Not Parallel:	I have learned three things: that one should not argue about legalisms, never expect miracles, and the impropriety of using a singular verb with a compound subject.
Parallel:	I have learned three things: never argue about legalisms, never expect miracles, and never use a singular verb with a compound subject.

Some Basic Grammatical Terms

Parts of Speech

Nouns: names of people, things, qualities, acts, ideas, relationships: *General Smith, Texas, aircraft, confusion, running, predestination, grandfather.*

Pronouns: words that refer indirectly to people, places, things, etc.: *he, she, which, it, someone.*

Adjectives: words that point out or indicate a quality of nouns or pronouns: *big, lowest, cold, hard.*

Prepositions: words that link nouns and pronouns to other words by showing the relationship between them: *to, by, between, above, behind, about, of, in, on from.*

Conjunctions: words used to join other words, phrases, and clauses: *and, but, however, because, although.*

Verbs: words that express action or indicate a state, feeling, or simply existence: go, hate, fly, feel, is.

Adverbs: words that tell how, where, when, or to what degree acts were performed, or indicate a degree of quality: *slowly, well, today, much, very.*

Note: Many of our words can serve as more than one part of speech. Some words may be used as nouns, adjectives, and verbs without any change in spelling: *Drinking* coffee is a popular pastime; He broke the *drinking* glass; The boy *is drinking* a glass of milk. Often they may be both adjectives and adverbs: *better, well, fast.* Ordinarily we add *-ly* to words to form adverbs, while adjectives may be formed by adding *-able, -ly, -ing, -al, -ese, -ful, -ish, -ous, -y,* etc. But these endings are not always necessary: *college* (noun); *college boy* (noun used as an adjective to modify the noun *boy*).

Other Grammatical Terms

Subject: a noun or pronoun (or word or phrase used as a noun) which names the actor in a sentence. The term may be used in a broader sense to include all of the words that are related to the actor.

Predicate: the verb with its modifiers and its object or complement.

Predicate complement: a noun completing the meaning of a linking verb and modifying the subject.

Jones is *chief* (noun). He was *pale* (adjective).

Linking verb: a verb with little or no meaning of its own that usually indicates a state of being or condition. It functions chiefly to connect the subject with an adjective or noun in the predicate. The most common linking verb is the verb *to be* (am, are, is, was, were, had been), but there are others.

He *feels* nervous.
He *acts* old.
He *seems* tired.

Clause: an element which is part of a complex or compound sentence and has a subject, a verb, and often an object. "Nero killed Agrippina" is a clause but is not ordinarily called one because it is the complete sentence. In the compound sentence, *"Nero killed Agrippina, but he paid the penalty,"* each italicized group of words is an independent clause. In the complex sentence, *"Because he killed Agrippina,* Nero paid the penalty," the italicized clause is made dependent or subordinate by the word *because;* it depends upon the rest of the sentence for the complete meaning.

Phrase: two or more words without a subject and predicate that function as a grammatical unit in a clause or sentence. A phrase may modify another word or may be used as a noun or verb. For example: beside the radiator, approaching the pier, to fly a kite.

Verbals: words made from verbs but used as other parts of speech:

Gerund: a verb used as a noun:
> *Swimming* was his favorite sport.

Participle: a verb used as an adjective:

> The aircraft *piloted* by Colonel Jones has crashed.

Infinitive: a verb used as a noun, adjective, or adverb:

> *To travel* is my greatest pleasure. (infinitive used as a noun)
> We have four days *to spend* at home. (infinitive used as an adjective)
> Bruce was glad *to have joined.* (infinitive used as adverb)

Common Grammar Errors Classified by Part of Speech

I. Nouns	CORRECTION
Incorrect form to express plural number: *He shot two deers.*	He shot two *deer*.
Incorrect form to express masculine or feminine gender: *She was a wizard.*	She was a *witch*.
Incorrect form of the possessive case: *Two boy's heads and two sheeps' heads.*	Two *boys'* heads and two *sheep's* heads.
Use of the objective case for the possessive: *I was sorry to hear of John doing wrong.*	I was sorry to hear of *John's* doing wrong.

II. Pronouns	
Pronoun *I* placed incorrectly: *I and my sister will attend the concert.*	My *sister* and *I* will attend the concert.
Use of compound personal pronoun for simple personal pronoun: *Sam and myself will do it.*	Sam and *I* will do it.
Incorrect choice of relative pronoun: *I have a dog who barks at night. This is the person which did the wrong. This is the house what Jack built. Columbus, that discovered America, was an Italian.*	I have a dog *which* barks at night. This is the person *who* did the wrong. This is the house *which* Jack built. Columbus, *who* discovered America, was an Italian. <u>CORRECTION</u>
Lack of agreement between pronoun and antecedent: *Every one of the pupils lost their books.*	Every one of the pupils lost *his* book.
Incorrect case form: *The book is your's or his'. I recognize it's cover.*	The book is *yours* or *his*. I recognize *its* cover.

Use of nominative case for objective:
Give it to Kate and I. I knew it to be she.

Give it to Kate and *me*. I knew it to be *her*.

Use of objective case for nominative:
Him and me are brothers. Whom do you suppose she is? It was her.

He and *I* are brothers. *Who* do you suppose she is? It was *she*.

Use of objective case for possessive:
There is no chance of me being chosen.

There is no chance of *my* being chosen.

Pleonastic use:
John, he tried, and then Mary, she tried.

John *tried* and then Mary *tried*.

Ambiguous use:
The man told his son to take his coat to the tailor's.

The man told his son to take *his (the man's)* coat to the tailor's.

III. VERBS AND VERBALS

Use of the indicative mood for the subjunctive:
I wish I was you.

I wish I *were* you.

Use of the subjunctive mood for the indicative:
If the cavern were of artificial construction, considerable pains had been taken to make it look natural.

If the cavern *was* of artificial construction, considerable pains had been taken to make it look natural.

Use of incorrect form to express tense:
I done it. He seen it. She come late yesterday. I see him last week. The boy has went home. My hands were froze. He teached me all I know. I ain't seen it.

I *did* it. He *saw* it. She *came* late yesterday. I *saw* him last week. The boy *has gone* home. My hands were *frozen*. He *taught* me all I know. I *haven't seen* it.

Error in sequence of tenses:
I meant, when first I came, to have bought all the parts. He did not know that mercury was a metal.

I meant, when first I came, *to buy* all the parts. He did not know that mercury *is* metal.

Lack of agreement between verb and subject:
Was you glad to see us? Neither he nor she have ever been there. It don't cost much.

Were you glad to see us? Neither he nor she *has* ever been there. It *doesn't* cost much.

Use of incorrect forms of principal parts of certain verbs; e.g., *sit* and *lie:*
The hen sets on the eggs. The book lays on the table. It laid there yesterday. It has laid there all week.

The hen *sits* on the eggs. The book *lies* on the table. It *lay* there yesterday. It *has lain* there all week.

Use of adjective participle without modified word:
Coming into the room, a great noise was heard.

Coming into the room, *I* heard a great noise.
CORRECTION

IV. ADJECTIVES

Omission of article:
The noun and pronoun are inflected.

The noun and *the* pronoun are inflected.

Use of superfluous article:
I do not like this kind of a story.

I do not like this *kind of* story.

Use of a for *an* and *an* for *a*:
This is an universal custom. I should like a apple.

This is *a* universal custom. I should like *an* apple.

Use of adverb for predicate adjective:
She looks nicely.

She looks *nice.*

Lack of concord between certain adjectives and the words they modify:
I do not like these kind of grapes.

I do not like *this kind* of grapes.

Incorrect forms of comparison:
His ways have become eviler.

His ways have become *more evil.*

Use of comparative form not accompanied by certain necessary words:
He is shorter than any boy in his class.

He is shorter than any *other* boy in the class.

Use of superlative form accompanied by certain superfluous words:
This is of all others the most important.

This is the most important.

Use of double comparative or superlative forms:
She is more kinder than you.

She is *kinder* than you.

Incorrect placing of adjective phrases and clauses:
The mariner shot the bird with an unfeeling heart.

With an unfeeling heart, the mariner shot the bird.

V. ADVERBS

Use of adjective for adverb:
She sings real well.

She sings *really* well.

Incorrect use of double negatives:
I cannot go no faster.

I cannot go *any* faster.

Incorrect placing of adverbs and of adverbial phrases and clauses:
I only came yesterday, and I go today.

I came *only* yesterday, and I go today.

VI. PREPOSITIONS

Incorrect choice of prepositions:
I walked from the hall in the room.
Divide this between the three boys.
I was to New York today.

I walked from the hall *into* the room.
Divide this *among* the three boys. I was *in* New York today.

Omission of preposition:
She is an example of what a person in good health is capable.

She is an example of what a person in good health is capable *of.*
<u>CORRECTION</u>

Use of a superfluous preposition:
The book in which the story appears in is mine.

The book in which the story appears is mine.

VII. CONJUNCTIONS

Incorrect choice of conjunctions, especially *like* for *as,* and *as* for *whether:*

I cannot write like you do. I don't know as I can go.

I cannot write *as* you do. I don't know *whether* I can go.

Incorrect choice of correlatives:

Neither this or that will do.

Neither this *nor* that will do.

Use of a superfluous conjunction:

I have no doubt but that he will come.
This is a fine picture and which all will admire.

I have no doubt *that* he will come.
This is a fine picture *which* all will admire.

Incorrect placing of correlatives:

He is neither disposed to sanction bloodshed nor deceit. (Place *neither* before *bloodshed.*)

He is disposed to sanction *neither* bloodshed nor deceit.

Part 2
Grammar and Usage Refresher

The following pages will be very helpful in your preparation for the Writing parts of the SAT. You will find in these pages a brief but to-the-point review for just about every type of Writing question that appears on the actual SAT.

These are the areas covered in this study section:

The Parts of Speech

Clauses and Phrases

The Sentence and Its Parts

Verbs

Nouns and Pronouns

Subject-Verb Relationship

Tense

Verbals

Mood and Voice

Adjective Modifiers

Adverbial Modifiers

Connectives

Correct Usage: Choosing the Right Word

Chapter 1: The Parts of Speech*

1a Noun

A **noun** is a word that names a **person, place, thing,** or **idea**.

Persons	Places	Things	Ideas
nurse	forest	banana	love
Henry	Miami	shoe	democracy
uncle	house	television	hunger
Chicano	airport	notebook	cooperation

A noun that is made up of more than one word is called a **compound noun**.

Persons	Places	Things	Ideas
Martin Luther King	high school	telephone book	energy crisis
cab driver	Puerto Rico	car key	arms race
movie star	dining room	park bench	light year
federal judge	Middle East	pork chop	market value

1b Pronoun

A **pronoun** is a word used **in place of a noun**.

Buy a newspaper and bring **it** home.
(The pronoun *it* stands for the noun *newspaper*.)

Marlene went to the party, but **she** didn't stay long.
(The pronoun *she* stands for the noun *Marlene*.)

A **pronoun** may be used **in place of a noun or a group of nouns**.
Pedro wanted to see the polar bears, camels, and tropical birds, **which** were at the zoo.
(The pronoun *which* stands for the nouns *polar bears, camels, and tropical birds*.)

When Mark, Steven, Teresa, and Barbara became eighteen, **they** registered to vote.
(The pronoun *they* stands for the nouns *Mark, Steven, Teresa, and Barbara*.)

The **noun that the pronoun replaces** is called the **antecedent** of the pronoun.

The **plates** broke when **they** fell.
(The noun "plates" is the antecedent of the pronoun "they.")

Avoid confusion by repeating the noun instead of using a pronoun if more than one noun might be considered to be the antecedent.

The lamp hit the table when **the lamp** was knocked over.
(**Not:** The lamp hit the table when **it** was knocked over.)

1c Verb

A **verb** is a word or group of words that **expresses action or being**.

The plane **crashed** in Chicago. (action)
Soccer **is** a popular sport. (being)

*An index to this entire Grammar Refresher section begins on page 79.

1d Adjective

An **adjective** is a word that **modifies a noun or pronoun**.

Note: In grammar, to modify a noun means to describe, talk about, explain, limit, specify, or change the character of a noun.

Susan brought us **red** flowers.
  (The adjective *red* describes the noun *flowers*.)

Everyone at the party looked **beautiful**.
  (The adjective "beautiful" describes the pronoun *everyone*.)

Several people watched the parade.
  (The adjective *several* does not actually describe the noun *people*; it limits or talks about how many *people* watched the parade.)

Those shoes are her **favorite** ones.
  (The adjective *favorite* defines or specifies which *ones*.)

They have **two** children.
  (The adjective *two* limits or specifies how many *children*.)

1e Adverb

An **adverb** is a word that **modifies** the meaning of **a verb, an adjective, or another adverb**.

The librarian spoke **softly**.
  (The adverb *softly* describes or explains how the librarian *spoke*.)

Jackie Onassis was **extremely** rich.
  (The adverb *extremely* talks about or specifies how *rich* Jackie Onassis was.)

The job is **very** nearly completed.
  (The adverb *very* limits or specifies how *nearly* the job is completed.)

1f Preposition

A **preposition** is a word that **connects a noun or pronoun to another word** in the sentence.

The mayor campaigned **throughout** the city.
  (The preposition *throughout* connects the noun *city* to the verb *campaigned*.)

A **preposition connects** a noun or pronoun to another word in the sentence **to show a relationship**.

The wife **of** the oil executive was kidnapped.

A friend **of** mine is a good lawyer.

The strainer **for** the sink is broken.

The floor **under** the sink is wet.

David wants to work **in** the city.

The accident occurred **about** eight o'clock.

1g   Conjunction

A **conjunction** is a word that **joins words, phrases, or clauses**.

Alan's father **and** mother are divorced. (two words joined)

Is your favorite song at the end **or** in the middle of the record? (two phrases joined)

You may swim in the pool, **but** don't stay long. (two clauses joined)

(See Chapter 12 for a discussion of how prepositions and conjunctions act as connectives.)

1h   Interjection

An **interjection** is a word (or group of words) that **expresses surprise, anger, pleasure, or some other emotion**.

Aha! I've caught you.

Oh no! What have you done now?

An **interjection** has **no grammatical relation** to another word.

Ouch! I've hurt myself.

1i   A word may belong to more than one part of speech, depending on its meaning.

Example 1

Everyone **but** Sam was invited to the wedding. (preposition)

The Orioles won the pennant, **but** the Angels came close to winning. (conjunction)

Harry has **but** ten dollars left in his bank account. (adverb)

Example 2

He lives **up** the street. (preposition)

It's time to get **up**. (adverb)

The sun is **up**. (adjective)

Every life has its **ups** and downs. (noun)

I'll **up** you five dollars. (verb)

Note: Just for fun—what is the part of speech of the word *behind* in this sentence?

Attempting to save Annie, the fireman ran for the door, dragging her **behind**.

Our answer is an adverb, meaning "at the rear." If your answer was a noun—oh my! The noun means a certain part of the human body. We won't tell you which part.

Chapter 2: Clauses and Phrases

2a **Clauses**
A **clause** is a **group of words** within a sentence.

From his room, **he could see the park**. (one clause)

The children loved the man who sold ice cream. (two clauses)

A clause contains **a subject and a verb**.

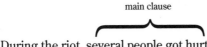

Before the race, **the jockeys inspected their horses**. (one clause)

When the rain stopped, the air was cooler. (two clauses)

2b There are two types of clauses: **main** and **subordinate**.*

main clause

During the riot, several people got hurt.

subordinate clause   main clause

When she won the lottery, Mrs. Ya-ching shouted with joy.

A **main clause** makes sense by itself.

We got the day off.

A **main clause** expresses a complete thought.

The fire was put out.
  (**Not:** When the fire was put out.)

It rained this morning.
  (**Not:** Because it rained this morning.)

A **subordinate clause** does not make sense by itself.

While the washing machine was broken, we couldn't wash anything.
  (The subordinate clause does not make sense without the rest of the sentence.)

Because a subordinate clause does not make sense by itself, a subordinate clause cannot stand as a complete sentence.

While the washing machine was broken…

A subordinate clause depends on a particular word in a main clause to make the subordinate clause mean something.

---

* A main clause may be called an independent clause. A subordinate clause may be called a dependent clause.

Jack abandoned the car **that had two flat tires**.
(The subordinate clause depends on the noun "car" in the main clause to describe the car.)

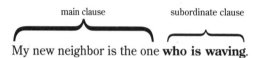

The job was offered to Ann **because she was best qualified**.

(The subordinate clause depends on the verb *was offered* in the main clause to explain **why** the job was offered.)

My new neighbor is the one **who is waving**.

(The subordinate clause depends on the pronoun *one* in the main clause to tell **who** is waving.)

A **subordinate clause** may be used in a sentence as an **adjective**, an **adverb**, or a **noun**.

Woody Allen's new film is the funniest movie **that he has made yet**.
(The subordinate clause acts as an adjective because it modifies—talks about—the noun *movie*.)

The child giggled **while he was asleep**.
(The subordinate clause functions as an adverb because it modifies the verb *giggled*.)

Please tell me **what this is all about**.

(The subordinate clause acts like a noun because it is the object of the action verb *tell*.)

2c Phrases

A phrase is a group of words within a sentence.

Thurmon Munson died **in a plane crash**. (one phrase)

Let's sit **under that apple tree**. (one phrase)

At the top   of the hill   there were some cows grazing. (two phrases)

The phrase itself **does not contain a subject or a verb**.

Many streets **in the city** need repairs.

A phrase **does not make sense by itself**.

Ellen has a collection **of beautiful earrings**.
(The phrase "of beautiful earrings" does not make sense by itself; therefore, the phrase cannot stand alone as a complete sentence.)

A phrase may begin with a preposition, a participle, a gerund, or an infinitive.

preposition
↓

Put the milk **into the refrigerator**. (prepositional phrase)

participle
↓

There are several people **waiting in line**. (participial phrase)

gerund
↓

Running ten miles a day is hard work. (gerund phrase)

infinitive
↓

To sing well takes a lot of practice. (infinitive phrase)

A **phrase** may be used as a **noun,** an **adjective,** or an **adverb**.

A doctor's job is **to heal people**.
(The infinitive phrase acts as a noun because it names the doctor's job.)

Raising his hands, the pope blessed the crowd.
(The participial phrase acts as an adjective because it describes the pope.)

Most stores close **at five o'clock**.
(The prepositional phrase acts as an adverb because it tells when most stores close.)

Chapter 3:
The Sentence and Its Parts

3a   A sentence is a group of words that has a subject and a verb.

subject   verb
↓   ↓

The **concert began** at midnight.

subject   verb
↓   ↓

During the storm, the **electricity was knocked out**.

3b   A sentence may be declarative, interrogative, or exclamatory.

A **declarative** sentence **states or asserts**.

Inflation is a serious problem.

An **interrogative** sentence **asks a question**.

How long must we suffer?

An **exclamatory** sentence **expresses emotion**.*

What a fool he is!

A **sentence** expresses a **complete thought**.

The price of gold has gone up.

Bus service will resume on Friday morning.

Note: Because a sentence expresses a complete thought, a sentence makes sense by itself.

Peter likes to tend his vegetable garden. (complete thought)

Peter likes. (incomplete thought—not a sentence)

The gasoline shortage created serious problems. (complete thought)

The gasoline shortage. (incomplete thought—not a sentence)

3c **The four types of sentences, according to structure, are the following:**

(1) **Simple**	Everyone likes music.
(2) **Compound**	The Simons put their house up for sale on Friday, and it was sold by Monday.
(3) **Complex**	If you want good Szechuan cooking, you should go to the Hot Wok Restaurant.
(4) **Compound-Complex**	Bob met Sally, who was in town for a few days, and they went to a museum.

* An "exclamatory sentence" is sometimes called an "imperative sentence."

3d Simple sentence

A **simple sentence** is made up of **one main clause** only.

I love you.

A simple sentence may be of any length.

The old man sitting on the park bench is the father of a dozen men and women besides being the grandfather of nearly forty children.

Note: A simple sentence **does not have a subordinate clause** in it.

3e Compound sentence

A **compound sentence** has **two or more main clauses**.

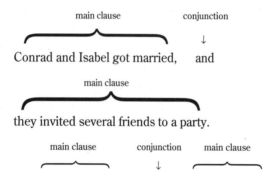

main clause conjunction

Conrad and Isabel got married, and

main clause

they invited several friends to a party.

main clause conjunction main clause

Stuart attended college, but he left after a year.

Each main clause in a compound sentence may stand by itself as a simple sentence—as long as the conjunction is left out.

conjunction
↓

Carlos will arrive by plane tonight, and Maria will go to the airport to meet him. (compound sentence)

Carlos will arrive by plane tonight. (simple sentence)

Maria will go to the airport to meet him. (simple sentence)

Note: A compound sentence does not have any subordinate clauses.

3f Complex sentence

A complex sentence contains only one main clause and one or more subordinate clauses.

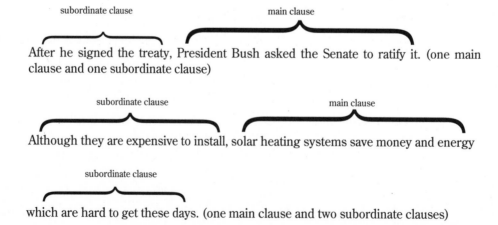

subordinate clause main clause

After he signed the treaty, President Bush asked the Senate to ratify it. (one main clause and one subordinate clause)

subordinate clause main clause

Although they are expensive to install, solar heating systems save money and energy

subordinate clause

which are hard to get these days. (one main clause and two subordinate clauses)

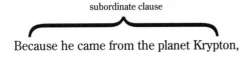

Because he came from the planet Krypton,

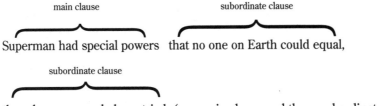

Superman had special powers that no one on Earth could equal,

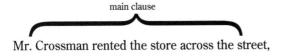

though many people have tried. (one main clause and three subordinate clauses)

3g Compound-complex sentence

A compound-complex sentence is made up of **two or more main clauses and one or more subordinate clauses**.

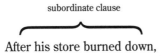

After his store burned down,

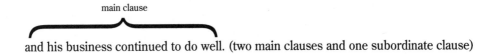

Mr. Crossman rented the store across the street,

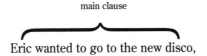

and his business continued to do well. (two main clauses and one subordinate clause)

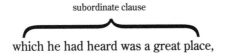

Eric wanted to go to the new disco,

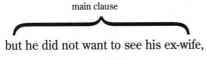

which he had heard was a great place,

main clause

but he did not want to see his ex-wife,

subordinate clause

who worked there. (two main clauses and two subordinate clauses)

3h The parts of a sentence

The basic parts of a sentence are a **subject,** a **verb,** and a **complement**.*

subject	verb	complement
↓	↓	↓

The   waiter   brought   the soup.

compound subject		verb		complement

Mason   and   Lucy   sold   me their   stereo.

3i Subject

A **subject** of a sentence is the word (or group of words) that **tells who or what is being talked about.**

> **Ann Landers** gives advice to millions of Americans.
>   (Because Ann Landers is being talked about, *Ann Landers* is the subject of the sentence.)

> High **taxes** caused many businesses to close.
>   (Because we are told that high taxes caused businesses to close, the noun *taxes* is the subject of the sentence.)

> **Whoever goes to bed last** should shut off the lights.
>   (Because we are told that whoever goes to bed last should do something, the noun clause *whoever goes to bed last* is the subject of the sentence.)

> **Brushing one's teeth and getting checkups regularly** are two important parts of good dental care.
>   (Because brushing one's teeth and getting checkups are discussed, the two gerund phrases are the **compound subject** of the sentence.)

3j A subject may be a noun, pronoun, verbal, phrase, or clause.

(1) A subject is usually a **noun**.

> Our **wedding** will be held outdoors.

> The **White House** is the home of the president.

> The **police** arrested the anti-nuclear energy demonstrators.

(2) A subject may be a **pronoun**.

> **He** always gets his way. (personal pronoun used as the subject)

> **Hers** is the tan raincoat. (possessive pronoun used as the subject)

> **What** did you do? (interrogative pronoun used as the subject)

> **That** is my car. (demonstrative pronoun used as the subject)

> **Everyone** was happy. (indefinite pronoun used as the subject)

(3) A subject may be a **verbal**.**

> **To begin** is the hardest part of the job. (infinitive used as the subject)

> **Jogging** is good exercise. (gerund used as a subject)

Note: A participle may not be used as a subject.

(4) A subject may be a **phrase**.

> **Smoking cigarettes** is unhealthy. (gerund phrase used as a subject)

> **To obey the law** is everyone's duty. (infinitive phrase used as a subject)

---

* The complement is discussed on pages 6–26.

**See Chapter 8.

(5) A subject may be a subordinate **clause**.

> **Whatever you decide** is all right.
>
> **That Danny had cancer** saddened his friends.
>
> **What will happen** is going to surprise you.
>
> **Who will star in the movie** will be announced.

3k   Verb

A verb is a word or group of words that **usually tells what the subject does**.

> Annie **skated** down the street.
>
> Your baby **has dropped** his toy.
>
> President Nixon **resigned**.
>
> The telephone **is ringing**.

Two or more verbs may have one subject.

> They **defeated** the Cubs but **lost** to the Pirates.
>
> Dick **works** during the day and **goes** to school at night.

A verb may **express a state or condition**.

> Lynn **appears** puzzled. (Or: Lynn **appears to be puzzled**.)
>
> The stew **tastes** delicious.
>
> Jason and Martha **are** good friends.

3l   The three kinds of verbs are **transitive, intransitive**, and **linking**.

3m A transitive verb tells what its subject does to someone or to something.

> The cat **caught** the mouse.
>
> Phil **washed** the dishes.
>
> Carol's mother **slapped** the boy.

3n   An intransitive verb tells what its subject does. The action of the intransitive verb does not affect someone or something else.

> The old man **slept** in his chair.
>
> The audience **applauded**.
>
> All of the job applicants **waited** patiently.

Note: Many verbs may be transitive or intransitive.

> He **will return** the book tomorrow. (transitive)
>
> The manager **will return** in an hour. (intransitive)

Whether a verb is transitive or intransitive depends on how it is used in the sentence.

> Chuck **opened** the package.
> (The verb is transitive because the action was carried out on something.)
>
> The door **opened** slowly.
> (The verb is intransitive because the action by the subject "door" did not affect anything else.)

3o   A linking verb links the subject with a noun, a pronoun, or an adjective.

"Jaws" was a terrifying **film**. (noun)

It's **I**.* (pronoun)

The child in this old photograph is **I**. (pronoun)

The girl who loves Peter is **she**. (pronoun)

The Beatles were **popular** in the 1960's. (adjective)

A linking verb may link the subject with an infinitive, a gerund, or a noun clause.

Stephanie's greatest pleasure is **to sing**. (infinitive)

Herb's mistake was **lying**. (gerund)

David's new job seemed **what he had hoped for**. (noun clause)

Linking verbs are **to be, to appear, to grow, to seem, to remain, to become,** and verbs that involve the senses, such as **to look, to smell, to feel, to sound,** and **to taste**.

Karen and Valerie **are** sisters.

Ben **is** strong.

Eric **appears** healthy.

The situation at the prison **remains** tense.

Gertrude **feels** better.

Jim **sounds** angry.

A verb that appears to be a sense-linking verb may not actually be a sense-linking verb.

The milk **smells** sour. (linking verb)

The dog **smells** the fire hydrant. (transitive verb)

Tony **looked** sad. (linking verb)

Rosie **looked** through the window. (intransitive verb)

Note: The use of a particular verb in a sentence determines whether that verb is sense-linking or transitive or intransitive.

Transitive verb	Intransitive verb	Linking verb
Expresses action	Expresses action	Does not express action
Is followed by a direct object that receives the action	Is not followed by a direct object	May be followed by a noun or an adjective
subject / trans. verb / direct object ↓ ↓ ↓ Keith shot a deer.	subject / intrans. verb ↓ ↓ Jimmy grinned.	subject / linking. verb / predicate noun ↓ ↓ ↓ Juanita is a nurse. subject / linking. verb / predicate adjective ↓ ↓ ↓ Lenny looks sick.

*In spoken English, it is acceptable to say "It's me" or "It's us." It is not acceptable, however, to say "It's him," or "It's them."

Chapter 4: Verbs

4a   **Five characteristics of every verb are number, person, tense, mood, and voice.**

4b   **Number shows whether the subject of the verb is singular or plural.**

Maggie **drives** well. (singular)

Adam and Peter **drive** dangerously. (plural)

Joan's grandmother **is** in Atlanta. (singular)

Arthur's parents **are** from Texas. (plural)

A verb must always agree in number with its subject.

subject   verb

Emily   **lives** alone. (subject and verb both singular)

subject   subject   verb

Dennis and Chuck **live** together. (subject and verb both plural)

4c   **Person tells whether the subject of the verb is speaking, being spoken to, or being spoken about.**

I **am** the person in charge. (first person)

You **are** my best friend. (second person)

Bill **is** not here. (third person)

I **swim** at the YMCA. (first person)

You **come** with me. (second person)

Rosa **speaks** Spanish and French. (third person)

All three persons may be singular or plural in number.

	Singular	**Plural**
First person	I run	we run
Second person	you run	you run
Third person	he runs	
	she runs	they run
	it runs	

Note: The same verb form is frequently used for different persons and different numbers.

I **love** ice cream. (first person singular)

We **love** ice cream. (first person plural)

They **love** ice cream. (third person plural)

4d Tense shows when the action of the verb takes place—whether in the present, the past, or the future.

A plane **is passing** over our house right now. (present)

Our guests **are** here. (present)

Two U.S. astronauts **walked** on the moon in 1969. (past)

The workmen **were** here yesterday. (past)

We'll **pay** you tomorrow. (future)

Many people **will be** at the party tomorrow. (future)

4e Mood indicates how a sentence is used—whether it is a statement or a question, a command or a request, a wish or a condition.

Dinner **is** ready. (statement)

Does Elizabeth **work** in New Jersey? (question)

Go away! (command)

Please **pass** me the bread. (request)

If it **doesn't** rain, we can go. (condition)

The three kinds of moods are indicative, imperative, and subjunctive.

The indicative mood is used to express a statement or a question.

Two firemen were injured in the blaze. (statement)

Are you going out tonight? (question)

The imperative mood expresses a command or a request.

Turn off that radio! (command)

May I have a menu? (request—not question)

Note: The imperative mood is frequently indicated by leaving out the pronoun "you."

(You) Stop that!

The subjunctive mood may be used to show that a wish rather than a fact is being expressed.

I wish I **were** ten years younger.

4f Voice indicates whether the subject acts or is acted upon.

The dog **barked** at the stranger.

The baby **was kissed** several times.

A verb in the active voice shows that the subject is doing something.

The thieves **wounded** the bank teller. (active voice)

The curtains **blocked** our view. (active voice)

A verb in the passive voice shows that something is being done to the subject.

The garbage **was picked up** this morning. (passive voice)

Tyrone's car **is being washed**. (passive voice)

4g Complement

A complement may be one or more words that come after either a transitive or a linking verb.

```
          complement
             |
             ▼
```
Fire destroyed the **building**. (transitive verb)

```
            complement
               |
               ▼
```
The cat seemed **startled**. (linking verb)

```
        complement      complement
           |               |
           ▼               ▼
```
Tony bought his **wife** a silver **necklace**. (transitive verb)

```
          complement
             |
             ▼
```
Adam will be **president** someday. (linking verb)

A complement completes the meaning of the verb.

The junta took **control of the government**.

A baseball broke the **window**.

4h The four ways that a complement may be used in a sentence are 1) as a direct object of the verb, 2) as an indirect object of the verb, 3) as a predicate noun,* and 4) as a predicate adjective.

Sally waters her **garden** every day. (direct object, receiving the action of the verb)

Vincent gave his **brother** a basketball. (indirect object, telling to whom the action of the verb was directed)

Note: The noun *basketball* is the direct object of the transitive verb *gave*; therefore, *basketball* is also a complement.

Arthur Fiedler was the **conductor** of the Boston Pops. (predicate noun, renaming the subject after the linking verb)

Alaska is **huge**. (predicate adjective, describing the subject after the linking verb)

4i A complement used as a direct object of the verb may be a noun, a pronoun, or a subordinate clause.

Uncle Nate plants **vegetables** each spring. (noun used as direct object)

You should see **her** now. (pronoun used as direct object)

Tell me **what you know about life insurance**. (subordinate clause used as direct object)

---

*A predicate noun is also called a predicate nominative.

4j **A complement used as an indirect object of the verb may also be a noun, a pronoun, or a subordinate clause.**

> The nurse sent the **patient** a bill. (noun used as indirect object)
>
> Will you do **me** a favor? (pronoun used as indirect object)
>
> Give **whoever calls today** this information. (subordinate clause used as indirect object)

Note: From the three examples above, you can see that **an indirect object must always be accompanied by a direct object.**

The three preceding sentences—which have indirect objects—may be expressed in a different way.

> The nurse sent a bill **to the patient.**
>
> Will you do a favor **for me**?
>
> Give this information to **whoever calls today.**

In these three sentences, the prepositional phrases serve the purpose of indirect objects.

4k **A complement that acts as a predicate noun may be a noun, a pronoun, a verbal, a phrase, or a clause.**

> Juan's uncle is **a bus driver**. (noun)
>
> It is **she**. (pronoun)
>
> Fred's favorite sport is **sailing**. (gerund)
>
> President Sadat's desire is **to make peace**. (infinitive phrase)
>
> Fixing cars is **what Tom does best**. (noun clause)

4l **A complement that acts like a predicate adjective may be an adjective or an adjective phrase.**

> Laverne and Shirley are **funny**. (adjective)
>
> The lecture was **about alcoholism**. (adjective phrase)

Note: Both predicate nouns and predicate adjectives may be called predicate complements.

Chapter 5: Nouns and Pronouns

5a Nouns

The five types of nouns are **1) proper, 2) common, 3) collective, 4) concrete,** and **5) abstract.***

5b A proper noun names a particular person, place, or thing.

> Cesar Chavez, San Clemente, Statue of Liberty
> (Proper nouns always begin with a capital letter.)

5c A common noun names a general sort of person, place, or thing.

> waitress, store, table

5d A collective noun names a group of individuals.

> congregation, class, political party
> (A collective noun is singular in form, but it refers to many people.)

5e A concrete noun names any material object that is inanimate.

> apple, hat, ball, box, desk, book, shirt

5f An abstract noun names a quality, state, or idea.

> truth, motion, beauty

5g Pronouns

The six kinds of pronouns are **1) personal, 2) relative, 3) interrogative, 4) indefinite, 5) demonstrative,** and **6) reflexive.**

5h A personal pronoun stands for the speaker, the person spoken to, or the person or thing spoken about.

> **I** am going out.
> (The first person "I" is speaking.)

> **You** should see the traffic jam downtown.
> (The second person "you" is being spoken to.)

> **She** wants to become a lawyer.
> (The third person "she" is being spoken about.)

The **personal pronouns** are the following:

> I, you, he, she, it, we, they, me, us, him, her, them

The **possessive** forms of the personal pronouns are the following:

> my, mine, yours, his, hers, its, our, ours, their, theirs

*A noun may be of more than one type. For example, *table* is both a common noun and a concrete noun.

A pronoun should be in the same person as the noun or pronoun it refers to.

The tree was damaged when lightning struck **it**. (noun and pronoun in third person)

Everyone knows that **he** should dress well to make a good impression. (both pronouns in third person)
(Not: **Everyone** knows that you should…)

5i The **relative pronouns** are the following:

who (whom), which, what, that, whose

A relative pronoun may begin a subordinate clause.

The child, **who** was alone, looked unhappy.

A relative pronoun connects the main clause to the subordinate clause.

The problem was in the gas line, **which** was rusty.
(The relative pronoun *which* joins the main clause to the subordinate clause it begins.)

A relative pronoun stands for a noun in the main clause.

Sharon gave me the money **that** I needed.
(The relative pronoun *that* stands for the noun *money* in the main clause.)

When to use the relative pronoun *whom*

Whom is the objective case form of *who*. We use *whom* as a **direct object,** an **indirect object,** or an **object of a preposition**.

The men **whom** you see are waiting for work.
(The relative pronoun *whom* is the direct object of the verb *see*.)

Hansen is the person to **whom** Wilmot gave the bribe money.
(The relative pronoun *whom* is the indirect object of the verb *gave*.)

The typewriter was stolen by the messenger about **whom** the office manager had been suspicious.
(The relative pronoun *whom* is the object of the preposition *about*.)

5j **An interrogative pronoun asks a question.**

Who wants to start first?

What did Richard do then?

Which should I take?

Whose is this jacket?

Whom do you want to speak to?

5k **An indefinite pronoun refers to a number of persons, places, or things in a general way.**

None of the dishes was broken.

Mark finds **everything** about boats interesting.

I'll bring you **another**.

Some of my friends buy lottery tickets.

Other commonly used indefinite pronouns are the following:

any, both, few, many, most, one, other, several, such

5l   A demonstrative pronoun points out a specific person or thing.

This is not my handwriting.

May I have two of **those?**

That is my brother.

These are my best friends.

Note: Interrogative, indefinite, and demonstrative pronouns may be used as adjectives.

Which dessert do you want? (interrogative adjective)

Every time I try to skate I fall down. (indefinite adjective)

That dress costs too much. (demonstrative adjective)

5m   A reflexive pronoun refers back to the noun it stands for.

I hurt **myself** while jogging.

Amy considers **herself** an adult.

A reflexive pronoun may be the **direct object of a verb,** the **indirect object of a verb,** the **object of a preposition,** or a **predicate noun.**

Kim pushed **himself** and finished the race. (direct object)

Ray bought **himself** a new watch. (indirect object)

Buffie likes to be by **herself.** (object of a preposition)

Mr. Thompson is just not **himself** lately. (predicate nominative)

Note: Do not use "hisself" for "himself," or "theirselves" for "themselves."

5n   Three characteristics shared by all nouns and pronouns are gender, number, and case.

5o   Gender indicates the sex of the person or thing named—whether masculine, feminine, or neuter.

Adam wants some ice cream, but **he** is on a diet.
("Adam" and the pronoun "he" are both masculine in gender.)

Alice said **she** was ready.
("Alice" and the pronoun "she" are both feminine in gender.)

The **movie** was good, but **it** was too long.
("Movie" and the pronoun "it" are neither masculine nor feminine; therefore, they are both neuter in gender.)

A pronoun should be in the same gender as the noun it refers to.

5p   Number indicates whether one or more than one person or thing is named.

Here is a **letter** for you.
(The one *letter* is singular in number.)

Many **cars** were involved in the accident.
(Many *cars* are plural in number.)

Note: A collective noun is singular in form but usually plural in meaning.

The audience was upset by the delay.
(*Audience* is singular in number, although many people are in the audience.)

A pronoun should be in the same number as the noun it refers to.

The **dishes** are not clean, so don't use **them**.
(*Dishes* and the pronoun *them* are both plural in number.)

Hockey is a lot of fun, but **it** is rough.
(*Hockey* and the pronoun *it* are both singular in number.)

A pronoun that refers to a collective noun that is considered as a unit should be singular in number.

The home team won its final game of the season.

A pronoun that refers to a collective noun that is considered as a group of individuals should be plural.

The visiting team felt they deserved to win.

A pronoun that refers to an indefinite pronoun antecedent must be singular.

Almost anyone can earn a good living if **he** or **she** works hard.

A pronoun must be singular if it refers to singular antecedents joined by *or* **or** *nor*.

Neither **Earle** nor **Jeff** could find **his** coat.

5q Case shows how a noun or pronoun is used in a sentence.

They stayed out all night.
(*They* is the subject.)

Natalie knew **him**.
(*Him* is the object of the transitive verb.)

Craig thinks this hat is **his**.
(*His* is a pronoun that shows ownership.)

The three cases are nominative, objective, and possessive.

5r The nominative case names the subject of a verb or the predicate noun of a linking verb.

Susan and **I** will call you tonight. (subjects)

My best friends are **Katherine** and **you**. (predicate nouns)

A noun in the nominative case is usually placed before a verb.

Mr. Garcia opened a dry cleaning business.

Ida answered the telephone.

Personal pronouns in the nominative case have the following forms:

I, you, he, she, it, we, they

The subject of a subordinate clause must be in the nominative case even if the clause itself acts as a direct object or an object of a preposition.

Show me **who** is waiting to see me. (subordinate clause as direct object)

Discuss this form with **whoever** applies for the job. (subordinate clause as object of a preposition)

5s **The objective case indicates that nouns and pronouns act as direct objects, indirect objects, or objects of prepositions**.

The storm forced **them** to stay home. (direct object)

Victor enjoyed meeting **her**. (direct object)

Sally called **us**, **Mary** and **me**, into her office. (direct objects)

The cab driver gave **me** good directions. (indirect object)

Our supervisor showed **him** and **me** some contracts. (indirect objects)

Annette had trouble teaching **them** how to type. (indirect object)

Several of **us** want more food. (object of the preposition)

Between **you** and **me,** I don't like our boss. (objects of the preposition)

Note: Each noun or pronoun in a compound object must be in the objective case.

A noun is in the objective case if it is placed after a transitive verb or after a preposition.

He saw **Greta Garbo**.

Ernie went into the **store**.

Personal pronouns in the objective case have the following forms:

me, you, him, her, it, us, them

5t Only two personal pronouns—*we* (*us*) and *you*—may also be used as **adjective pronouns**.

We women have responded to the challenge of the 2000's.

They are discriminating against **us** women.

You boys should play more quietly.

Note: The adjective pronoun *we* is in the nominative case when it modifies a subject. The adjective pronoun *us* is in the objective case when it modifies an object of a verb or an object of a preposition.

We Republicans support President Bush's bid for re-election. (nominative case, modifying subject)

Mom sent **us** children to bed. (objective case, modifying direct object of verb)

Won't you give **us** boys a chance to earn some money? (objective case, modifying indirect object of verb)

Many children were on the plane with **us** adults. (objective case, modifying object of a preposition)

5u **The objective case is used for nouns and pronouns that are the subject of an infinitive**.

Paul's father wants **him** to help paint the house.

Should Fred ask **her** to join the club?

A noun or pronoun following the infinitive **to be** must, like its subject, be in the objective case.

Pat didn't expect my friend to be **him**.

Note: If the infinitive **to be** has no subject, the noun or pronoun that comes after the infinitive is in the nominative case.

My twin brother is often thought to be **I**. (nominative case)

5v The possessive case indicates ownership.

Martha's home is in Ohio.

This book is **mine**.

Possession is generally shown by using an apostrophe:

Bumbry's error   men's room

child's toy   ship's crew

Ownership may be shown by an "of" phrase.

The handle **of the door** is broken.

The "of" phrase is used in formal English to show possession by inanimate things or to avoid awkward constructions.

The passage **of the bill** now in Congress will mean lower taxes.
(Not: The bill's passage…)

The sister **of my uncle's wife** is eighty years old.
(Not: My uncle's wife's sister…)

Personal and relative pronouns have distinct forms to show the possessive case.

The following are personal pronouns (possessive form):

mine, yours, his, hers, ours, theirs, its*

That dress is **hers**.

Ours is the house on the left.

"Whose" is a relative pronoun. (possessive form)[†]

No one knows **whose** it is.

The possessive forms **my, your, his, our, their,**[‡] and **whose** are called adjective pronouns because they modify nouns.

Your shirt has a button missing.

My family is very large.

Their apartment costs a lot of money.

The woman **whose** typewriter I borrowed gave it to me.

The possessive case is used by nouns and pronouns that come before a gerund.

Bubba's shouting attracted a large crowd. (noun)

My being sick caused me to miss an important lecture. (pronoun)

---

*_Its_ is the possessive form of the personal pronoun _it_. _It's_ is a contraction of _it is_.
[†]_Whose_ is the possessive form of the relative pronoun _who_; _who's_ is a contraction of _who is_.
[‡]_Their_ is the possessive form of the relative pronoun _they_; _they're_ is a contraction of _they are_.

The possessive case of a compound noun is indicated by adding *-s* to the **last word of the compound noun**.

A **movie star's** life is glamorous.

The **Governor of California's** speech attacked the president.

Pope John Paul II's visit to the United States pleased millions.

Note: The plural of a compound noun is formed by adding *-s* to the principal noun.

chief of police (singular)   chief of police's (singular possessive)

chiefs of police (plural)   chiefs of police's (plural possessive)

5w An **appositive** is a **noun or pronoun** usually placed next to another noun or pronoun to rename it.

Two guys, **Nestar and his cousin**, were already there. (identifies the subject)

Clarinda's dog **Sonya** eats only hamburgers. (renames the subject)

Note: An appositive must always be in the same case as the noun it renames.

We, **my brother and I,** are going hunting together. (both subject and appositive in nominative case)

Uncle Joe gave us, **Stuart and me,** tickets to the World Series. (both object and appositive in case)

5x **Direct address** and **nominative absolute** constructions are **always in the nominative case**.

Direct address consists of a noun (or pronoun) that names a particular person when someone else addresses that person.

Willy, please come here immediately.

A nominative absolute consists of a noun plus a participle.

The money having been spent, the boys decided to go home.

Chapter 6: Subject-Verb Relationship

6a **A verb must agree with its subject in number and in person.**

> Dr. Shu has office hours from 8 until 4.
>   (The third person singular form of "to have" agrees with the subject "Dr. Shu.")

> Robin and I **play** squash every Tuesday.
>   (The first person plural form of "to play" agrees with the compound subject "Robin and I.")

6b **Collective nouns are followed by singular or plural verbs according to the sense of the sentence.**

> The jury **has** asked for more time.
>   (The third person singular is used because the jury is considered to be a unified body.)

> The jury **are** unable to agree.
>   (The third person plural is used because the jury is considered to be a group of twelve persons.)

To summarize, a **collective noun** is **singular** when it refers to a group as a single unit.

A minority in Congress **is** delaying passage of the bill.

A **collective noun** is **plural** when it refers to the individual members of the group.

A minority of Congressmen **want** to defeat the bill.

6c **Some indefinite pronouns are always singular in meaning.**

> **Each** of the candidates **wants** an opportunity to discuss his beliefs.

> **Anyone is** allowed to use the public beach.

> **Any one** of us **is** willing to help.

Some indefinite pronouns are always plural in meaning.

> **Many** of the drawings **were** beautiful.

> A **few** of the windows **were** broken.

> **Several** of Joe's friends **are** sorry that he left.

6d A verb should be **singular** if its subject has **"every"** or **"many a"** just before it.

> **Many a woman feels** entitled to more in life than just housework.

> **Every man, woman, and child wants** to be happy.

Some **indefinite pronouns** may be **singular or plural,** depending on the meaning of the sentence.

Some of the books **have** been lost.

Some of the work **was** completed.

All of the ice cream **is** gone.

All of the men **have** left.

Most of the talk **was** about football.

Most of the people **were** dissatisfied.

6e **When singular subjects are joined by "or" or "nor," the subject is considered to be singular.**

Neither the mother **nor** her daughter **was** ever seen again.

One or the **other** of us **has** to buy the tickets.

6f **When one singular and one plural subject are joined by "or" or "nor," the subject closer to the verb determines the number of the verb.**

Neither the plumber nor the painters **have** finished.

Either the branch offices or the main office **closes** at 4.

6g **When the subjects joined by "or" or "nor" are of different persons, the subject nearer the verb determines the person.**

She or you **are** responsible.

You or she **is** responsible.

To avoid such awkward sentences, place a verb next to each subject.

Either she **is** responsible or you **are.**

Either you **are** responsible or she **is.**

6h **Even if the verb comes before the subject, the verb agrees with the true subject in number and person.**

Are the cat and the dog fighting? (The cat and the dog are…)

Coming at us from the left **was** an ambulance. (An ambulance was…)

There **are** two things you can do.* (Two things are…)

There **is** only one bottle left.* (Only one bottle is…)

---

*In this sentence, *there* is an expletive. An expletive is a word that gets a sentence started, but it is not a subject. Another expletive is *it.*

6i **Interrogative pronouns and the adverbs** *where,* *here,* **and** *there* **do not affect the number or person of the verb when they introduce a sentence.**

subject
↓
What **is** the **name** of your friend?

subject
↓
What **are** the **addresses** of some good restaurants?

subject
↓
Who **is** the **man** standing over there?

subject
↓
Who **are** those **people?**

subject
↓
Here **comes** my **friend.**

subject
↓
Here **come** my **parents.**

6j **When a predicate noun (following a linking verb) differs in number from the subject, the verb must agree with the subject.**

Our biggest problem **is** angry customers.

More gas guzzlers **aren't** what this country needs.

6k **Parenthetical phrases** or other modifiers that come between the subject and verb **do not change the number or person of the true subject**—which the verb agrees with.

The amount shown, plus interest, **is** due on Friday.

The president, together with his advisers, **is** at Camp David.

Chapter 7: Tense

7a   **Tense specifies the moment of an action or condition.**

We **are walking** to the park. (present moment)

We **will walk** to the park tomorrow. (future moment)

We **walked** to the park yesterday. (past moment)

I **have worked** here for three years. (action begun in the past and continued into the present)

I **had worked** in Chicago for four years before I left. (past action completed **before** another past action)

I **will have worked** here six months next Friday. (past action to be completed sometime in the future)

7b   **The six tenses are present, past, future, present perfect, past perfect, and future perfect.**

7c   The **present tense** shows that an action is **happening in the present** or that a condition exists now.

I **live** here. (action)

He **is** busy now. (condition)

The **present tense** forms of **to work, to have,** and **to be** follow:

to work	to have	to be
I work	I have	I am
you work	you have	you are
he ⎫ she ⎬ works it ⎭	he ⎫ she ⎬ has it ⎭	he ⎫ she ⎬ is it ⎭
we work	we have	we are
you work	you have	you are
they work	they have	they are

The present tense may indicate **habitual action** or **habitual condition,** or **a general truth**.

Judy **leaves** her office every day at 5 o'clock. (habitual action)

Dana **is** allergic to chocolate. (habitual condition)

Two and two **are** four. (general truth)

The present tense may express **future time with the help of an adverb**.

adverb
↓
Gary flies to Washington **tomorrow**.

adverb
↓
We are going to see a movie **tonight**.

7d   The **present perfect tense** shows that an action which **began in the past** is **still going on in the present**.

Betsy and I **have been** in New York for two years. (and are still in New York)

The Johnson family **has owned** a plumbing supply company for sixty years. (and still owns it)

The **present perfect tense** may show that an action **begun in the past was just completed at the present time**.

Our men **have worked** on your car until now.

Charlayne **has** just **walked** in.

The **present perfect tense** is formed with **have or has and a past participle**.

I **have eaten** too much.

Nina **has** always **loved** music.

7e   The **past tense** shows that an action **occurred some time in the past** but has **not continued into the present**.

Laura's doctor **advised** her to lose weight.

The plane **landed** on time.

Susan **was living** in Philadelphia then. (progressive form)

We **went** along for the ride.

If the verb in the main clause is in the past tense, the verb in the subordinate clause must also be in the past tense.

The surgeon told his patient that an operation **was** necessary.
   (**Not:** The surgeon told his patient that an operation **will be** necessary.)

Lenny said that he **would meet** Frank at 7:30.
   (**Not:** Lenny said that he **will meet** Frank at 7:30.)

The past tense (first, second, and third person—singular and plural) is often formed by adding "ed" to the infinitive (without "to.")

Jim **helped** us many times.

We **called** you last night.

7f   The **past perfect tense** indicates that an **action was completed before another action began**.

I remembered the answer after I **had handed in** my exam.

Kenny **had bought** the tickets before he met Ruth.

Margaret **had worked** very hard, so she took a vacation.

Note: The **past tense** shows that an event happened at any time in the past, but the **past perfect tense** indicates that an event happened before another event in the past.

Paula **had finished** dressing before I woke up.
(Not: Paula **finished** dressing before I woke up.)

Jake **had** already **left** by the time I arrived.)
(Not: Jake already **left** by the time I arrived.)

The past perfect tense is formed with "had" and a past participle.

Peter **had said** he would call before twelve.

7g The **future tense** indicates that an **action is going to take place sometime in the future**.

All of us **will pay** more for heat this winter.

The weatherman says it **will rain** tomorrow.

Will you **join** us for lunch, Eric?

I'll go away this weekend.

The future tense is formed with "will" and the infinitive (without "to").

Don **will take** you to the airport.

7h The **future perfect tense** is used to express a **future action that will be completed before another future action**.

By the time we get home, my parents **will have gone** to bed.

We'll start eating after you **(will) have washed** your hands.
Helena **will have finished** her work when we meet her at the office.

The future perfect tense is formed with "will have" and a past participle.

Patty **will have quit** her job by Christmas.

7i **All six tenses may be expressed in a progressive form by adding the present participle of a verb to the appropriate form of "to be."**

The Cosmos **are winning**. (present progressive)

The Cosmos **were winning**. (past progressive)

The Cosmos **have been winning**. (present perfect progressive)

The Cosmos **had been winning**. (past perfect progressive)

The Cosmos **will be winning**. (future progressive)

The Cosmos **will have been winning**. (future perfect progressive)

7j **Principal parts of irregular verbs**

We call a verb like "eat" an irregular verb. Any verb that changes internally to form the past participle is an irregular verb.

Present Tense	Past Tense	Past Participle	Present Participle
eat	ate	eaten	eating
begin	began	begun	beginning
blow	blew	blown	blowing
break	broke	broken	breaking
burst	burst	burst	bursting
catch	caught	caught	catching
choose	chose	chosen	choosing
come	came	come	coming
do	did	done	doing
drink	drank	drunk	drinking
drive	drove	driven	driving
fall	fell	fallen	falling
find	found	found	finding
fly	flew	flown	flying
freeze	froze	frozen	freezing
give	gave	given	giving
go	went	gone	going
grow	grew	grown	growing
know	knew	known	knowing
lay (place)	laid	laid	laying
lie (rest)	lay	lain	lying
ring	rang	rung	ringing
raise	raised	raised	raising
rise	rose	risen	rising
run	ran	run	running
set	set	set	setting
sit	sat	sat	sitting
speak	spoke	spoken	speaking
steal	stole	stolen	stealing
swim	swam	swum	swimming
take	took	taken	taking
throw	threw	thrown	throwing
wear	wore	worn	wearing
write	wrote	written	writing

Chapter 8: Verbals

8a   **A verbal is a word formed from a verb**.

    Skiing can be dangerous.

    We could hear our neighbors **arguing**.

    Bonnie and Clyde worked hard **to succeed**.

8b   The **three kinds of verbals** are **gerunds, participles,** and **infinitives**.

8c   **A gerund acts like a noun**.

    Smoking is not allowed in many stores.

    Traveling by train can be fun.

    Mark's favorite sport is **boating**.

    A gerund ends in *-ing*.

    Nureyev's **dancing** is terrific.

    Flying is the fastest way to get there.

    A phrase that begins with a gerund is called a gerund phrase.

    Paying bills on time is a good habit.

    Leaving my friends made me sad.

8d   **A participle acts like an adjective**.

    The police stopped the **speeding** car.

    The **tired** children were sent to bed.

    A present participle ends in *-ing*.

    A priest comforted the **dying** woman.

    Running, the girl caught up with her friends.

    Note: A present participle looks like a gerund because they both end in *-ing*. **A present participle, however, is used as an adjective, not as a noun.**

    A past participle usually ends in *-d, -ed, -t, -n,* **or** *-en*.

    Used clothing is cheaper than new clothes.

    Woody left **written** instructions for his assistant.

A phrase that begins with a participle is called a participial phrase.

Getting off the elevator, I met a friend.

Questioned by the police, several witnesses described the robbery.

8e **An infinitive is used as a noun, an adjective, or an adverb.**

Franz loves **to dance**. (noun)

Our candidate has the ability **to win**. (adjective)

Lisa practices every day **to improve**. (adverb)

An infinitive usually begins with "to," but not always.

Sally wants **to know** if you need a ride.

Help me wash my car. (Or: Help me **to wash** my car.)

A phrase introduced by an infinitive is called an infinitive phrase.

His only desire was **to save money**. (infinitive phrase used as a noun)

There must be a way **to solve this problem**. (infinitive phrase used as an adjective)

The doctor is too busy **to see you now**. (infinitive phrase used as an adverb)

8f **Gerunds may be present or perfect.**

Good **cooking** is her specialty. (present)

Your **having arrived** on time saved me. (perfect)

A gerund in the present form refers to an **action happening at the same time as the action of the main verb.**

Swimming is fun.

Running a mile tired him out.

Taking driving lessons will help you drive better.

A gerund in the perfect form refers to an **action that was completed before the time of the main verb.**

He believes his recovery is a result of his **having prayed**.

Our **having read** the book made the movie boring.

8g **Participles may be present, past, or perfect.**

The woman **sitting** on the couch is my mother. (present)

Warned by his doctor, Jack began to exercise. (past)

Having been recognized, Elton John was mobbed by his fans. (perfect)

A present participle refers to **action happening at the same time as the action of the main verb.**

present
↓
Smiling broadly, the president **answers** questions from the audience.

past
↓
Smiling broadly, the president **answered** questions from the audience.

present
↓

Holding up his hands, the teacher **is asking** for silence.

past
↓

Holding up his hands, the teacher **asked** for silence.

A past participle sometimes refers to action happening at the same time as the action of the main verb.

> **Irritated** by his sister, Raphael yelled at her.

> **Dressed up,** Tom looks like a new man.

A past participle sometimes refers to action that happened before the action of the main verb.

> **Burned** by the sun, Mary is suffering.

> **Awakened** by the noise, we looked outside.

The perfect participle always refers to action occurring before the action of the main verb.

> **Having finished** work, we can leave.

> **Having seen** that movie, we went somewhere else.

> **Having left** home in a hurry, Michael forgot his raincoat.

8h Infinitives may be present or perfect.

> Albert likes **to read** all day. (present)

> Tina was supposed **to have brought** the money. (perfect)

The present infinitive shows an action occurring at the same time as the action of the main verb.

> I **am trying to finish** this puzzle. (both present)

> Jerry **looked** around **to see** who was there. (both past)

> Dana **will call to ask** you for some advice. (both future)

The present infinitive may indicate action or a state of being at some future time.

> I hope **to see** you again.

> I expect **to be** there in an hour.

> He intended **to write** to us.

An infinitive is never used in a subordinate clause which begins with "that."

> I expect everyone to remain seated.

> I expect that everyone will remain seated.
>   (**Not:** I expect that everyone to remain seated.)

The perfect infinitive expresses action occurring before that of the main verb.

> I am sorry not **to have met** you before.

> He claims **to have seen** a flying saucer.

Avoid using the perfect infinitive after main verbs in the past or past perfect tense.

I had expected **to receive** my mail today.
(**Not:** I had expected **to have received**...)

They hoped **to join** us for dinner.
(**Not:** They hoped **to have joined** us...)

Mike would have liked to **ask** Alice for a date, but he was too shy.
(**Not:** Mike would have like **to have asked** Alice...)

Chapter 9: Mood and Voice

9a   Mood

The **three moods** that a verb may express are **indicative, imperative,** and **subjunctive**.

9b   The indicative mood indicates that the action or state is something believed to be true.

> I **am** the greatest.
>
> She **sings** beautifully.

The **indicative** mood is **used in asking a question**.

> **Are** you Mr. Feldman?
>
> **Does** Tom **want** to watch "Saturday Night Live?"

9c   The imperative mood expresses a command or a request or a suggestion.

> **Answer** the telephone. (command)
>
> **Give** me a napkin, please. (request)
>
> **Try** turning the handle the other way. (suggestion)

The imperative mood is not only more emphatic than the indicative mood—it is more quickly and easily understood.

> **Give** me that letter. (imperative)
>
> I **would appreciate** it if you would give me that letter. (indicative)

9d   The subjunctive mood is often used to express a wish or a condition that is not real—that is, contrary to fact.

> I wish the weather **were** nicer.
>
> If this paint **were** dry, we could sit on the bench.
>
> Debbie suggested that Carol **stay** at her apartment.
>
> Carl asked that Stan **agree** to pay for the damage.

The subjunctive mood is also used to express purpose or intention.

> Connie said that she **would visit** her mother at Easter.
>   (**Not:** Connie said that she **will visit** her mother at Easter.)
>
> We made box lunches so that we **would have** food for the trip.
>   (**Not:** We made box lunches so that we **had** food for the trip.)

The subjunctive mood is mainly indicated by **two forms of the verb "to be."** The forms are **"be"** and **"were."**

> **Be** good.
>
> If I **were** president, I'd nationalize the oil industry.

The present subjunctive uses "be" for all three persons, both singular and plural.

I be, you be, he be, we be, they be

I have one wish—that I **be** president some day.

Mrs. Diggs insists that you **be** given a bonus.

I asked that the child not **be** punished.

The judge ordered that the tenants **be** allowed to stay.

The more common form of the subjunctive is the past subjunctive form "were" for all three persons, both singular and plural.

$$\text{If} \left\{ \begin{array}{l} \text{I} \\ \text{you} \\ \text{he} \\ \text{we} \\ \text{they} \end{array} \right\} \textbf{were} \text{ here, everything would be all right.}$$

The subjunctive mood for verbs other than "to be" is formed by using the present tense first person singular form for all persons.

Mary suggested that Ronald **keep** an extra pair of eyeglasses.

The umpire insisted that the manager **leave** the field.

9e   Choosing between the subjunctive and indicative mood

One should show how he sees a situation: **contrary to fact or within the realm of possibility**. He does this by choosing either the subjunctive mood or the indicative mood.

If his statement **be** true, this is a case of fraud. (subjunctive)
(The writer thinks it is highly improbable that the statement is true.)

If his statement **is** true, this may be a case of fraud. (indicative)
(The writer indicates that it is quite possible that the statement may be true.)

If he **were** at the meeting, he would… (subjunctive)
(The speaker tells the listener that the man is not at the meeting.)

If he **was** at the meeting, he would have been able to speak to the point. (indicative)
(Perhaps the man **was** at the meeting; one doesn't know.)

Had the first payment been made in April, the second would be due in September. (subjunctive)
(The speaker indicates that the payment was **not** made in April.)

If the first payment **was** made in April, the second will be due in September. (indicative)
(Perhaps it was made; perhaps not—the speaker doesn't know.)

Do not use "would have" instead of "had" in "if" clauses to express the past perfect tense of the subjunctive.

If he **had worked** harder, he would have a better job.
(**Not:** If he **would have worked** harder…)

9f   Voice

A verb is either in the active voice or in the passive voice.

9g A verb in the active voice indicates that the subject performs an action.

Maggie **reads** every night before going to sleep.

The fire **burned** the entire house.

A verb in the active voice stresses the subject or actor rather than the action.

9h A verb in the passive voice indicates that something is being done to the subject.

The children **were given** lunches to take to school.

The television **was turned** off by my dad.

A verb in the passive voice stresses the action rather than the actor.

9i All transitive verbs—verbs whose action affects something or someone—**can be used in the passive voice.**

Johnny Bench **caught** the ball. (active)

The ball **was caught** by Johnny Bench. (passive)

9j To form the passive, the object of the transitive verb in the active voice is moved ahead of the verb, thus becoming the subject. A form of "to be" is added to the main verb. The subject of the active sentence is either left out or expressed in a prepositional phrase.

The **tow truck pulled** the **car** out of the ditch. (active voice)

The **car was pulled** out of the ditch **by the tow truck.** (passive voice)

9k If the active sentence has an indirect object as well as a direct object, either the indirect object or the direct object may be the subject of the passive sentence.

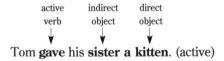

Tom **gave** his **sister a kitten.** (active)

A **kitten was given** by Tom to his sister. (passive)

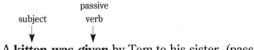

Tom's **sister was given** a kitten by Tom. (passive)

9l The passive voice is appropriate to express an action **when the actor is unknown.**

The door **had been locked** before we arrived.

Note: In general, avoid the passive voice for clearer, more forceful sentences.

Chapter 10: Modifiers—Adjectives, Adjective Phrases, and Clauses

10a Modifiers

A modifier adds information to another word in the sentence.

> **Blue** flowers were growing in the field.
> (The adjective *blue* adds color to the noun *flowers*.)

> Vera paints **beautifully**.
> (The adverb *beautifully* tells how Vera paints.)

10b Modifiers may be a word, a phrase, or a clause.

> Billy put on a **clean** shirt. (word)

> The wristband of **her watch** was broken. (phrase)

> Andy liked the painting **that was done by his friend**. (clause)

There are **various types** of modifiers.

> Jill brought us **fresh** fruit. (adjective as modifier)

> Bob's friends greeted him **warmly**. (adverb as modifier)

> Rudy enjoyed the ride **from Birmingham to Atlanta**. (adjective phrase as modifier)

> The rent will increase **after this month**. (adverb phrase as modifier)

> Louise holds two jobs **because she supports her sons in college**. (subordinate clause as adverbial modifier)

> The houses **where American presidents were born** are museums. (subordinate clause as adjectival modifier)

10c Adjectives modify nouns.

The six kinds of adjectives are the following:

> **Limiting: Many** children are bused to school.

> **Numerical: Four** days have passed since I saw her.

> **Descriptive: Striped** wallpaper hung in the hall.

> **Proper: American** and **Russian** flags lined the parade route.

> **Pronoun: My** book has a torn cover.

> **Article: A** letter has arrived.

10d Articles

The **articles** *a* and *an* (indefinite articles) indicate that the **noun they modify is an example of a general type**.

A dove symbolizes peace. (any dove)

A doctor saves lives. (any doctor)

An ambulance brings people to hospitals. (any ambulance)

Note: Do not use the articles *a* or *an* after "kind of," "type of," or "sort of."

A mango is **a kind of fruit**.

(Not:…**a kind of a fruit**.)

The Citation is **a new type of car**.
(Not:…**a new type of a car**.)

That sound gives me **a sort of weird feeling**.
(Not:…**a sort of a weird feeling**.)

The article *the* **(definite article) indicates that the noun it modifies is a particular noun.**

The winner received ten thousand dollars. (specific person)

The lamp over there is sold. (specific thing)

10e Single adjectives and compound adjectives

A single adjective usually comes immediately before the word it modifies.

Help me carry this **heavy** package.

A compound adjective consists of **two or more words serving as a single adjective**.

The drought made the earth **bone dry**.

My dictionary is **up to date**.

When a **compound adjective** comes **before a noun,** the words are **joined by a hyphen**.

Woody Allen was my **next-door** neighbor.

A **large-scale** map is hanging on the wall.

When the modifying words follow a noun, they are not hyphenated, unless they are normally hyphenated compounds.

This book is **well written**.

My new watch is **self-winding**. (normally hyphenated)

When two or more adjectives come before a noun but do not act jointly, they are not hyphenated.

Jim was wearing a **white silk** shirt.

I've had a **long, hard** day.

Note: If the word *and* can be inserted between two adjectives that come before a noun without destroying the meaning of the sentence, put a comma in between the two adjectives; otherwise, do not.

Miss Cameron is a **kind, generous** person. (kind **and** generous)

Show us your **new suit**.
(**Not:**…your, new suit.)

10f Two or more adjectives may follow the word they modify to make the sentence read more smoothly.

> The children, **tired and hungry,** were difficult to control.

10g Most adjectives may show greater or lesser degrees of their characteristic quality.

> Today was **cold**. (characteristic quality)
>
> Tomorrow will be **colder** than today. (greater)
>
> The day after will be **the coldest**. (still greater)
>
> Yesterday was **less cold** than today. (lesser)
>
> The day before was **the least cold** this week. (lesser still)

Some adjectives do not show comparison.

> Jennifer is **pregnant**.
> (She cannot be **more** pregnant or **less** pregnant.)
>
> This salad dressing is **perfect**.
> (**Not:**…is **more** perfect or **less** perfect.)

10h The three degrees of comparison are positive, comparative, and superlative.

> Tania is **happy**. (positive degree)
>
> Lenny is **happier** than Frank. (comparative degree)
>
> Wayne is **the happiest** of all. (superlative degree)

The positive degree simply names the quality expressed by an adjective.

> I like **spicy** food.

The comparative degree indicates that the quality described by an adjective exists in one person to a **greater or lesser degree** than in another person or thing.

> Susan looks **older** than Liz. (greater)
>
> Marlo was **more excited** than her brother. (greater)
>
> This street is **less clean** than the one where I live. (lesser)

The greater form of the comparative degree is formed by adding *-er* to the positive degree or by inserting "more" before the positive form.

> **rich + er = richer**
>
> **rich + more = more rich**

The lesser form of the comparative degree is formed by inserting "less" before the positive form.

> **rich + less = less rich**

Note: Use the comparative degree when comparing only two things.

The superlative degree indicates that the quality described by an adjective exists in the **greatest or least degree** in one person or thing.

> Rufus is **the friendliest** dog I know. (greatest)
>
> Florence seems **the least nervous** of us all. (least)

Note: Use the superlative degree when comparing more than two things.

10i **Some adjectives do not follow the regular methods of forming their comparative and superlative degrees.**

Positive degree	Comparative degree	Superlative degree
good	better	best
bad	worse	worst
little	less, lesser	least

(A dictionary will provide the irregular comparisons of such adjectives.)

Most adjectives of three syllables or more are compared by the use of "more" and "most," rather than by the endings -*er* and -*est*.

Tim is **more capable** of managing a business than Jon.

Alma is **the most wonderful** girl I know.

10j **Avoid double comparisons, which are formed by adding both "more" or "most" and -*er* or -*est*.**

Alan is **the brightest** little boy.
(**Not:**...the **most brightest**...)

Eric is a **better** eater than his brother.
(**Not:**...a **more better** eater...)

10k **When two things are compared, both things should be clearly accounted for.**

These clothes look cleaner than **those (clothes)**.

George looks older than **he** used to.

An **ellipsis** is the leaving out of one or more words that are grammatically important but that are understood by the reader.

Harvey plays soccer better than I (do).

While (he was) waiting for the pitch, Al Bumbry clenched the bat tightly.

Incomplete subordinate clauses that cause confusion, similar to the confusion caused by **dangling modifiers,** may be corrected by supplying the missing words.

Margaret's dress was torn while **she was** climbing over the fence.
(**Not:** Margaret's dress was torn while climbing over the fence.)

Use the word *other* or *else* to separate the thing being compared from the rest of the group of which the word is a part.

This car gets better mileage than all the **other** cars.

Mary Beth is more beautiful than anyone **else** around.

10l **Infinitives, infinitive phrases, participles, and participial phrases may act as adjectives.**

Mr. Garcia is the man **to know** if you want a bank loan. (infinitive as adjective)

This is a day **to remember always**. (infinitive phrase as adjective)

Screaming, Nancy woke up from her nightmare. (present participle as adjective)

Covering his face, the defendant walked past the reporters. (participial phrase as adjective)

10m **Infinitive and participial phrases that begin a sentence must be able to refer, both logically and grammatically, to the subject of the main clause.**

> **To qualify for the job, you** need a high school diploma.
> (**Not:** To qualify for the job, a high school diploma is needed. A "high school diploma" cannot apply for the job.)

> **Rushing to finish, Tina** made some errors.
> (**Not:** Rushing to finish, some errors were made by Tina. "Errors" cannot rush to finish.)

10n **Infinitive and participial phrases are called dangling modifiers if they cannot logically and grammatically attach to the subject of the main clause.**

> **To apply for a credit card,** an application form must be filled out. (infinitive phrase as dangling modifier)

> **Being an only child,** my parents spoiled me. (participial phrase as dangling modifier)

Sentences with dangling modifiers may be corrected either by supplying the subject that the phrase can sensibly modify or by changing the phrase to an introductory adverbial clause.

> To apply for a credit card, **one** must fill out an application. (Or: **When one applies for a credit card,** an application form must be filled out.)

> Being an only child, **I** was spoiled by my parents. (Or. **Because I am an only child,** I was spoiled by my parents.)

10o **A prepositional phrase may act as an adjective.**

> The violent storm damaged the roof **of our house**.

> Her leaving **without saying a word** irritated me.
> (also considered a **gerund phrase**)

10p **A subordinate clause may act as an adjective.**

> Thanks for the present **that you gave me**.

> The woman **who can help you** is not at her desk.

> This ring, **which belonged to my grandmother,** is valuable.

> The building **where they used to live** is being torn down.

> There is never a time **when Ed isn't busy.**

Subordinate clauses that act as adjectives may state essential information or nonessential information.

> The train **that you need to take** is leaving from Track 12. (information essential to describe which train)

> Peter loves his car, **which he hasn't finished paying for.** (information that is nonessential to describe which car)

10q **Restrictive and nonrestrictive clauses**

Restrictive clauses, which contain essential information, are not set apart by commas.

> The secondhand radio **that I bought for five dollars** works beautifully. (restrictive clause)

Nonrestrictive clauses, which contain secondary information that is not essential to the sentence, are set off by commas.

My friend Dina, **whom I've known for years,** wants me to visit her. (nonrestrictive clause)

10r **"Whose" is the possessive form for the relative pronouns "who," "which," and "that."**

The boy **whose** father died had to get a job.

The dog **whose** leg was broken runs well now.

Mr. Temple, **whose** wife is a ballerina, teaches French.

The book **whose** cover is damaged is half price.

10s A word, phrase, or clause should be placed as close as possible to the word it modifies.

Give me a glass of **cold** beer.
    (**Not:** Give me a cold glass…)

We need someone **with experience** to cook breakfast.
    (**Not:** We need someone to cook breakfast with experience.)

Grant wore a felt hat **that was obviously too small on his head.**
    (**Not:** Grant wore a felt hat on his head that was obviously too small.)

10t **A misplaced modifier is a word, phrase, or clause that is misplaced in the sentence so that it modifies the wrong word.**

Wrong: Mrs. Kent was injured while preparing her husband's dinner **in a horrible manner**.

Right: Mrs. Kent was injured **in a horrible manner** while preparing her husband's dinner.

Wrong: The old farmer went to the barn to milk the cow **with a cane**.

Right: The old farmer **with the cane** went to the barn to milk the cow.

Wrong: The flames were extinguished before any damage was done **by the Fire Department**.

Right: The flames were extinguished **by the Fire Department** before any damage was done.

10u **Squinting modifiers** are modifiers that are misplaced so that the reader cannot tell if the word, phrase, or clause modifies the words immediately before the modifier or immediately after.

Wrong: Henry said **today** he would wash his car.

Right: **Today** Henry said he would wash his car. (**Or:** Henry said he would wash his car **today**.)

Wrong: The dentist told him **frequently** to use dental floss.

Right: The dentist **frequently** told him to use dental floss. (**Or:** The dentist told him to use dental floss **frequently**.)

Chapter 11: Modifiers (Continued)—Adverbs, Adverbial Phrases, and Clauses

11a Adverbs modify verbs, adjectives, and adverbs.

Don runs **slowly**. (modifies verb)

Emily is an **extremely** gifted pianist. (modifies adjective)

Eric Heiden skates **incredibly** well. (modifies adverb)

11b The five kinds of adverbs are classified by the questions they answer.

How? Adverbs of manner.

She sings **well**. He speaks **clearly**.

Where? Adverbs of place or direction.

Take me **home**. She was just **here**. He went **out**.

When? Adverbs of time.

Bring it **immediately**. I'll see you **tomorrow**.

How much? Adverbs of degree or measure.

That's **enough**. A little **more,** please.

Why? Adverbs of cause, reason, or purpose.

He left **because** he was afraid.

I have ten dollars, **so** we can go out.

11c The following words can be either adjectives or adverbs, depending on their use.

above	fast	only
better	first	slow
cheap	hard	well
deep	long	
early	much	

The sign said to drive **slow**. (adverb)

Slow drivers can be dangerous. (adjective)

Mark Spitz can swim **better** than I can. (adverb)

Lucy feels **better** now. (adjective)

11d Distinguish carefully **when an adverb should follow a linking verb** and **when a predicate adjective should be used** to follow the linking verb.

Sharon looks **bad**. (predicate adjective meaning that Sharon doesn't look healthy)

Miguel looks **badly**. (adverb meaning that Miguel is doing a poor job looking for something)

Carmen smells **sweet**. (predicate adjective meaning that Carmen has a sweet scent)

Roses smell **sweetly**. (adverb **incorrectly** meaning that roses sniff the air sweetly!)

11e While speaking, one may incorrectly drop the *-ly* ending from common adverbs.

I'm **real** glad you called.
    (**Correct:** I'm **really** glad you called.)

He **sure** is lucky.
    (**Correct:** He **surely** is lucky.)

Do not drop the *-ly* ending unless a shorter form is correct.

I bought it **cheaply**. (**Or:** I bought it **cheap**.)

Come **quickly**! (**Or:** Come **quick**!)

The adverbs *hardly*, *scarcely*, *only*, **and** *barely* **should not be used with a negative verb construction**.

Ernie has hardly any free time.
    (**Not:** Ernie **hasn't** hardly any free time.)

Rose and I have scarcely worked this week.
    (**Not:** Rose and I **haven't** scarcely worked this week.)

11f **An adverb may show greater or lesser degrees** of its characteristic quality.

Peter arrived **early**.

Adam came **earlier** than Peter.

Amy came **earliest** of all.

The positive degree simply names the quality expressed by an adverb.

Stephanie runs **quickly**.

The **comparative degree** indicates that the quality described by an adverb exists for one person or thing to **a greater or lesser degree** than for another person or thing.

New air conditioners run **more efficiently** than old ones.

Nat draws **less well** than Monica.

The **comparative degree** of adverbs is formed by inserting **"more" or "less" before the positive degree form,** unless there is an irregular form for the comparative degree.

Charles works **more diligently** than Mark.

Barbara gets angry **less often** than Steven.

This stereo sounds **better** than mine. (irregular form)

The **superlative degree** indicates the quality described by the adverb exists in the **greatest or least degree** for one person or thing.

Ben works **most carefully** when someone is watching.

Elaine explained the problem the **most clearly**.

His was the **least carefully** written report.

The **superlative degree** of adverbs is formed by inserting **"most" or "least" before the positive degree form**.

Who was voted "**most likely** to succeed"?

Tracy Austin played **least skillfully** during the first set.

When two persons or things are being compared, the comparison should be clear.

I love chocolate more than **Umberto** does.
> (**Not:** I love chocolate more than Umberto. Such an incomplete comparison might be interpreted to mean "I love chocolate more than I love Umberto.")

11g An infinitive or an infinitive phrase may be used as an adverb.

Robert was willing **to go**. (infinitive used as adverb)

I am writing **to explain my behavior last night**. (infinitive phrase used as adverb)

11h A prepositional phrase may be used as an adverb.

We left **for the weekend**.

The old man sat **on the park bench**.

The coach supported his team **in every way**.

11i A subordinate clause may be used as an adverb.

Mrs. Maurillo forgot her umbrella **when she left**.

Because they cooperated with him, the president thanked several members of Congress.

11j **An adverb or an adverbial phrase should be placed as close as possible to the word it modifies.**

Joanne worked **without complaining** while her husband went to school.
> (**Not:** Joanne worked while her husband went to school **without complaining**.)

Note how an adverbial misplacement may change the meaning of a sentence.

The room can be painted **only** by me.
> (not by anyone else)

The room can **only** be painted by me.
> (not wallpapered)

Only the room can be painted by me.
> (not the outside of the house)

11k An adverbial clause may be placed either at the beginning of a sentence or, in its natural order, after the main clause.

> **After you have read this letter,** you will understand my reasons.
>
> You will understand my reasons **after you have read this letter.**

Note: An adverbial clause is followed by a comma when it is used to introduce a sentence.

11l Adverbial phrases and clauses should be placed so that only one meaning is possible.

> **After the movie** we all agreed to go for some ice cream. (**Or:** We all agreed to go for some ice cream **after the movie.**)
>   (**Not:** We all agreed **after the movie** to go for some ice cream.)
>
> Ask Kay to call me **when she gets in**. (**Or: When she gets in,** ask Kay to call me.)
>   (**Not:** Ask Kay **when she gets in** to call me.)

Chapter 12: Connectives

12a A connective joins one part of a sentence to another part.

Phillip **and** Dennis are giving a concert tonight.
(The connective *and* joins the two parts of the compound subject.)

Did you go out, **or** did you stay home last night?
(The connective *or* joins the two independent clauses.)

The banks are closed **because** today is a holiday.
(The connective *because* joins the main clause to the subordinate clause.)

The investigation **of** the robbery has been completed.
(The connective *of* joins the noun *robbery* to the noun *investigation*.)

12b A connective may be a preposition, a conjunction, an adverb, or a pronoun.

Josie left her scarf **on** the bus. (preposition)

Mr. Fernandez campaigned for the presidency, **but** he lost. (conjunction)

Kevin looked back **because** someone was shouting. (conjunction)

Ernie left his home an hour ago; **therefore,** he should be here any minute. (adverb)

The letter **that** was mailed this morning should arrive tomorrow. (pronoun)

12c Prepositions as connectives

A preposition may be **a word or a compound**. A compound consists of two or more words that function as one word.

Come **over** here. (word)

Women live longer than men, **according to** statistics. (compound)

12d A preposition joins a noun or pronoun to the rest of the sentence.

prep.
One of the **windows** is broken. (noun)

prep.
Josh is worried about his **health**. (noun)

prep.
These bags have nothing in **them**. (pronoun)

Choosing the correct preposition is often based on **idiomatic usage**—that is, the way English is used, whether or not it contradicts strict grammatical rules.

12e Some commonly used prepositional idioms are the following:

absolve	from	[blame]
abstain	from	[drinking]
accede	to	[a request]
accommodate	to	[a situation]
accompanied	by	[a lady (**a person**)]
accompanied	with	[applause (**a thing**)]
account	for	[one's actions]
account	to	[one's superior]
acquit	of	[a crime]
adapted	to	[his requirements]
adapted	from	[a novel]
adept	in	[selling a product]
adequate	to	[the demand]
adequate	for	[her needs]
agree	to	[a proposal (**an idea**)]
agree	with	[the teacher (**a person**)]
amenable	to	[an offer]
angry	with	[my cousin (**a person**)]
angry	at	[a remark (**a thing**)]
annoyed	by	[the noise (**a thing**)]
annoyed	with	[the child (**a person**)]
appreciative	of	[their efforts]
averse	to	[hard work (**an idea**)]
basis	for	[agreement]
capable	of	[getting high marks]
concur	with	[the mayor (**a person**)]
concur	in	[the decision (**an idea**)]
confer	with	[someone (**a person**)]
confer	about	[something (**a thing**)]
conform	to	[the rules]
correspond	to	[what I said (**a thing**)]
correspond	with	[his lawyer (**a person**)]
differs	from	[her sister (**a person**)]
differs	with	[what was done (**a thing**)]
disappointed	in	[you (**a person**)]
disappointed	with	[the result (**a thing**)]
enter	into	[an agreement]
enter	upon	[a career]
excepted	from	[further responsibility]
exempt	from	[taxes]
expect	from	[your investment (**a thing**)]
expect	of	[his assistant (**a person**)]
familiar	to	[me (**a person**)]
familiar	with	[the proceedings (**a thing**)]
free	of	[his wife (**a person**)]
free	from	[her nagging (**a thing**)]
identical	with	[something else]
ignorant	of	[his rights]
incompatible	with	[fellow workers]
independent	of	[his relative]
infer	from	[a statement]
involved	in	[a project (**a thing**)]
involved	with	[a friend (**a person**)]
liable	to	[damages (**a thing**)]
necessity	for	[food (**a thing**)]
necessity	of	[avoiding trouble (**doing something**)]
proficient	in	[a skill]

profit	by	[knowledge]
responsible	to	[the owner (**a person**)]
responsible	for	[paying a debt (**a thing**)]
talk	to	[the group (**one person talks**)]
talk	with	[my friends (**all talk**)]
variance	with	[another]
wait	at	[the church (**a place**)]
wait	for	[your uncle (**a person**)]
worthy	of	[consideration]

12f   Prepositions should not be used needlessly.

> Where is your brother?
>> (**Not:** Where is your brother **at?**)

> Where are you going?
>> (**Not:** Where are you going **to?**)

> Pete started on another project.
>> (**Not:** Pete started **in** on another project.)

> We agreed to divide the housework.
>> (**Not:** We agreed to divide **up** the housework.)

Prepositions are sometimes left out by mistake.

> Irene talked to me **about** her new job and **about** why she left her old one.
>> (**Not:** Irene talked to me about her new job and why…)

> Dr. Rosen was puzzled **by** and concerned **about** Ellen's nightmares.
>> (**Not:** Dr. Rosen was puzzled and concerned about…)

Note: Two different prepositions are needed for this last sentence.

12g   Conjunctions as connectives

A conjunction is a word that joins words, phrases, clauses, or sentences.

> Nixon **and** Agnew ended their political careers by resigning. (words joined)

> The mouse ran out of the kitchen **and** into the living room. (phrases joined)

> Casino gambling in Atlantic City has helped some, **but** it has hurt others. (clauses joined)

> Sally has the ability to do the job; **however,** she has too many personal problems. (sentences joined)

12h   Conjunctions are coordinate, correlative, or subordinate.

A coordinate conjunction and a **correlative conjunction** connect grammatical elements of equal rank. **A subordinate conjunction** connects grammatical elements of unequal rank.

12i   Coordinate conjunctions connect two equal elements. They include the following words.

> and, but, or, nor, so, yet

> On our vacation, we will go to Boston **or** to Cape Cod. (two phrases)

> My two favorite colors are blue **and** green. (two words)

> I told Stanley that I couldn't leave my house, **so** he should come over tonight. (two subordinate clauses)

> Phil was eager to try the new restaurant, **but** he moved away before trying it. (two independent clauses)

12j Correlative conjunctions include the following **word pairs**. Correlative conjunctions connect **two equal elements**.

either…or, neither…nor, not only…but also, both…and, if…then, since…therefore

Take **either** the dark meat **or** the light meat. (two words)

Not only has Rick quit school, **but** he has **also** left town. (two independent clauses)

Both the Baltimore Orioles **and** the Pittsburgh Pirates won the pennant in 1979. (two noun phrases)

I have seen her **neither** in the movies **nor** on television. (two phrases)

Note: The correlative conjunctions "neither…nor" should never be written "neither…or."

Each member of the pair of correlative conjunctions must be followed by the same grammatical construction.

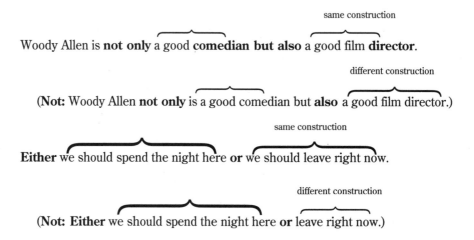

same construction

Woody Allen is **not only** a good **comedian but also** a good film **director**.

different construction

(**Not:** Woody Allen **not only** is a good comedian but **also** a good film director.)

same construction

Either we should spend the night here **or** we should leave right now.

different construction

(**Not: Either** we should spend the night here **or** leave right now.)

12k Conjunctive adverbs

A **conjunctive adverb** may be considered a **type of coordinate conjunction**.

Conjunctive adverbs include the following words, which **serve to connect two equal elements**.

therefore, however, consequently, accordingly, furthermore, besides, moreover, nevertheless, still

Although the clause introduced by a conjunctive adverb is grammatically independent, it is logically dependent on the preceding clause for complete meaning.

A storm knocked down our electric wires; **therefore,** we had to eat by candlelight.

A bad traffic accident ahead of us caused us to be delayed; **nevertheless,** we made the party on time.

You have not paid your rent for six months; **accordingly,** I am going to see a lawyer.

Independent clauses joined by a conjunctive adverb should be separated by a semicolon (;) or a period.

Frank and Marty delayed their vacation one week; **consequently,** I was able to join them.

The judge awarded custody of the child to its mother. **Moreover,** the judge set strict guidelines for visiting privileges.

Certain phrases may act as conjunctive adverbs.

Eunice wanted to buy a fur coat; **on the other hand,** she was trying to save money for a car.

We saw many interesting towns and cities on our tour. **In addition,** we met several nice people.

12l Join only the **same parts of speech** with coordinate conjunctions or with correlative conjunctions. **Faulty parallelism will result if different parts of speech are combined**.

Correct: Jim's day consisted of waking up early, working all day, **and** going back to bed. (three gerund phrases)

Faulty: Jim's day consisted of waking up early, working all day, **and** then to go back to bed. (two gerund phrases combined with an infinitive phrase)

Correct: The president's plan was a disappointment **not only** to the leaders of big business, **but also** to the leaders of organized labor. (two prepositional phrases)

Faulty: The president's plan was a disappointment **not only** to the leaders of big business, but also the leaders of organized labor. (one prepositional phrase and one noun)

12m Connecting elements of unequal rank

A less important idea should be put into a subordinate clause; the more important idea should be expressed in the main or independent clause.

main idea   subordinate idea

Bill is going to work for his father, although he was offered other jobs.

12n Subordination may be introduced by a subordinate conjunction, by a relative pronoun, or by a relative adverb.

Eva will want to go straight to bed **after** she comes back from her exercise class. (subordinate conjunction)

I bought the sneakers **that** you wanted. (relative pronoun)

We saw the house **where** they filmed *Gone with the Wind*. (relative adverb)

A subordinate conjunction introduces an adverbial clause.

My mother can knit a sweater **while** she watches television. (adverbial clause tells **when**)

Tell me what he looks like **so that** I'll recognize him. (adverbial clause tells **why**)

12o Some relative pronouns introduce adjective clauses.

Everyone wants a job **that** he likes.

The woman **who** walked across the United States has written a book about her experience.

Bobby gave Connie a new tennis racket, **which** she needed.

Other relative pronouns introduce noun clauses.

Tell me **what** you did.

This book has **whatever** you want to know about scuba diving.

Invite **whomever** you like.

12p A relative adverb introduces an adjective clause.

Do you remember the night **when** we locked ourselves out of the house?

Chris will be at the place **where** we met him last time.

Chapter 13: Correct Usage: Choosing the Right Word

"The difference between the right word and the almost-right word is the difference between the lightning and the lightning-bug [firefly]."

—Mark Twain

A, an.   The indefinite article *a* is used before a consonant sound; the indefinite article *an* is used before a vowel sound. Say *a plan, an idea*.

Accept, except.   *Accept* means *to receive; except* when used as a verb means *to leave out*. (We *accepted* the gift. Pedro's name was *excepted* from the honor roll.) The word *except* is used most often as a preposition. *Everyone went except me.*

Affect, effect.   *Affect* is a verb which means to *influence*. (Winning the sweepstakes will *affect* his attitude.) *Effect,* as a noun, means *an influence*. (Smoking has an *effect* on one's health.) *Effect,* as a verb, means to *bring about*. (The teacher's praise *effected* a change in the student.)

Affected, as an adjective, has the meaning of *false*. (She had an *affected* way of speaking.)

Aggravate, irritate.   *Aggravate* means to make worse. (Drinking iced water will *aggravate* your cold.) *Irritate* means to *annoy* or *exasperate*. (Mary's continuous chattering *irritated* me.)

Ain't.   Do not use this expression.

Already, all ready.   *Already* means *before* or *by a certain time*. (Mike said that he had *already* done the job.) *All ready* means *completely ready*. (When the buzzer sounded, the horses were *all ready* to start running.)

All right, alright.   The only correct spelling is *all right*.

Altogether, all together.   *Altogether* means *entirely, wholly*. (Jane is *altogether* too conceited to get along with people.) *All together* means *as a group*. (After the explosion, the boss was relieved to find his workers *all together* in front of the building.)

Among, between.   *Among* is used with more than two persons or things. (The manager distributed the gifts *among* all of the employees.) *Between* is used only with two persons or things. (The steak was divided *between* the two children.)

Amount, number.   *Amount* is used to refer to things in bulk. (The war costs a great *amount* of money.) *Number* is used to refer to things that can be counted. (A large *number* of pupils attend this school.)

And etc.   This is incorrect. The abbreviation *etc.* stands for the Latin *et cetera*. The *et* means *and;* the *cetera* means *other things*. It is wrong to say *and etc.* because the idea of *and* is already included in the *etc.*

Anyways, anywheres, everywheres, somewheres.   These expressions are not correct. Omit the final *s* after each.

As, like.   *As,* used as a conjunction, is followed by a verb. (Please do it *as* I told you to.) *Like* may not be used as a conjunction. If it is used as a preposition, it is not followed by a verb. (This ice cream looks *like* custard.)

Awful.   See **Terrific, terrible**.

Being that. *Being that* is incorrect for *since* or *because.* (*Since* you are tired, you ought to rest.)

Beside, besides. *Beside* means *alongside of; besides* means *in addition to.* (Nixon sat *beside* Autry at the baseball game.) (There is nobody *besides* her husband who understands Ann.)

Between. See **Among**.

Bring, take. Consider the speaker as a starting point. *Bring* is used for something carried in the direction of the speaker. (When you return from lunch, please *bring* me a ham sandwich.) *Take* is used for something carried away from the speaker. (If you are going downtown, please *take* this letter to the post office.)

Bunch. *Bunch* means cluster. Do not use *bunch* for *group* or *crowd.* (This is a large *bunch* of grapes.) (A *crowd* of people was at the scene of the accident.)

But that, but what. Do not use these expressions in place of *that* in structures like the following: I do not question *that* (not *but that*) you are richer than I am.

Can't hardly. Don't use this double negative. Say *can hardly.*

Continual, continuous. *Continual* means happening at intervals. (Salesmen are *continually* walking into this office.) *Continuous* means going on without interruption. (Without a moment of dry weather, it rained *continuously* for forty days and forty nights.)

Could of. Do not use for *could have.*

Data. Although *data* is the plural of *datum,* idiom permits the use of this word as a singular. Some authorities still insist on *Data are gathered* rather than *Data is gathered* or *these data* rather than *this data.* Most persons in computer programming now say *Data is gathered* or *this data.*

Deal. Do not use this term for *arrangement* or *transaction.* (He has an *excellent arrangement* (not *deal*) with the manager.)

Different from, different than. *Different from* is correct. *Different than* is incorrect. (His method of doing this is *different from* mine.)

Discover, invent. *Discover* means to see or learn something that has not been previously known. (They say the Vikings, not Columbus, *discovered* America.) *Invent* means to create for the first time. (William S. Burroughs *invented* the adding machine.)

Disinterested, uninterested. *Disinterested* means without bias. (An umpire must be *disinterested* to judge fairly in a baseball game.) *Uninterested* means not caring about a situation. (I am totally *uninterested* in your plan.)

Doesn't, don't. *Doesn't* means *does not; don't* means *do not.* Do not say *He don't* (*do not*) when you mean *He doesn't* (*does not*).

Due to. At the beginning of a sentence, *due to* is always incorrect. Use, instead, *on account of, because of,* or a similar expression. (*On account of* bad weather, the contest was postponed.) As a predicate adjective construction, *due to* is correct. His weakness was *due to* his hunger.

Each other, one another. *Each other* is used for two persons. (The executive and his secretary antagonize *each other.*) *One another* is used for more than two persons. (The members of the large family love *one another.*)

Effect. See **Affect**.

Enthuse. Do not use this word. Say *enthusiastic.* (The art critic was *enthusiastic* about the painting.)

Equally as good. This expression is incorrect. Say, instead, *just as good.* (This car is *just as good* as that.)

Farther, further.   *Farther* is used for a distance that is measurable. (The farmer's house is about 100 yards *farther* down the road.) *Further* is used to express the extension of an idea. (A *further* explanation may be necessary.)

Fewer, less.   *Fewer* applies to what may be counted. (Greenwich Village has *fewer* conservatives than liberals.) *Less* refers to degree or amount. (*Less* rain fell this month than the month before.)

Flout, flaunt.   *Flout* means to mock or insult. (The king *flouted* the wise man when the latter offered advice.) *Flaunt* means to make a pretentious display of. (The upstart *flaunted* his diamond ring.)

Further.   See **Farther.**

Get.   *Get* means *to obtain* or *receive*. Get should not be used in the sense of *to excite, to interest,* or *to understand*. Say: His guitar playing *fascinates* (not *gets*) me. Say: When you talk about lifestyles, I just don't *understand* (not *get*) *you*.

Good, well.   Do not use the adjective *good* in place of the adverb *well* in structures like the following: John works *well* (not *good*) in the kitchen. Jim Palmer pitched *well* (not *good*) in last night's game.

Graduate.   One *graduates from,* or *is graduated from,* a school. One does *not graduate a school*. (The student *graduated* [or was graduated] from high school.)

Had of.   Avoid this for *had*. Say: My father always said that he wished he *had* (not *had of*) gone to college.

Hanged, hung.   When a person is *executed,* he is *hanged*. When anything is *suspended* in space, it is *hung*.

Hardly.   See **Can't hardly.**

Healthful, healthy.   *Healthful* applies to *conditions that promote health*. *Healthy* applies to *a state of health*. Say: Stevenson found the climate of Saranac Lake very *healthful*. Say: Mary is a very *healthy* girl.

If, whether.   Use *whether*—not *if*—in structures that follow verbs like *ask, doubt, know, learn, say*. Say: Hank Aaron didn't know *whether* (not *if*) he was going to break Babe Ruth's home-run record.

Imply, infer.   The speaker *implies* when he suggests or hints at. (The owner of the store *implied* that the patron stole a box of toothpicks.) The listener *infers* when he draws a conclusion from facts or evidence. (From what you say, I *infer* that I am about to be discharged.)

In, into.   *In* is used to express a location, without the involvement of motion. (The sugar is *in* the cupboard.) *Into* is used to express motion from one place to another. (The housekeeper put the sugar *into* the cupboard.)

In regards to.   This is incorrect. Say *in regard to* or *with regard to*.

Invent.   See **Discover.**

Irregardless.   Do not use *irregardless*. It is incorrect for *regardless*. (You will not be able to go out tonight *regardless* of the fact that you have done all of your homework.)

Its, it's.   *Its* is the possessive of *it; it's* is the contraction for *it is*.

Kind of, sort of.   Do not use these expressions as adverbs. Say: Ali was *quite* (not *kind of* or *sort of*) witty in his post-fight interview.

Kind of a, sort of a.   Omit the *a*. Say: What *kind of* (not *kind of a* or *sort of a*) game is lacrosse?

Lay, lie.   See "Principal Parts of Irregular Verbs"—pages 47–48.

Learn, teach. *Learn* means *to gain knowledge. Teach* means *to impart knowledge.* Say: He *taught* (not *learned*) his brother how to swim.

Leave, let. The word *leave* means *to depart.* (I *leave* today for San Francisco.) The word *let* means to allow. (*Let* me take your place.)

Less, fewer. See **Fewer, less**.

Liable, likely. *Liable* means exposed to something unpleasant. (If you speed, you are *liable* to get a summons.) *Likely* means probable, with reference to either a pleasant or unpleasant happening. (It is *likely* to snow tomorrow.)

Locate. Do not use *locate* to mean *settle* or *move to.* Say: We will *move to* (not *locate in*) Florida next year.

Might of, must of. Omit the *of.*

Myself, himself, yourself. These pronouns are to be used as intensives. (The Chairman *himself* will open the meeting.) Do not use these pronouns when *me, him,* or *you* will serve. Say: We shall be happy if Joe and *you* (not *yourself*) join us for lunch at the Plaza.

Nice. See **Terrific, terrible**.

Number, amount. See **Amount, number**.

Of, have. Do not use *of* for *have* in structures like *could have.*

Off of. Omit the *of.* Say: The book fell *off* (not *off of*) the shelf.

Pour, spill. When one *pours,* he does it deliberately. (He carefully *poured* the wine into her glass.) When one *spills,* he does it accidentally. (I carelessly *spilled* some wine on her dress.)

Practical, practicable. *Practical* means *fitted for actual work. Practicable* means *feasible* or *possible.* Say: My business partner is a *practical man.* Say: The boss did not consider the plan *practicable* for this coming year.

Principal, principle. *Principal* applies to a *chief* or the *chief part* of something. *Principle* applies to a *basic law.* Say: Mr. Jones is the *principal* of the school. Professor White was the *principal* speaker. Honesty is a good *principle* to follow.

Raise, rise. See "Principal Parts of Irregular Verbs"—pages 47–48.

Reason is because. Do not use the expression *reason is because*—it is always incorrect. Say the *reason is that.* (The *reason* Jack failed the course *is that* he didn't study.)

Regardless. See **Irregardless**.

Respectfully, respectively. *Respectfully* means *with respect,* as in the complimentary close of a letter, *respectfully yours. Respectively* means that each item will be considered *in the order given.* Say: This paper is *respectfully* submitted. Say: The hero, the heroine, and the villain will be played by Albert, Joan, and Harry *respectively.*

Rise, raise. See "Principal Parts of Irregular Verbs"—pages 47–48.

Said. Avoid the legalistic use of *said,* like *said letter, said plan, said program,* except in legal writing.

Should of. Do not use for *should have.*

Sit, set. See "Principal Parts of Irregular Verbs"—pages 47–48.

Some. Do not use *some* when you mean *somewhat.* Say: I'm confused *somewhat* (not *some*).

Spill, pour. See **Pour, spill**.

Suspicion. Do not use *suspicion* as a verb when you mean *suspect.*

Take, bring. See **Bring, take**.

Teach, learn.   See **Learn, teach**.

Terrific, terrible.   Avoid "lazy words." Many people don't want to take the trouble to use the exact word. They will use words like *terrific, swell, great, beautiful,* etc., to describe anything and everything that is favorable. And they will use words like *terrible, awful, lousy, miserable,* etc., for whatever is unfavorable. Use the exact word. Say: We had a *delicious* (not terrific) meal. Say: We had a *boring* (not *terrible*) weekend.

This kind, these kind.   *This kind* is correct—as is *that kind, these kinds,* and *those kinds.* (My little brother likes *this kind* of pears.) *These kind* and *those kind* are incorrect.

Try and.   Do not say *try and.* Say *try to.* (*Try to* visit me while I am in Florida.)

Uninterested.   See **Disinterested**.

Wait for, wait on.   *Wait for* means *to await; wait on* means *to serve.* Say: I am waiting *for* (not *on*) Carter to call me on the telephone.

Way, ways.   Do not use *ways* for *way.* Say: It is a long *way* (not *ways*) to Japan.

Where.   Do not use *where* in place of *that* in expressions like the following: I see in the newspaper *that* (not *where*) a nuclear reactor may be built a mile away from our house.

Would of.   Do not use for *would have.*

Chapter 14: Grammar and Usage Index

* This Index does not include items listed in Chapter 13 (Correct Usage: Choosing the Right Word). Since these Correct Usage items are in alphabetical order, it will be easy for you to locate any Correct Usage explanation whatsoever.

Part 3
The SAT
Writing Test

The Writing Test will include a direct writing sample and multiple-choice questions that require recognition of the conventions of standard written English, appropriate diction, and effective and logical expression.

The SAT Writing Test will include:

- An essay that will provide a direct measure of writing ability;

- Essay topics that will not assume any specific subject-matter knowledge;

- Revision-in-context passages, which will present a context larger than a discrete sentence and therefore permit questions on logic, coherence, and organization;

- Revision-in-context tasks that are similar to common in-class exercises in which students revise their own essays;

- Usage questions, which will require students to recognize errors. Sentence-correction questions will require recognition of errors and selection of the correct rephrasing.

The SAT Writing Section

The SAT Writing section will measure a student's mastery of developing and expressing ideas effectively. It will include both multiple-choice items and an essay. The multiple-choice component of the writing section will measure the student's understanding of how to use language in a clear, consistent manner and how to improve a piece of writing through revision and editing. Students will be asked to recognize sentence errors, to choose the best version of a piece of writing, and to improve paragraphs within a writing context. However, students will not be asked to define or to use grammatical terms, and spelling or capitalization will not be tested.

For the essay, students will have 25 minutes to write a first draft of an original essay. This will be a direct measure of their ability, under timed conditions, to do the kind of writing required in most college courses—writing that emphasizes precise use of language, logical presentation of ideas, development of a point of view, and clarity of expression.

The combination of the multiple-choice items and the essay will provide an assessment of writing that takes into account both the student's understanding of the conventions of language and his or her ability to develop ideas in a thoughtful, coherent, and cogent essay.

The scores for the SAT Writing section will range from 200 to 800. Two subscores will be given for the writing section: a multiple-choice subscore that will range from 20 to 80 and an essay subscore that will range from 2 to 12. Essays not written on the essay assignment will be given a score of zero. The essay component will count toward one-third of the total writing score, and the multiple-choice component will count toward two-thirds of the total writing score.

Content of the Writing Test

Multiple-Choice Questions: 35 Minutes, 49 Questions*

- Usage—Identifying Sentence Errors: 18 questions

- Sentence Correction—Improving Sentences: 25 questions

- Revision in Context—Improving Paragraphs: 6 questions

Essay (Writing Exercise): 25 Minutes
Scoring the Writing Test

All essays will be scored holistically. Two readers will independently read each essay and score according to agreed-upon criteria.

Essay Reporting Service

Students may request that copies of essays be sent to high schools and/or colleges.

*The PSAT will include items in this multiple-choice writing section.

The Essay on the SAT Writing Test

On the SAT, you will be required to write an essay. Here's an example of the directions to the Essay:

SECTION 2	Time—25 minutes 1 Question	ESSAY

Directions: Consider carefully the following excerpt and the assignment below it. Then plan and write an essay that explains your ideas as persuasively as possible. Keep in mind that the support you provide—both reasons and examples—will help make your view convincing to the reader.

Please note the essays are considered "first drafts" and are scored holistically. This means readers will award a score according to the overall quality of the essay. They will take into account aspects of writing such as the development of ideas, supporting examples, organization, word choice, and sentence structure.

> The principle is this: each failure leads us closer to deeper knowledge, to greater creativity in understanding old data, to new lines of inquiry. Thomas Edison experienced 10,000 failures before he succeeded in perfecting the lightbulb. When a friend of his remarked that 10,000 failures was a lot, Edison replied, "I didn't fail 10,000 times, I successfully eliminated 10,000 materials and combinations that didn't work."
>
> *Myles Brand, "Taking the Measure of Your Success"*
>
> **Assignment:** What is your view on the idea that it takes failure to achieve success? In an essay, support your position using an example (or examples) from literature, the arts, history, current events, politics, science and technology, or your experience or observation.

WHEN THE SUPERVISOR ANNOUNCES THAT 25 MINUTES HAVE PASSED, YOU MUST STOP WRITING THE ESSAY. DO NOT GO ON TO ANY OTHER SECTION IN THE TEST.

YOU MAY MAKE NOTES ON THIS PAGE, BUT YOU MUST WRITE YOUR ESSAY ON THE ANSWER SHEET.

Here are some more sample essay topics:

Consider carefully the following statement and the assignment below it. Then, plan and write your essay as directed.

"Outrageous behavior is instructive. It reveals to us the limits of our tolerance."

Assignment: The quotation implies that those who go beyond accepted standards help us to clarify our own standards. Do you agree or disagree with the quotation? Discuss, supporting your position with examples from current affairs, literature, history, or your own experience.

Consider carefully the following quotation and the assignment following it. Then, plan and write your essay as directed.

"People seldom stand up for what they truly believe; instead they merely go along with the popular view."

Assignment: Do you agree or disagree with this statement? Write an essay in which you support your opinion with specific examples from history, contemporary affairs, literature, or personal observation.

Consider carefully the following statement and the assignment below it. Then, plan and write your essay as directed.

"Everything has its cost."

Assignment: Choose an example from literature, current affairs, history, or from personal observation in which a cause, an ideal, or an object had to be paid for at some cost. What was that cost? Was what was gained worth it, or was the cost too high? Give reasons for your position.

A Few Words About Scoring the Essay. Even with some errors in spelling, punctuation, and grammar, a student can get a top score on the essay. The highly trained high school and college composition teachers who score the essays will follow a rubric that focuses upon content, organization, and language usage and sentence structure. Each essay will be scored independently by two such readers on a 1–6 scale. If the readers' scores differ by more than two points, the test will be evaluated by a third reader. We know from our experience with the SAT II: Writing test that fewer than 2 percent of all scored essays require a third reader.

The rubric for the SAT Writing section is similar to the one used for the previous SAT II: Writing Test, which follows.

The SAT Essay Scoring Guide

Score of 6	Score of 5	Score of 4
An essay in this category is *outstanding*, demonstrating *clear and consistent mastery*, although it may have a few minor errors. A typical essay	An essay in this category is *effective*, demonstrating *reasonably consistent mastery*, although it will have occasional errors or lapses in quality. A typical essay	An essay in this category is *competent*, demonstrating *adequate mastery*, although it will have lapses in quality. A typical essay
• effectively and insightfully develops a point of view on the issue and demonstrates outstanding critical thinking, using clearly appropriate examples, reasons, and other evidence to support its position	• effectively develops a point of view on the issue and demonstrates strong critical thinking, generally using appropriate examples, reasons, and other evidence to support its position	• develops a point of view on the issue and demonstrates competent critical thinking, using adequate examples, reasons, and other evidence to support its position
• is well organized and clearly focused, demonstrating clear coherence and smooth progression of ideas	• is well organized and focused, demonstrating coherence and progression of ideas	• is generally organized and focused, demonstrating some coherence and progression of ideas
• exhibits skillful use of language, using a varied, accurate, and apt vocabulary	• exhibits facility in the use of language, using appropriate vocabulary	• exhibits adequate but inconsistent facility in the use of language, using generally appropriate vocabulary
• demonstrates meaningful variety in sentence structure	• demonstrates variety in sentence structure	• demonstrates some variety in sentence structure
• is free of most errors in grammar, usage, and mechanics	• is generally free of most errors in grammar, usage, and mechanics	• has some errors in grammar, usage, and mechanics

Score of 3	Score of 2	Score of 1
An essay in this category is *inadequate*, but demonstrates *developing mastery*, and is marked by ONE OR MORE of the following weaknesses:	An essay in this category is *seriously limited*, demonstrating *little mastery*, and is flawed by ONE OR MORE of the following weaknesses:	An essay in this category is *fundamentally lacking*, demonstrating *very little* or *no mastery*, and is severely flawed by ONE OR MORE of the following weaknesses:
• develops a point of view on the issue, demonstrating some critical thinking, but may do so inconsistently or use inadequate examples, reasons, or other evidence to support its position	• develops a point of view on the issue that is vague or seriously limited, demonstrating weak critical thinking, providing inappropriate or insufficient examples, reasons, or other evidence to support its position	• develops no viable point of view on the issue, or provides little or no evidence to support its position
• is limited in its organization or focus, or may demonstrate some lapses in coherence or progression of ideas	• is poorly organized and/or focused, or demonstrates serious problems with coherence or progression of ideas	• is disorganized or unfocused, resulting in a disjointed or incoherent essay
• displays developing facility in the use of language, but sometimes uses weak vocabulary or inappropriate word choice	• displays very little facility in the use of language, using very limited vocabulary or incorrect word choice	• displays fundamental errors in vocabulary
• lacks variety or demonstrates problems in sentence structure	• demonstrates frequent problems in sentence structure	• demonstrates severe flaws in sentence structure
• contains an accumulation of errors in grammar, usage, and mechanics	• contains errors in grammar, usage, and mechanics so serious that meaning is somewhat obscured	• contains pervasive errors in grammar, usage, or mechanics that persistently interfere with meaning

Essays not written on the essay assignment will receive a score of zero.

The Writing Sample

Writing sample essays are read and scored by "readers," high school and college teachers who have experience with the writing demonstrated by students at the end of high school. They do not expect polished compositions. Two readers score each essay on a 6-point scale, with 6 as the highest score and 1 as the lowest. The total writing sample score is the sum of the two readers' scores. It is weighted to equal one-third of the total SAT Writing Test score. If the two readers' scores are more than two points apart, a third reader resolves the discrepancy.

Sample Essays

Reproduced below is a topic used on an SAT Writing Test. You will also see the Scoring Guide for Readers of Student Responses to the Writing Subject Test and actual students' essays. The Scoring Guide is used to instruct essay readers. The directions that follow are identical to those in the test.

You have twenty-five minutes to write an essay on the topic assigned below. DO NOT WRITE ON ANOTHER TOPIC. AN ESSAY ON ANOTHER TOPIC IS NOT ACCEPTABLE.

The essay is assigned to give you an opportunity to show how well you can write. You should, therefore, take care to express your thoughts on the topic clearly and effectively. How well you write is much more important than how much you write, but to cover the topic adequately you will probably need to write more than one paragraph. Be specific.

Your essay must be written on the lines provided on your answer sheet. You will receive no other paper on which to write. You will find that you have enough space if you write on every line, avoid wide margins, and keep your handwriting to a reasonable size. It is important to remember that what you write will be read by someone who is not familiar with your handwriting. Try to write or print so that what you are writing is legible to the reader.

Consider carefully the following statement. Then plan and write your essay as directed.

Nothing requires more discipline than freedom.

Assignment: In an essay, discuss your view of the statement above. Support your view with an example or examples from literature, the arts, history, politics, science and technology, current events, or your experience or observation.

Essays with a Total Score of 12

(Each reader gave the essay a score of 6.)

Although essays in this category differ in approach, style, and opinion, and have slight differences in quality, they all demonstrate the *clear and consistent competence* specified in the scoring guide. These essays are characterized by good organization, good command of the language, pertinent support for the ideas being developed, and an effective presentation. These essays are not perfect, nor are they expected to be, for each is only a first draft written in the twenty minutes allotted. The essay below is representative of essays in this category.

The ultimate freedom does not require discipline because to be entirely free, one must have no restrictions created by them or the world around them. But ultimate freedom exists only as a concept and while humans can strive to be free, in reality it can never be achieved. Discipline is therefore inescapable.

In William Shakespeare's *King Lear,* the theme of madness plays a major role in Lear's life. Lear's madness becomes his freedom from the rules around him. In the first scene, Lear gives up his land and therefore, power to his daughters, supposedly freeing himself from obligations in his old age. Yet Lear soon finds that his life and the people in his life are not as he once thought them to be. His daughters Regan and Goneril each display cruelty towards him and place restrictions of Lear. By giving up his power, Lear was in fact giving away his freedom. He can no longer do as he pleases, for example, he must beg each daughter to let him live with them. If discipline is taken to mean restrictions and rules placed upon oneself, then Lear in fact has more as a free man than a powerful man. Lear's freedom, or rather his lack of power, ends up promoting his madness. This madness removes him from obligations, but at the same time creates a different kind of restriction on him. Lear in his mad state may not have restrictions and discipline in the sense generally thought of, but he does in a new sense. The discipline of madness consumes him.

Lear, in both his powerful state and his weakened yet free state has freedom and discipline. And while the concept of ultimate freedom is without discipline, Lear's freedom in both cases is an example of how imperfect freedom does involve discipline. When Lear had power, he was free to make decisions, but these decisions were disciplined choices. When Lear had madness instead of power, he had freedom to do what he wanted, without concern of the consequences, but he had discipline forced upon him by his situation. Because ultimate freedom cannot be attained, freedom as we see it and refer to daily does involve discipline. Only the unachievable, ultimate freedom does not require discipline.

Essays with a Total Score of 10

(Each reader gave the essay a score of 5.)

Essays in this category demonstrate the *reasonably consistent competence* described in the scoring guide. They present pertinent examples and a developed argument. These essays, however, do contain lapses that keep them out of the top category. These lapses range from an awkward sentence or two to a failure to maintain a consistent tone. Still, whatever the flaws, they do not detract from the overall impression that the writing is well done.

In society today, as well as histories past, we have seen that "nothing requires more discipline than freedom." Freedom was a principle that people fought and died for. It was an undisputable right that was sometimes put to the test. However, Adeline Yen Mah and Martin Luther King Jr. prove that nothing isn't worth fighting for.

In "Falling Leaves" by Adeline Yen Mah, we can easily sympathize with her struggle for freedom and rights of passage. Ever since she was a young Chinese girl growing up in a male-dominated world, Adeline had to prove to herself and others that she deserved the praise, affection, and education that her three brothers easily attained. With much determination and introspective spirit, she soon learned the power of her will. By speaking out for her wanting to be rid of her provincial education and moving on to higher learning through attending England's Universities did she recognize that "nothing requires more discipline than freedom."

In addition to Adeline's opposition, Martin Luther King Jr. was a prominent figure in America's history that proved that his efforts were not wasted. He was a firm believer of equal rights for his fellow African American people. Without Martin's unerring attempts at breaking the barriers, there would not have been such a great uproar to stop the injustices.

From time to time, people have felt the restraint and oppression, but Adeline and Martin proved that their voices could not go on unheard. They attacked all obstacles and grew strong enough to realize the importance of their cause. The attainment of freedom have bonded these figures into our nation.

Essays with a Total Score of 8

(Each reader gave the essay a score of 4.)

As the scoring guide describes, essays in this category demonstrate *adequate competence* with occasional errors and lapses in quality. Although the papers show that the writers have adequate command of the skills needed for good writing, the papers have the kinds of flaws that keep them out of the top ranges.

In today's world almost all people are granted certain freedoms in relation to behavior or emotions. In the United States of America this priviledge is especially prevelant through it's democratic government and the constitution it provides to protect the people's rights. Because too much unrestricted freedom can hurt a nation, the freedoms granted to the people must be regulated by each person's self-discipline. As with most things in life, freedom can be taken for granted if responsibility is not taken for one's own actions.

One major freedom given to most teenagers is the priviledge to go away from home for college. This is a major commitment and responsibility because in many cases a student will be living away from his/her parents for the first time. His/her mother and father are no longer around to hassle the youth about homework, going to sleep, or other decisions. It is a beginning college student's own discipline or practicality that must aid the teen in making such lifestyle choices. In order to succeed and keep the new freedom of living away from home, the student must prove that he or she is mature enough to handle it. The student must organize his/her time apropriately, take care of himself/herself, and act like an adult.

Many personal freedoms and liberties are granted to people in life. In exchange for these rights, human beings must show they are worthy of receiving them by showing discipline and maturity in their actions and decision. If people were to live carelessly without regard for the preciousness of their freedom, the world would be full of chaos and injustice.

Important Tips on How to Write the Best Essay

Making Your Sentences Effective

What Is Style?

Many good ideas are lost because they are expressed in a dull, wordy, involved way. We often have difficulty following—we may even ignore—instructions that are hard to read. Yet we find other instructions written in such a clear and simple way that a child could easily follow them. This way of writing—the words we choose and the way we use them—we call style.

No two people write exactly alike. Even when writing about the same thing, they probably will say it differently. Some will say it more effectively than others, of course; what they say will be more easily read and understood. But there is seldom any one best way to say something. Rather, there are usually several equally good ways. This flexibility is what makes English such a rich language.

Style can't be taught; each person's style is like personality—it is unique to him or her. But we can each improve our style. Let us consider how we can improve our writing style by improving our sentences.

How to Write Effective Sentences

We speak in sentences; we write in sentences. A single word or phrase sometimes carries a complete thought, but sentences are more often the real units of thought communication.

Writing good sentences takes concentration, patience, and practice. It involves much more than just stringing words together, one after another, as they tumble from our minds. If writers aren't careful, their sentences may not mean to the reader what they want them to; they may mean what they *didn't* want them to—or they may mean nothing at all.

This section discusses five things writers can do to write better sentences—or improve sentences already written. These are:

1. Create interest.
2. Make your meaning clear.
3. Keep your sentences brief.
4. Make every word count.
5. Vary your sentence patterns.

Let's consider interest first.

1. Create Interest.

We can make our writing more interesting by writing in an informal, conversational style. This style also makes our writing easier to understand and our readers more receptive to our thoughts.

Listen to two men meeting in the coffee shop. One tells the other, "Let me know when you need more paper clips." But how would he have written it? Probably as follows:

Request this office be notified when your activity's supply of paper clips, wire, steel gem pattern, large type 1, stock No. 7510-634-6516, falls below 30-day level prescribed in AFR 67-1, Vol. II, Section IV, subject: Office Supplies. Requisition will be submitted as expeditiously as possible to preclude noncompliance with appropriate directives.

Judging from the formal, academic style of much of our writing, we want to *impress* rather than *express*. There seems to be something about writing that brings out our biggest words, our most complex sentences, and our most formal style. Obviously this is not effective writing. We wouldn't dare say it aloud this formally for fear someone would laugh at us, but we will write it.

WRITE TO EXPRESS

One of the best ways to make our writing more interesting to the reader—and, hence, more effective—is to write as we talk. Of course we can't write *exactly* as we talk, and we shouldn't want to. We usually straighten out the sentence structure, make our sentences complete rather than fragmentary or run-on, substitute for obvious slang words, and so on. But we can come close to our conversational style without being folksy or ungrammatical or wordy. This informal style is far more appropriate for the kind of writing we do and for the kind of readers we have than the old formal style. And it certainly makes better reading.

BE DEFINITE, SPECIFIC, AND CONCRETE

Another way—and one of the surest—to arouse and hold the interest and attention of readers is to be definite, specific, and concrete.

2. Make Your Meaning Clear.

You do not need to be a grammarian to recognize a good sentence. After all, the first requirement of grammar is that you focus your reader's attention on the meaning you wish to convey. If you take care to make your meaning clear, your grammar will usually take care of itself. You can, however, do three things to make your meaning clearer to your reader: (1) emphasize your main ideas, (2) avoid wandering sentences, and (3) avoid ambiguity.

EMPHASIZE THE MAIN IDEAS

When we talk we use gestures, voice changes, pauses, smiles, frowns, and so on to emphasize our main ideas. In writing we have to use different methods for emphasis. Some are purely mechanical; others are structural.

Mechanical devices include capital letters, underlining or italics, punctuation, and headings. Printers used to capitalize the first letter of a word they wanted to emphasize. We still occasionally capitalize or use a heavier type to emphasize words, phrases, or whole sentences. Sometimes we underline or italicize words that we want to stand out. Often we label or head main sections or subdivisions, as we have done in this book. This effectively separates main ideas and makes them stand out so that our reader doesn't have to search for them.

But mechanical devices for emphasizing an idea—capitalization, particularly—are often overused. The best way to emphasize an idea is to place it effectively in the sentence. The most emphatic position is at the end of the sentence. The next most emphatic position is at the beginning of the sentence. The place of least importance is anywhere in the middle. Remember, therefore, to put the important clause, phrase, name, or idea at the beginning or at the end of your sentences, and never hide the main idea in a subordinate clause or have it so buried in the middle of the sentence that the reader has to dig it out or miss it altogether.

Unemphatic: People drive on the left side instead of the right side in England.
Better: Instead of driving on the right side, people in England drive on the left.

AVOID WANDERING SENTENCES

All parts of a sentence should contribute to one clear idea or impression. Long, straggling sentences usually contain a hodgepodge of unrelated ideas. You should either break them up into shorter sentences or put the subordinate thoughts into subordinate form. Look at this sentence:

The sergeant, an irritable fellow who had been a truck driver, born and brought up in the corn belt of Iowa, strong as an ox and 6 feet tall, fixed an angry eye on the recruit.

You can see that the main idea is "The sergeant fixed an angry eye on the recruit." That he was an irritable fellow, strong as an ox, and 6 feet tall adds to the main idea. But the facts that he had been a truck driver and had been born in Iowa add nothing to the main thought, and the sentence is better without them.

The sergeant, an irritable fellow who was strong as an ox and 6 feet tall, fixed an angry eye on the recruit.

AVOID AMBIGUITY

If a sentence can be misunderstood, it will be misunderstood. A sentence that says that "The truck followed the jeep until its tire blew out" may be perfectly clear to the writer, but it will mean nothing to the reader until the pronoun *its* is identified.

MAKE SURE THAT YOUR MODIFIERS SAY WHAT YOU MEAN

"While eating oats, the farmer took the horse out of the stable." This sentence provides little more than a laugh until you add to the first part of the sentence a logical subject ("the horse"): "While the horse was eating oats, the farmer took him out of the stable." Sometimes simple misplacement of modifiers in sentences leads to misunderstanding: "The young lady went to the dance with her boyfriend wearing a low-cut gown." You can clarify this sentence by simply rearranging it: "Wearing a low-cut gown, the young lady went to the dance with her boyfriend."

3. Keep Your Sentences Brief.

Sentences written like 10-word advertisements are hard to read. You cannot get the kind of brevity you want by leaving out the articles (*a, an,* and *the*). You can get brevity by dividing complex ideas into bite-size sentences and by avoiding unnecessary words and phrases and needless repetition and elaboration. Here are some suggestions that will help you to write short, straightforward sentences.

USE VERBS THAT WORK

The verb—the action word—is the most important word in a sentence. It is the power plant that supplies the energy, vitality, and motion in the sentence. So use strong verbs, verbs that really *work* in your sentences.

USE THE ACTIVE VOICE

Sentences written in the basic subject-verb-object pattern are said to be written in the *active voice.* In such sentences someone or something *does* something to the object—there is a forward movement of the idea. In sentences written in the *passive voice,* the subject merely receives the action—it has something done to it by someone or something, and there is no feeling of forward movement of the idea.

The active voice, in general, is preferable to the passive voice because it helps to give writing a sense of energy, vitality, and motion. When we use the passive voice predominantly, our writing doesn't seem to have much life, the actor in the sentences is not allowed to act, and verbs become weak. So don't rob your writing of its power by using the passive voice when you can use the active voice. Nine out of ten sentences will be both shorter (up to 25 percent shorter) and stronger in the active voice.

Let's compare the two voices:

Active: The pilot flew   the aircraft.
          (*Actor*) (*action*) (*acted upon*)

Passive: The aircraft was flown by the pilot.
           (*Acted upon*) (*action*) (*actor*)

Now let's see some typical passive examples:

The committee will be appointed by the principal.
Reports have been received…
Provisions will be made by the manager in case of a subway strike.

Aren't these familiar? In most of these we should be emphasizing the actor rather than leaving out or subordinating him or her.

See how much more effective those sentences are when they are written in the active voice.

The principal will appoint the committee.
We have received reports…
The manager will make provisions in case of a subway strike.

AVOID USING THE PASSIVE VOICE

The passive voice always takes more words to say what could be said just as well (and probably better) in the active voice. In the passive voice the subject also becomes less personal and may seem less important, and the motion of the sentence grinds to a halt.

There are times, of course, when the passive voice is useful and justified—as when the person or thing doing the action is unknown or unimportant.

When we use the lifeless passive voice indiscriminately, we make our writing weak, ineffective, and dull. Remember that the normal English word order is subject-verb-object. There may be occasions in your writing when you feel that the passive voice is preferable. But should such an occasion arise, think twice before you write; the passive voice rarely improves your style. Before using a passive construction, make certain that you have a specific reason. After using it, check to see that your sentence is not misleading.

TAKE A DIRECT APPROACH

Closely related to passive voice construction is indirect phrasing.

It is requested…
It is recommended…
It has been brought to the attention of…
It is the opinion of…

Again, this is so familiar to us that we don't even question it. But who requested? Who recommended? Who knows? Who believes? No one knows from reading such sentences!

This indirect way of writing, this use of the passive voice and the indirect phrase, is perhaps the most characteristic feature of the formal style of the past. There are many explanations for it. A psychiatrist might say the writer was afraid to take the responsibility for what he or she is writing or merely passing the buck. The writer may unjustifiably believe this style makes him or her anonymous, or makes him or her sound less dogmatic and authoritarian.

Express your ideas immediately and directly. Unnecessary expressions like *it is, there is,* and *there are* weaken sentences and delay comprehension. They also tend to place part of the sentence in the passive voice. *It is the recommendation of the sales manager that the report be forwarded immediately* is more directly expressed as *The sales manager recommends that we send the report immediately.*

Change Long Modifiers

Mr. Barnes, who is president of the board, will preside.

Vehicles that are defective are…

They gave us a month for accomplishment of the task.

to Shorter Ones

Mr. Barnes, the board president, will preside.

Defective vehicles are…

They gave us a month to do the job.

Break Up Long Sentences

There is not enough time available for the average executive to do everything that might be done and so it is necessary for him to determine wisely the essentials and do them first, then spend the remaining time on things that are "nice to do."

The average executive lacks time to do everything that might be done. Consequently, he must decide what is essential and do it first. Then he can spend the remaining time on things that are "nice to do."

4. Make Every Word Count.

Don't cheat your readers. They are looking for ideas—for meaning—when they read your letter, report, or directive. If they have to read several words that have little to do with the real meaning of a sentence, or if they have to read a number of sentences to get just a little meaning, you are cheating them. Much of their time and effort is wasted because they aren't getting full benefit from it. They expected something that you didn't deliver.

MAKE EACH WORD ADVANCE YOUR THOUGHT

Each word in a sentence should advance the thought of that sentence. To leave it out would destroy the meaning you are trying to convey.

"Naturally," you say. "Of course!" But reread the last letter you wrote. Aren't some of your sentences rather wordy? Couldn't you have said the same thing in fewer words? And finally, how many times did you use a whole phrase to say what could have been said in one word, or a whole clause for what could have been expressed in a short phrase? In short, try tightening up a sentence like this:

The reason that prices rose was that the demand was increasing at the same time that the production was decreasing.

Rewritten:
Prices rose because the demand increased while production decreased.

Doesn't our rewrite say the same thing as the original? Yet we have saved the reader some effort by squeezing the unnecessary words out of a wordy sentence.

Now try this one:

Wordy: The following statistics serve to give a good idea of the cost of production.
Improved: The following statistics give a good idea of the production costs.

or

These statistics show production costs.

And this one:

Wordy: I have a production supervisor who likes to talk a great deal.
Improved: I have a talkative production supervisor.

In all of those rewritten sentences we have saved our reader some time. The same thing has been said in fewer words.

Of course, you can be *too* concise. If your writing is too brief or terse, it may "sound" rude and abrupt, and you may lose more than you gain. You need, then, to be politely concise. What you are writing, what you are writing about, and whom you are writing for will help you decide just where to draw the line. However, the general rule, make every word count, still stands. Say what you have to say in as few words as clarity *and tact* will allow.

CONSOLIDATE IDEAS

A second way to save the reader's effort is to consolidate ideas whenever possible. Pack as much meaning as possible into each sentence *without making the sentence structure too complicated.*

Each sentence is by definition an idea, a unit of thought. Each time the readers read one of these units they should get as much meaning as possible. It takes just about as much effort to read a sentence with a simple thought as it does to read one with a strong idea or with two or three strong ideas.

There are several things we can do to pack meaning into a sentence. In general, they all have to do with summarizing, combining, and consolidating ideas.

Some people write sentences that are weak and insignificant, both in structure and thought. Ordinarily several such sentences can be summarized and the thought put into one good, mature sentence. For example:

We left Wisconsin the next morning. I remember watching three aircraft. They were F-4s. They were flying very low. I felt sure they were going to crash over a half a dozen times. The F-4 is new to me. I hadn't seen one before.

Rewritten:
When we left Wisconsin the next morning, I remember watching three F-4s, a type of aircraft I had never seen before. They were flying so low that over a half dozen times I felt sure they were going to crash.

When summarizing like this, be sure to emphasize the main action. Notice in the next example how we have kept the main action as our verb and made the other actions subordinate by changing them to verbals.

Poor: It was in 1959 that he *retired* from teaching and he *devoted* his time to *writing* his autobiography. (three verbs, one verbal)

Improved: In 1959 he *retired* from teaching to *devote* his time to *writing* his autobiography. (one verb, two verbals)

Here is an example similar to ones we might find in a directive:

Poor: The evaluation forms will be picked up from your respective personnel office. You should have these completed by 1700 hours, 18 May. They will be delivered immediately to the security section.

Notice that in the above instructions all of the actions are to be performed by the reader or "you." Now let's put these into one sentence, placing the things to be done in a series and using a single subject.

Improved: Pick up the evaluation forms from your personnel office; complete and deliver them to the security section by 1700 hours, 18 May. (The subject [*you*] is understood.)

The same thing can be done with subjects or predicates:

Poor: Horror stories shown on television appear to contribute to juvenile delinquency. Comic books with their horror stories seem to have the same effect. Even the reports of criminal activities which appear in our newspapers seem to contribute to juvenile delinquency.

Improved: Television, comic books, and newspapers seem to contribute to juvenile delinquency by emphasizing stories of horror and crime.

There is one more thing we can do to make our sentences better. We can vary their length and complexity. The following paragraphs suggest ways to do this.

5. *Vary Your Sentence Patterns.*

We should, as a general rule, write predominantly short sentences. Similarly, we should keep our sentences simple enough for our readers to understand them easily and quickly.

But most people soon get tired of nothing but simple, straightforward sentences. So, give your reader an occasional change of pace. Vary both the length and the construction of your sentences.

VARY SENTENCE LENGTH

Some writers use nothing but short, choppy sentences ("The road ended in a wrecked village. The lines were up beyond. There was much artillery around.") In the hands of a Hemingway, from whom this example is taken, short sentences can give an effect of purity and simplicity; in the hands of a less skillful writer, choppy sentences are usually only monotonous.

The other extreme, of course, is just as bad. The writer who always writes heavy sentences of 20 to 30 words soon loses the reader. Some great writers use long sentences effectively, but most writers do not.

The readability experts suggest that, for the most effective *communication*, a sentence should rarely exceed 20 words. Their suggestion is a good rule of thumb, but sentence length should vary. And an occasional long sentence is not hard to read if it is followed by shorter ones. A fair goal for most letter-writers is an average of 21 words per sentence, or less. For longer types of writing, such as regulations and manuals, sentences should average 15 words or less. The sentences in opening paragraphs and in short letters may run a little longer than the average.

VARY SENTENCE CONSTRUCTION

Just as important as varied sentence length is variety of construction. Four common sentence categories are simple, compound, complex, and compound-complex.

A *simple sentence* consists of only one main (independent) clause:

Rain came down in torrents.
Rain and hail started falling. (Simple sentence with compound subject)
The storm began and soon grew in intensity. (Simple sentence with compound predicate)

A *compound sentence* has two or more main clauses:

Rain started falling, and all work stopped.
The storm began; all work stopped.

The storm began, the workers found shelter, and all work stopped.

A *complex sentence* has one main clause and at least one subordinate (dependent) clause. (Subordinate clauses are underlined in the following sentences.)

They were just starting their work <u>when the rain started</u>.
<u>Before they had made any progress</u>, the rain started falling.
The storm, <u>which grew rapidly in intensity</u>, stopped all work.

A *compound-complex sentence* has two or more main clauses and at least one subordinate clause. (Subordinate clauses are underlined in the following sentences.)

Rain started falling, and all work stopped <u>before they had made any progress</u>.
<u>Although the workers were eager to finish the job</u>, the storm forced them to stop, and they quickly found shelter.
They had made some progress <u>before the storm began</u>, but, <u>when it started</u>, all work stopped.

The names of the categories are really not important except to remind you to vary your sentence construction when you write. But remember that sentence variety is not just a mechanical chore to perform after your draft is complete. Good sentence variety comes naturally as the result of proper coordination and subordination when you write.
For example, if two or more short sentences have the same subject, combine them into one simple sentence with a compound verb.

The men were hot. They were tired, too. They were also angry.
The men were hot and tired and angry.

If you have two ideas of equal weight or parallel thought, write them as two clauses in a compound sentence.

The day was hot and humid. The men had worked hard.
The men had worked hard, and the day was hot and humid.
The day was hot and humid, but the men had worked hard.

If one idea is more important than others, put it in the main clause of a complex sentence:

Poor: The men were tired, and they had worked hard, and the day was hot.

Better: The men were tired because they had worked hard on a hot day.
                                or
Although the day was hot and the men were tired, they worked hard.

If the adverbial modifier is the least important part of a complex sentence, put it first and keep the end position for the more important main clause:

Instead of: The men finished the job in record time, even though the day was hot and humid and they were tired.

Better: Even though the day was hot and humid and the men were tired, they finished the job in record time.

But be careful about having long, involved subordinate clauses come before the main clause. The reader may get lost or confused before getting to your main point or give up before getting to it. Also beware of letting too many modifying words, phrases, or clauses come between the subject and the verb. This is torture for the reader. The subject and the verb are usually the most important elements of a sentence; keep them close together whenever possible.

Other Types of Questions on the SAT Writing Test

Following are some directions with samples of some of the other question types on the SAT Writing Test. Following the questions are explanatory answers with comments for all the wrong answers. Pay attention to the explanation in the answer that you got wrong.

Improving Sentences

The following sentences test correctness and effectiveness of expression. Part of each sentence or the entire sentence is underlined; beneath each sentence are five ways of phrasing the underlined material. Choice A repeats the original phrasing; the other four choices are different. If you think the original phrasing produces a better sentence than any of the alternatives, select choice A; if not, select one of the other choices.

In making your selection, follow the requirements of standard written English; that is, pay attention to grammar, choice of words, sentence construction, and punctuation. Your selection should result in the most effective sentence—clear and precise, without awkwardness or ambiguity.

EXAMPLE:

Laura Ingalls Wilder published her first book <u>and she was sixty-five years old then</u>.

(A) and she was sixty-five years old then
(B) when she was sixty-five
(C) at age sixty-five years old
(D) upon the reaching of sixty-five years
(E) at the time when she was sixty-five

Sample Questions with Answers

1. In 1926 historian Carter G. Woodson proposed that the achievements of African Americans <u>being celebrated every February, the month when</u> both Frederick Douglass and President Abraham Lincoln were born.

    (A) being celebrated every February, the month when
    (B) be celebrated every February, the month in which

    (C) ought to be celebrated every February for when
    (D) should be celebrated in every February when
    (E) have a February celebration, which is the month

2. <u>Seeking both protection from predators and opportunities to hunt cooperatively</u>, many fish congregate in schools.

   (A) Seeking both protection from predators and opportunities to hunt cooperatively,
   (B) Seeking protection from predators and to hunt with cooperation;
   (C) Protection from predators and opportunities to hunt cooperatively are sought by
   (D) To seek protection from predators and cooperative hunting opportunities is why
   (E) While seeking both protection from predators and opportunities to hunt, then

3. <u>Crickets produce their characteristic chirp</u> by scraping its right forewing across a series of ridges on its left forewing.

   (A) Crickets produce their characteristic chirp
   (B) A cricket produces their characteristic chirp
   (C) The characteristic chirp of crickets are produced
   (D) The cricket's characteristic chirp, produced
   (E) The cricket produces its characteristic chirp

4. Clara Barton, who founded the American Red Cross, <u>and became the first woman to be paid a salary equal to that of a man</u> by the United States government.

   (A) and became the first woman to be paid a salary equal to that of a man
   (B) became the first woman to be paid a salary equal to that paid a man
   (C) became the first woman receiving equal pay with a man
   (D) would become the first woman who was paid equal to a man
   (E) and would become the first woman paid equal to a man

5. <u>Since he is hungry and having no money</u>, Jean Valjean steals a loaf of bread early in Victor Hugo's novel.

   (A) Since he is hungry and having no money
   (B) Hungry and with the lack of money
   (C) Being hungry and he has no money
   (D) Because he is hungry and has no money
   (E) Motivated by being hungry and no money

6. Increasingly aware of the mosquito's role in transmitting certain <u>diseases, and fearing of an epidemic</u>, the mayor finally decided to drain the town pond.

   (A) diseases, and fearing of an epidemic
   (B) diseases and because of being fearful about an epidemic
   (C) diseases and fearful of an epidemic
   (D) diseases, while fearing an epidemic
   (E) diseases, the fear of an epidemic

7. <u>By failing to resolve the city's fiscal crisis is why</u> the mayor lost his bid for reelection.

   (A) By failing to resolve the city's fiscal crisis is why
   (B) Because he failed to resolve the city's fiscal crisis,
   (C) Due to his failure at resolving the city's fiscal crisis,
   (D) He failed to resolve the city's fiscal crisis is the reason that
   (E) His failure to resolve the city's fiscal crisis resulted in that

8. <u>The prices of either of the cars seem to be well worth it.</u>

   (A) The prices of either of the cars seem to be well worth it.
   (B) The price of either of the cars seems to be well worth it.
   (C) Either of the cars seems to be well worth its price.
   (D) Either of the cars seems to be well worth their prices.
   (E) Either of the cars seem to be well worth the price.

Identifying Errors

The following sentences test your ability to recognize grammar and usage errors. Each sentence contains either a single error or no error at all. No sentence contains more than one error. The error, if there is one, is underlined and lettered. If the sentence contains an error, select the one underlined part that must be changed to make the sentence correct. If the sentence is correct, select choice E. In choosing answers, follow the requirements of standard written English.

EXAMPLE:

The other delegates and him immediately accepted the resolution drafted by the
   A   B   C   D
neutral states. No error.
           E

Sample Questions with Answers

9. If one spends much time with children, you should
    A   B
realize that a promise made to a child is a serious
                  C
matter because the child will never forget it.
                       D
No error.
 E

10. Unlike Roman art, which depicted human beings as
             A
naturalistically as possible, the Egyptians depicted
          B   C
them in a deliberately stylized manner. No error.
        D   E

11. Either Caroline or her twin sister Catherine were
  A   B
outdoors shoveling snow for a neighbor yesterday
afternoon and would have seen anyone who passed
          C   D
by. No error.
    E

12. The illuminated manuscripts in the rare-books
collection, all more than five hundred years old,
        A
are the products of a scribal art long since lost.
 B   C   D
No error.
 E

13. In the middle of the eighteenth century, American
surveyors such as George Washington created
      A
maps that were much more accurate than
         B
previous mapmakers because of dramatic improve-
     C   D
ments in surveying techniques. No error.
              E

14. Before he found his current job, Edward had spent
                       A
several miserable years working in a large
commercial bakery where the expression of
outrageously offensive opinions were as common
  B   C
as saying "hello." No error.
  D   E

Improving Paragraphs

> **Directions:** The following passage is an early draft of an essay. Some parts of the passage need to be rewritten.
>
> Read the passage and select the best answers for the questions that follow. Some questions are about particular sentences or parts of sentences and ask you to improve sentence structure or word choice. Other questions ask you to consider organization and development. In choosing answers, follow the requirements of standard written English.

Questions 15–16 refer to the following passage.

¹Have you ever been to a poetry slam? ²I saw the event listed on the schedule of the Downtown Summer Festival, and I decided to go just to satisfy my curiousity. ³Even before sitting down, the decision was to stay only for a few minutes. ⁴I have always loved poetry, but even good poems can sound dull when people read them aloud in a flat, singsong voice.

15. Which of the following sentences is best to insert between sentences 1 and 2?

    (A) Sometimes people who don't like to read poetry find out that they enjoy listening to it when it is read aloud.
    (B) The first one I attended was in my own hometown.
    (C) People from all around the state come to the Downtown Summer Festival.
    (D) Students, in particular, are attracted to poetry readings.
    (E) The range of events offered this year at the Downtown Summer Festival was more impressive than ever.

16. Which of the following revisions is most needed in sentence 3 (reproduced below)?

    Even before sitting down, the decision was to stay only for a few minutes.

    (A) Delete "down."
    (B) Insert "Furthermore" at the beginning.
    (C) Change "only" to "merely."
    (D) Change "the decision was" to "I had decided."
    (E) Insert "at the poetry slam" after "stay."

Explanatory Answers with Comments for All Wrong Answers

Improving Sentences

1.

(A) You propose that something be done. That it <u>be</u> celebrated, not <u>being</u> celebrated.

(B) This is correct. You propose that something be done. That it <u>be</u> celebrated, not <u>being</u> celebrated.

(C) The word "ought" changes the tone and meaning of the sentence by weakening the proposal.

(D) "Should be" is not as direct as "be" and changes the meaning of the sentence.

(E) This is too roundabout—should be "be celebrated."

2.

(A) This is correct.

(B) The parts of the sentence do not connect properly. "Seeking…to hunt." Also, the semicolon is incorrect here.

(C) "…are sought by many fish congregate in schools." Does not make sense.

(D) "To seek…is why" is awkward.

(E) This is not an "if" and "then" type sentence. The word "then" does not connect properly with "while."

3.

(A) "Crickets [they] produce by scraping <u>their</u>…" <u>They</u> has to tie in with <u>their</u>.

(B) A cricket produces <u>its</u> characteristic chirp, not <u>their</u> characteristic chirp, since <u>cricket</u> is singular.

(C) "The characteristic chirp of crickets <u>is</u> produced…," not <u>are</u> produced since <u>chirp</u> is singular.

(D) "The cricket's characteristic chirp <u>is</u> produced…" The word "is" must be included.

(E) This is correct. "The cricket produces its characteristic chirp by scraping its…" "Its" is singular.

4.

(A) The clause "who founded the American Red Cross" can be left out for this grammar evaluation. The sentence would then read: "Clara Barton and became the first woman…" It should read: "Clara Barton became the first woman…" Also, the clause "that of a man" should be "that paid a man."

(B) This is correct. The clause "who founded the American Red Cross" can be left out for this grammar evaluation. The sentence should then read: "Clara Barton became the first woman…" Also, the clause "that of a man" should be "that paid a man."

(C) It should be "became the first woman to receive," not "receiving."

(D) It should read "paid a salary equal to that paid a man."

(E) The "and" is redundant and "paid equal to a man" should be "paid a salary equal to that paid a man."

5.

(A) You say "he is hungry and has no money," not "he is hungry and having no money."

(B) If we leave out the "and with lack of money," this will read: "Hungry, Jean Valjean…" It should read, "Because he is hungry, Jean Valjean…"

(C) You should be able to make two sentences with the word "and." "Being hungry, Jean Valjean…" "He has no money, Jean Valjean…" This second sentence does not make sense. This should read: "Having no money, Jean Valjean…"

(D) This is correct. "Because he is hungry and [because he] has no money…"

(E) This is like having two sentences: "Motivated by being hungry, Jean Valjean…" This is OK, but the second sentence, "No money, Jean Valjean…" should read: "Having no money, Jean Valjean…"

6.

(A) You don't say "fearing an epidemic," you say "fearful of an epidemic."

(B) You don't need the "because of being" part.

(C) This is correct. You say: "fearful of an epidemic."

(D) You don't need "while fearing an epidemic." You can just say "fearful of an epidemic."

(E) The clause "the fear of an epidemic" does not connect with "the mayor finally decided…"

7.

(A) You don't say "By failing…is why…" You say "Because he failed."

(B) This is correct. "because…the mayor…" (cause and effect).

(C) You don't start out with "Due to," you say "Because of."

(D) You don't say "He failed to resolve…is the reason…" You say "His failure to resolve…is the reason that…"

(E) "The <u>mayor's</u> failure to resolve the city's fiscal crisis resulted in the mayor's <u>losing</u> his bid for reelection." In choice E, the word "his" does not necessarily refer to "mayor." You also have to use the word "losing" here.

8.

(A) The clause "of either of the cars" can be taken out to analyze the grammar. Look at the statement: "The prices seem to be well worth it." That doesn't make sense. It's not the prices that are well worth it, it's the cars that are worth the prices. Also, you wouldn't say "the prices of either of the cars," you would say "the price of either of the cars," since you are talking about one or the other car (singular).

(B) The clause "of either of the cars" can be taken out to analyze the grammar. Look at the statement: "The price seems to be well worth it." That doesn't make sense. It's not the price that is well worth it, it's the car that is worth the price.

(C) It's the car that is worth the price, so this choice is correct. "Either" refers to one or the other car, so you are dealing with a singular situation. You would say "Either of the cars [it] seems to be well worth its price." Notice that it's not "the price" but "its price," because you are talking about the price of one or the other car.

(D) "Either" refers to one or the other car, so you are dealing with a singular situation. So you should say "Either of the cars seems to be well worth its price."

(E) "Either" refers to one or the other car, so you are dealing with a singular situation. You would say "Either of the cars [it] seems to be well worth its price." Notice that it's not "the price" but "its price" because you are talking about the price of one or the other car.

Identifying Errors

9.

(A) Correct. One spends should be you spend to link to "you should realize…"
(B) Much is OK. Did you think it should be more?
(C) Made to is OK. Did you think it should be made for?
(D) Will never is OK. Did you think it should be never will or would never?
(E) No. See A.

10.

(C) Correct. The Egyptians should be Egyptian art, since we are talking about art, not people.
(A) Which depicted is OK. Did you think it should be that depicted or depicted?
(B) As possible is OK.
(D) Deliberately is OK.
(E) No. See C.

11.

(B) Correct. "Either…or" refers to one. So were should be was. (Caroline was, her sister was).
(A) OK.
(C) Would have is OK. Did you think it should be will have or had?
(D) Anyone who is OK. Did you think it should be anyone whom?
(E) No. See B.

12.

(E) No error is correct.
(A) All more than is OK. Did you think it should be more than?
(B) Are is OK. Did you think it should be is?
(C) OK.
(D) OK.

13.

(C) Correct. George Washington created maps that were much more accurate than the maps of previous mapmakers—not the previous mapmakers!
(A) OK.
(B) OK.
(C) OK.
(D) See C.

14.

(C) Correct. The clause "of outrageously offensive opinions" can be left out of the grammar analysis here. So the sentence would read: "…where the expression were as common…" But expression is singular, so it would read: "…the expression…was…"
(A) Had spent is OK. Did you think it should be have spent or spent?
(B) Outrageously is OK. Did you think it should be outrageous? It's "outrageously offensive," not "outrageously opinions." The word outrageously modifies the word offensive, not the word opinions.
(D) Saying is OK. Did you think it should be to say? It is the act of saying, not to say.
(E) No. See C.

Improving Paragraphs

15.

(B) Correct. Look at a connecting sentence that links sentence 1 and sentence 2. It makes sense that after the speaker asks about ever being to a "poetry slam," and before he mentions that he saw the event listed in his hometown, that the second sentence would be related to the first time he has been to one.
(A) This doesn't link to sentence 2.
(C) This doesn't make sense after sentence 1.
(D) This doesn't link to sentence 2.
(E) This doesn't make sense after sentence 1.

16.

(D) Correct. Since the speaker is always talking in first person, he would not use the language "the decision." He would keep it consistent and say "I had decided."
(A) This is not a necessary change.
(B) This is not a necessary change.
(C) This is not a necessary change.
(E) This is not a necessary change.

Additional Questions

Following are some directions and samples of some of the other question types on the SAT Writing Test.

Improving Sentences

Directions: The following sentences test correctness and effectiveness of expression. In choosing answers, follow the requirements of standard written English; that is, pay attention to grammar, choice of words, sentence construction, and punctuation.

In each of the following sentences, part of the sentence or the entire sentence is underlined. Beneath each sentence you will find five ways of phrasing the underlined part. Choice A repeats the original; the other four are different.

Choose the answer that best expresses the meaning of the original sentence. If you think the original is better than any of the alternatives, choose it; otherwise choose one of the others. Your choice should produce the most effective sentence—clear and precise, without awkwardness or ambiguity.

EXAMPLE:

Laura Ingalls Wilder published her first book
and she was sixty-five years old then.

(A) and she was sixty-five years old then
(B) when she was sixty-five
(C) being age sixty-five years old
(D) upon the reaching of sixty-five years
(E) at the time when she was sixty-five

SAMPLE ANSWER

Sample Questions with Answers

1. Such of his novels as was humorous were successful.

    (A) Such of his novels as was humorous were successful.
    (B) Such of his novels as were humorous were successful.
    (C) His novels such as were humorous were successful.
    (D) His novels were successful and humorous.
    (E) Novels such as his humorous ones were successful.

2. Being that the plane was grounded, we stayed over until the next morning so that we could get the first flight out.

    (A) Being that the plane was grounded, we stayed over
    (B) In view of the fact that the plane was grounded, we stayed over
    (C) Since the plane was grounded, we stayed over
    (D) Because the plane was grounded, we stood over
    (E) On account of the plane being grounded, we stayed over

3. <u>He never has and he never will</u> keep his word.

    (A) He never has and he never will
    (B) He has never yet and never will
    (C) He has not ever and he will not
    (D) He never has or will
    (E) He never has kept and he never will

4. The teacher <u>felt badly because she had scolded the bright child</u> who was restless for want of something to do.

    (A) felt badly because she had scolded the bright child
    (B) felt badly why she had scolded the bright child
    (C) felt bad because she had scolded the bright child
    (D) felt bad by scolding the bright child
    (E) had felt badly because she scolded the bright child

5. This book <u>does not describe the struggle of the blacks to win their voting rights that I bought</u>.

    (A) does not describe the struggle of the blacks to win their voting rights that I bought
    (B) does not describe the black struggle to win their voting rights that I bought
    (C) does not, although I bought it, describe the struggle of the blacks to win their voting rights
    (D) which I bought does not describe the struggle to win for blacks their voting rights
    (E) that I bought does not describe the struggle of the blacks to win their voting rights

6. <u>Barbara cannot help but think</u> that she will win a college scholarship.

    (A) Barbara cannot help but think
    (B) Barbara cannot help but to think
    (C) Barbara cannot help not to think
    (D) Barbara can help but think
    (E) Barbara cannot but help thinking

7. In spite of <u>Tom wanting to study</u>, his sister made him wash the dishes.

    (A) Tom wanting to study
    (B) the fact that Tom wanted to study
    (C) Tom's need to study
    (D) Tom's wanting to study
    (E) Tom studying

8. The old sea captain <u>told my wife and me</u> many interesting yarns about his many voyages.

    (A) my wife and me
    (B) me and my wife
    (C) my wife and I
    (D) I and my wife
    (E) my wife along with me

9. A great many students from several universities <u>are planning to, if the weather is favorable, attend next Saturday's mass rally in Washington</u>.

    (A) are planning to, if the weather is favorable, attend next Saturday's mass rally in Washington
    (B) are planning, if the weather is favorable, to attend next Saturday's mass rally in Washington
    (C) are planning to attend, if the weather is favorable, next Saturday's mass rally in Washington
    (D) are planning to attend next Saturday's mass rally in Washington, if the weather is favorable
    (E) are, if the weather is favorable, planning to attend next Saturday's mass rally in Washington

10. Jane's body movements are <u>like those of a dancer</u>.

    (A) like those of a dancer
    (B) the same as a dancer
    (C) like a dancer
    (D) a dancer's
    (E) like those of a dancer's

Identifying Errors

Sample Questions with Answers

11. <u>Even before</u> he became the youngest player to win
    A
the Wimbledon men's <u>singles</u> championship, Boris
                  B
Becker <u>had sensed</u> that his life would <u>no longer</u> be
       C   D
the same. <u>No error.</u>
         E

12. If any signer of the Constitution <u>was</u> to return to life
                          A
<u>for a day</u>, his opinion <u>of</u> our amendments <u>would be</u>
  B   C   D
interesting. <u>No error.</u>
           E

13. The dean <u>of the college</u>, together <u>with</u> some other
         A   B
faculty members, <u>are</u> planning a conference for
            C
the purpose of <u>laying</u> down certain regulations.
              D
<u>No error.</u>
  E

14. If one <u>lives</u> in Florida <u>one day</u> and in Iceland the
        A   B
next, he is <u>certain</u> to feel the change in temperature.
  C   D
<u>No error.</u>
  E

15. <u>Now</u> that the stress of examinations and interviews
  A
<u>are</u> over, we can <u>all</u> <u>relax</u> for a while. <u>No error.</u>
  B   C   D   E

16. The industrial <u>trend</u> <u>is</u> in the direction of <u>more</u>
           A B   C
machines and <u>less</u> people. <u>No error.</u>
         D   E

17. The American standard of living <u>is</u> still <u>higher</u>
                     A   B
<u>than most</u> of the <u>other countries</u> of the world.
  C   D
<u>No error.</u>
  E

18. <u>At last,</u> <u>late</u> in the afternoon, a long line of flags and
    A   B

    colored umbrellas <u>were</u> seen moving <u>toward</u> the
                     C   D

    gate of the palace. <u>No error.</u>
                       E

19. <u>Due to</u> the failure of the air-cooling system, many in
    A

    the audience <u>had left</u> the meeting <u>before</u> the principal
              B   C

    speaker <u>arrived</u>. <u>No error.</u>
          D   E

20. Psychologists and psychiatrists <u>will tell</u> us that it is
                            A

    of utmost importance that a <u>disturbed</u> child <u>receive</u>
                        B   C

    professional attention <u>as soon as</u> possible.
                     D

    <u>No error.</u>
      E

21. After we were waiting in line <u>for three hours,</u>
         A   B

    much to our disgust, the tickets had been sold out
                      C

    <u>when</u> we reached the window. <u>No error.</u>
      D   E

22. That angry outburst of <u>Father's</u> last night was so
                   A

    annoying that it resulted in our <u>guests</u> <u>packing up</u>
                         B   C

    and leaving <u>this</u> morning. <u>No error.</u>
           D   E

23. <u>Sharp</u> advances last week in the wholesale price of
    A

    beef <u>is</u> a strong indication of higher meat <u>costs</u> to
       B   C

    come, but so far retail prices continue <u>favorable</u>.
                             D

    <u>No error.</u>
      E

24. An acquaintance with the memoirs of Elizabeth

    Barrett Browning and Robert Browning <u>enable</u> us
                                        A

    to appreciate the <u>depth of influence</u> that two people
                       B

    of talent can have <u>on</u> <u>each other</u>. <u>No error.</u>
                 C   D   E

25. The supervisor <u>was advised</u> to give the assignment
                 A

    to <u>whomever</u> <u>he believed</u> had a strong sense of
          B   C

    responsibility, and the courage <u>of</u> his convictions.
                            D

    <u>No error.</u>
      E

26. If he <u>would have</u> <u>lain</u> quietly as instructed by the
          A   B

    doctor, he <u>might not</u> <u>have had</u> a second heart
             C   D

    attack. <u>No error.</u>
          E

27. The founder and, <u>for many years</u>, the <u>guiding spirit</u>
                    A   B

    of the *Kenyon Review* is John Crowe Ransom, <u>who</u>
                                   C

    you must know <u>as</u> an outstanding American critic.
                D

    <u>No error.</u>
      E

28. <u>Though</u> you may not <u>agree with</u> the philosophy of
    A   B

    Malcolm X, you must admit that he <u>had</u> tremendous
                          C

    influence <u>over</u> a great many followers. <u>No error.</u>
           D   E

29. There is no objection to <u>him</u> joining the party
                             A
<u>provided</u> he is willing to <u>fit in with</u> the plans of the
    B   C
group and is <u>ready and</u> able to do his share of the
                  D
work. <u>No error</u>.
       E

30. <u>Ceremonies</u> <u>were opened</u> by a drum and bugle
    A   B
corps of Chinese children parading <u>up</u> Mott Street
                                    C
<u>in colorful uniforms</u>. <u>No error</u>.
          D   E

31. The reason <u>most</u> Americans <u>don't</u> pay much atten-
               A   B
tion to <u>rising</u> African nationalism is <u>because</u> they
        C   D
really do not know modern Africa. <u>No error</u>.
                                   E

32. There <u>remains</u> many reasons for the <u>animosity</u> that
          A   B
<u>exists</u> <u>between</u> the Arab countries and Israel.
C   D
<u>No error</u>.
E

33. The Federal Aviation Administration <u>ordered</u> an
                                        A
emergency inspection <u>of several</u> Pan American
                     B
planes <u>on account of</u> a Pan American Boeing 707
       C
<u>had crashed</u> on Bali, in Indonesia. <u>No error</u>.
D   E

34. A gang <u>of armed thieves</u>, directed by a young
           A
woman, <u>has raided</u> the mansion of a <u>gold-mining</u>
       B   C
millionaire <u>near Dublin</u> late last night. <u>No error</u>.
            D   E

35. I <u>had</u> a male <u>chauvinist pig dream</u> that the women
     A   B
of the world <u>rose up</u> and denounced the <u>women's</u>
             C   D
liberation movement. <u>No error</u>.
                     E

Explanatory Answers

1. Choice B is correct. Choice A is incorrect because the plural verb ("were") is necessary. The reason for the plural verb is that the subject "as" acts as a relative pronoun whose antecedent is the plural noun "novels." Choice B is correct. Choice C is awkward. Choice D changes the meaning of the original sentence—so does Choice E.

2. Choice C is correct. Choice A is incorrect—never start a sentence with "being that." Choice B is too wordy. Choice D is incorrect because we "stayed"—not "stood." Choice E is incorrect because "on account of" may never be used as a subordinate conjunction.

3. Choice E is correct. Avoid improper ellipsis. Choices A, B, C, and D are incorrect for this reason. The word "kept" must be included since the second part of the sentence uses another form of the verb ("keep").

4. Choice C is correct. Choice A is incorrect because the copulative verb "felt" takes a predicate adjective ("bad")—not an adverb ("badly"). Choice B is incorrect for the same reason. Moreover, we don't say "felt bad why." Choice D is incorrect because the verbal phrase "by scolding" is awkward in this context. Choice E is incorrect because of the use of "badly" and because the past perfect form of the verb ("had felt") is wrong in this time sequence.

5. Choice E is correct. Choices A, B, and C are incorrect because the part of the sentence that deals with the buying of the book is in the wrong position. Choice D is incorrect because the meaning of the original sentence has been changed. According to this choice, others besides blacks have been struggling.

6. Choice A is correct. The other choices are unidiomatic.

7. Choice D is correct. Choice A is incorrect because the possessive form of the noun ("Tom's") must be used to modify the gerund ("wanting"). Choice B is too wordy. Choice C changes the meaning of the original sentence. Choice E is incorrect for the same reason that Choice A is incorrect. Also, Choice E changes the meaning of the original sentence.

8. Choice A is correct. Choice B is incorrect because "wife" should precede "me." Choice C is incorrect because the object form "me" (not the nominative form "I") should be used as the indirect object. Choice D is incorrect for the reasons given above for Choices B and C. Choice E is too roundabout.

9. Choice D is correct. Choices A, B, C, and E are incorrect because of the misplacement of the subordinate clause ("if the weather is favorable").

10. Choice A is correct. Choices B and C are incorrect because of improper ellipsis. The words "those of" are necessary in these choices. Choice D is incorrect because the "body movements" are not "a dancer's." The possessive use of "dancer's" is incorrect in Choice E.

11. Choice E is correct. All underlined parts are correct.

12. Choice A is correct. "If any signer of the Constitution *were* to return to life…" The verb in the "if clause" of a present contrary-to-fact conditional statement must have a past subjunctive form (*were*).

13. Choice C is correct. "The dean of the college… *is* planning…" The subject of the sentence (*dean*) is singular. Therefore, the verb must be singular (*is planning*).

14. Choice E is correct. All underlined parts are correct.

15. Choice B is correct. "Now that the stress…*is* over…" The subject of the subordinate clause is singular (*stress*). Accordingly, the verb of the clause must be singular (*is*—not *are*). Incidentally, *examinations* and *interviews* are not subjects—they are objects of the preposition *of*.

16. Choice D is correct. "…of more machines and *fewer* people." We use *fewer* for persons and things that may be counted. We use *less* for bulk or mass.

17. Choice C or D is correct. "…than *that of most* of the other countries of the world." We must have parallelism so that the word *standard* in the main clause of the sentence acts as an antecedent for the pronoun *that* in the subordinate clause. As the original sentence reads, the American standard of living is still higher than the countries themselves. You could also have said, "The American Standard of living is still higher than most of the other countries' standard of living of the world," making Choice D also correct.

18. Choice C is correct. "…a long line of flags…*was* seen…" The subject of the sentence is singular (*line*). Therefore, the verb must be singular (*was seen*).

19. Choice A is correct. "*Because of* the failure…" Never start a sentence with *Due to*.

20. Choice E is correct. All underlined parts are correct.

21. Choice C is correct. "After we were waiting in line for three hours, the tickets had, *much to our disgust*, been sold out when we reached the window." Avoid squinting constructions—that is, modifiers that are so placed that the reader cannot tell whether they are modifying the words immediately preceding the construction or the words immediately following the construction. As the sentence initially reads, we don't know whether *much to our disgust* modifies *after we were waiting in line for three hours* or *the tickets had been sold out when we reached the window.*

22. Choice B is correct. "...resulted in our *guests'* packing up..." A noun or pronoun immediately preceding a gerund is in the possessive case. Note that the noun *guests* followed by an apostrophe is possessive.

23. Choice B is correct. "Sharp advances...*are*..." Since the subject of the sentence is plural (*advances*), the verb must be plural (*are*).

24. Choice A is correct. "An acquaintance with the memoirs...*enables* us..." Since the subject of the sentence is singular (*acquaintance*), the verb must be singular (*enables*).

25. Choice B is correct. "...to *whoever*...had a strong sense..." The subject of the subordinate clause is *whoever*, and it takes a nominative form (*whoever*—not *whomever*) since it is a subject. Incidentally, the expression *he believed* is parenthetical, so it has no grammatical relationship with the rest of the sentence.

26. Choice A is correct. "If he *had lain*..." The verb in the "if clause" of a past contrary-to-fact conditional statement must take the *had lain* form—not the *would have lain* form.

27. Choice C is correct. "...John Crowe Ransom, *whom* you must know as an outstanding American critic." The direct object of the subordinate clause—or of any clause or sentence—must be in the objective case and, accordingly, must take the objective form (*whom*—not *who*).

28. Choice E is correct. All underlined parts are correct.

29. Choice A is correct. "There is no objection to *his* joining..." We have here a pronoun that is acting as the subject of the gerund *joining*. As a subject of the gerund, the pronoun must be in the possessive case (*his*).

30. Choice D is correct. "...of Chinese children parading *in colorful uniforms* up Mott Street." In the original sentence, *in colorful uniforms* was a misplaced modifier.

31. Choice D is correct. "The reason...is *that*..." We must say *the reason is that*—not *the reason is because.*

32. Choice A is correct. "There *remain* many reasons..." The word "There" in this sentence is an expletive or introductory adverb. The subject of the sentence ("reasons") must agree with the verb ("remain") in number.

33. Choice C is correct. "...*because* a Pan American Boeing 707 had crashed..." The word group *on account of* has the function of a preposition. We need a subordinate conjunction (*because*) here in order to introduce the clause.

34. Choice B is correct. "...*raided* the mansion..." The past tense (*raided*)—not the present perfect tense (*has raided*)—is necessary because the sentence has a specific past time reference (*last night*).

35. Choice E is correct. All underlined parts are correct.

Improving Paragraphs
Revision-in-Context
Passage with Questions

One part of the Writing Test is the Improving Paragraphs section. This is by far the most difficult part of the Writing Test, and thus the reason I am including extensive instructional and practice material. Here are typical directions to that item-type on the test:

Directions: The following passage is an early draft of an essay. Some parts of the passage need to be rewritten. Read the passage and select the best answers for the questions that follow. Some questions are about particular sentences or parts of sentences and ask you to improve sentence structure and word choice. Other questions refer to parts of the essay or the entire essay and ask you to consider organization and development. In making your decisions, follow the conventions of standard written English.

Now in the passage you are given, the weaknesses in the passage may apply to the classifications listed below:

1. **Sentence Order.** The selection of the best order for the sentences in the passage.

2. **Diction.** The use of an appropriate word or words to express the meaning intended in a sentence, or to be consistent with the style of the passage.

3. **Sentence Relationship.** The use of a transitional word or words to establish the relationship between sentences.

4. **Irrelevancy.** A statement or part of a statement which is not related to the rest of the passage.

5. **Economy.** The combining of ideas by fusing two sentences into one. Also, the elimination of unnecessary words.

6. **Clarity.** The reconstruction of a sentence or the addition of an idea to make the sentence or the passage perfectly clear.

7. **Paragraphing.** The division of the passage into the logical number of paragraphs.

Sentence Order

In order to bake a cake, a cook must take a certain number of steps in a certain order. To rearrange the order in which these steps are taken would be disastrous. No one would consider baking the ingredients before mixing them or buttering the pan.

Like baking a cake, writing a paragraph demands a certain kind of logic. The sentences must be arranged in an order which makes sense. When one writes a paragraph or a short selection, he must do so in an orderly manner. The sentences must appeal in the right order. They must fit together properly so that the whole passage is easy to understand and agreeable to read.

In the passages, your job will be to recognize when the order of a sentence in a passage is illogical. If your attention is directed to a particular sentence, determine whether that sentence logically follows the sentence that precedes it and logically leads into the sentence that follows it.

To answer a *sentence order* question correctly, you should be aware of certain clues:

1. The opening sentence should introduce the main idea of the passage or grab the reader's attention.

2. The closing sentence should sum up the information presented in the passage, draw a conclusion, or present the final step in a logically developed process.

3. Two sentences that are closely connected in meaning or closely related in some other way should be placed one after the other.

The following passage will illustrate the way in which poor sentence order can be recognized and corrected.

---

[1]John Joseph Haley, who played the Tin Man in the film version of *The Wizard of Oz*, began charming audiences as a 6-year-old singer in a church festival in Boston, where he was born in 1899. [2]He began in professional show business as a song-plugger in Philadelphia, then turned to song—comedy routines in vaudeville. [3]After graduating from high school, the youth bowed to his parents' wishes and began learning to be an electrician. [4]After saving up some of his earnings as an apprentice electrician, he ran away from home. [5]Moving to New York in the '20's, he finally began getting Broadway roles. [6]In the year s that followed, Mr. Haley's bright blue eyes, his wavy hair, and his inexhaustible good humor made him sought after to fill some of the many light comic roles provided by the bountiful crops of musical comedies that Broadway produced.

QUESTION

Sentence 2 should be

(A) left where it is
(B) moved to precede sentence 1
(C) moved to follow sentence 3
(D) moved to follow sentence 4
(E) omitted from the passage

ANSWER

This passage, we should note as we read it, is organized on the principle of a chronology—that is, steps in time. The facts are presented in the order in which they occurred. The question directs our attention to sentence 2. Choice A suggests that sentence 2 is in the correct order as it stands. To check, reread sentence 1, then sentence 2, then sentence 3. Is this the logical order in which these sentences should be presented? No. Sentence 1 introduces the actor, his birth date, and his earliest experience as a performer. Sentence 2 jumps ahead to Mr. Haley's professional acting career in Philadelphia, while sentence 3 returns to his earlier days as a high school student. Such jumping around is not appropriate in a passage using a chronological time sequence. Accordingly, Choice A is incorrect.

Choice B suggests we move sentence 2 to precede sentence 1. We need not reread the sentences to check this. Sentence 1 begins the passage with the actor's earliest days and no sentence dealing with his later days should precede it. Choice B is incorrect and so we consider Choice C. Choice C would move sentence 2 to follow sentence 3. To check, we read sentence 3, then sentence 2, then sentence 4. Sentences 3 and 4 are closely related sentences, discussing Mr. Haley's early training after high school and his decision to leave Boston. These sentences should not be separated by sentence 2, which discusses a later event in Philadelphia. Having read sentence 4, we have already begun to check Choice D. The young man ran away from home. We are now ready for a sentence that shifts location. Reading sentence 4, then sentence 2, then sentence 5, we finally find the logical place for sentence

2. In chronological order, Mr. Haley ran away from home, began working as a performer in Philadelphia, then moved to New York and Broadway. Choice D is, therefore, the correct choice. Choice E, suggesting sentence 2 be omitted, is not correct as it would eliminate an important phase in Mr. Haley's life and career.

Diction

Diction refers to the choice of words—their exact meanings, their overtones, their force.

A writer should, first and foremost, know the precise meanings of the words he uses. He should make every effort to use the best possible word in order to convey exactly what he wants to express. There are sometimes many words available from which a writer may choose that one word which best conveys the meaning he wishes to express.

In selecting the right word, a writer should take into account the intended tone of his writing. There are basically three tones a writer may use: a *formal* tone, a *semi-formal* tone, and an *informal* tone. A writer uses a formal tone when, for example, he is writing about a technical matter. Textbooks, legal documents, and instruction manuals are ordinarily written in a formal tone. The vocabulary tends to be formal or technical in nature. A semi-formal tone is used when a writer wants to express an idea in a way that will interest the average reader. The vocabulary will be less technical; certain informal or conversational expressions may be used occasionally. A writer uses an informal tone when his style is conversational throughout—when he writes as if he is talking to the reader. Colloquial expressions—and sometimes slang—are appropriate in an informally written passage.

In a passage, you should be aware of the tone in which the passage is written. Diction problems commonly arise when the writer is inconsistent, using words that are inappropriate to the overall tone of the passage.

Another type of diction problem occurs when a writer selects a word that does not accurately convey his intended meaning. You can judge the intended meaning from the context of a sentence or from the entire passage.

A third type of diction error may be the unintended use of an ungrammatical word or expression. Such nonstandard forms as "The boy *couldn't hardly* see in the fog," or "The teacher should *of knowed* I would be late to class" are hardly ever appropriate in conversation or writing.

Below you will find a passage, followed by a question which directs your attention to a diction problem in a sentence.

---

[1]In theory, bail is designed to ensure the presence of the defendant in court. [2]But a seemingly low bail—say $1000—for a person with fifty cents in his pocket is the same thing as preventive detention. [3]And although judges will deny in public that they do so, many admit in private that the real reason they set high bail is a deep feeling that the suspect is dangerous and guilty of a crime. [4]The alternative to bail is the clink. [5]It ensures that a defendant cannot flee the jurisdiction, tamper with the evidence, or threaten witnesses.

QUESTION

In sentence 4, the clink should be

(A) left as it is
(B) the slammer
(C) entombment
(D) captivity
(E) incarceration

To answer a diction question like the one above, you are advised to use the substitution method. After having judged the general tone of the passage, substitute the possibly wrong word or expression given in the stem (beginning) of the question with the word or expression given in the choices.

ANSWER

In the question given, our attention is directed to the expression <u>the clink</u>. Is <u>the clink</u> appropriate here? No. We are not dealing with a conversational passage so a slang expression is not appropriate. Therefore, Choice A is incorrect. Accordingly, Choice B (<u>the slammer</u>) is also incorrect since the expression is also slang.

Consider Choice C. The word <u>entombment</u> does not provide the meaning needed to replace <u>the clink</u>. Therefore Choice C is incorrect.

Consider Choice D. The word <u>captivity</u> does not provide the meaning needed to replace the <u>clink</u>. Therefore, Choice D is incorrect.

Consider Choice E. The word <u>incarceration</u> is the appropriate replacement for <u>the clink</u>. Therefore, Choice E is correct.

Sentence Relationship

When a writer makes use of a number of different thoughts to illustrate his point in writing, he must be sure to make the relationship between these ideas clear. A good writer should move from one idea to the next, or from one sentence to the next, logically and smoothly. He uses *transitional elements* to achieve *coherence* in his writing.

Transitional elements make the relationship between ideas clear while at the same time they bring ideas together. Special *transitional words* are used to indicate the different types of relationships possible between ideas and sentences. Some examples are listed below.

FOR COMPARING

similarly, likewise, in the same way, in a like manner

FOR CONTRASTING

nevertheless, yet, but, still, however, on the other hand, after all, in spite of, although, on the contrary

FOR GIVING AN EXAMPLE

that is, for example, as a matter of fact, for instance, in fact, specifically, in other words

FOR GIVING A RESULT

consequently, therefore, accordingly, thus, as a result, hence

FOR SHOWING A TIME RELATIONSHIP

afterward, since while, soon, finally, immediately, shortly, meanwhile, until

Transitional elements are quite important in writing. They help us to understand what the writer is leading to. Connecting words and phrases act as signposts on a road. They direct us to our destination. To the traveler; his purpose is to get to a place. To the reader, his purpose is to understand what the writer is trying to convey. If traditional elements are misplaced or poorly placed, they cause the same problem that a misplaced or poorly placed road sign would cause—pointing us in the wrong direction. We, as a consequence, lose our sense of what the writer is try ing to say, of where he is trying to lead us.

In passages, you will have to be able to identify a misplaced or a poorly chosen transitional element. Watch out for such an element , be it a word or phrase which tends to confuse the reader by creating illogical relationships between sentences or within parts of a sentence. The transitional element should be clear and specific to do its job well.

Below you will find an example of a passage which contains a poor sentence relationship. The question following the passage will ask you to correct the error.

---

[1]Fine liquor was flowing in a foreign Embassy—down the drain. [2]Recently, the embassy dumped $22,000 worth of brand-name liquor found in its basement. [3]Under the embassy's last ambassador, the embassy entertained lavishly. [4]But the new government is strict and forbids drinking or selling liquor, so it directed the embassy to get rid of its stock. [5]Local dealers refused to buy the liquor back because the sales had been made more than three months before. [6]Next the embassy simply had eight to ten of its people methodically attack a huge stack of liquor cases. [7]They uncapped each bottle and poured its contents into a sewer.

QUESTION

Sentence 6 should begin

(A) the way it begins now
(B) with Afterward
(C) with Presently
(D) with Finally
(E) with Consequently

ANSWER

Consider Choice A. Next introduces sentence 6. Next is a transitional element which merely indicates a shift in time. First one thing happens. Next something else happens. The word Next is not a logical connective after sentence 5. Therefore, Choice A is wrong.

An appropriate transitional element would be one which indicated that sentence 6 was the result of or the consequence of sentence 5. Test the other choices by substituting a better connective for Next. Of the four choices remaining, only Choice E suggests an opening word which conveys not only a shift in time, but also a cause and effect relationship. Choice E, beginning sentence 6 with Consequently, is therefore the correct choice.

Irrelevancy

Every time a person writes, he has a reason for writing. This reason may be to inform, entertain, or persuade the reader. The point that the author wants to make should be made clearly. To do this, he must stick to his point: Only sentences that are necessary to express an idea exactly belong in the passage. All other sentences are irrelevant; they should be omitted.

In the Improving Paragraphs section of the test, a question may direct your attention to a particular sentence in the passage. When you reread that sentence, test it for relevancy. Ask yourself, "Does this sentence belong in this passage? Does it add to the information offered in the passage or does it distract my attention from the point being made? Is the sentence relevant or irrelevant?"

Here is an example of a passage followed by one question:

---

[1]On May 6, 1954, Roger Bannister, an English medical student, became the first person to run a mile in under 4 minutes. [2]It was one of history's great sports achievements. [3]To some people of that era, breaking the 4-minute record for the mile was one of humanity's great feats. [4]Many people in the United States have taken up running, just for fun and recreation.

QUESTION

What should be done with sentence 4?

(A) It should be left where it is.
(B) It should be moved to follow sentence 1.
(C) It should be moved to follow sentence 2.
(D) It should precede sentence 1.
(E) It should be omitted.

ANSWER

Consider Choice A. Sentence 4 does not make much sense if it is placed after sentence 3. It is clearly irrelevant after sentence 3. Therefore, Choice A is incorrect.

Consider Choice B. Read sentence 1—then read sentence 4—then read sentence 2. These three sentences obviously do not belong together. Sentence 4 is out of place in this combination—it is an irrelevant sentence. Therefore, Choice B is incorrect.

Consider Choice C. Read sentence 2—then read sentence 4—then read sentence 3. Again, we find that sentence 4 is irrelevant. Therefore, Choice C is incorrect.

Consider Choice D. Read sentence 4—then read sentence 1. Once more we find that sentence 4 is irrelevant. Therefore, Choice D is incorrect.

Consider Choice E which tells us to omit sentence 4. Since we have placed sentence 4 in every possible position in the passage and found it irrelevant in every case, we can conclude that sentence 4 should be omitted from the passage. Therefore, Choice E is correct.

Economy

A writer should include only those words or phrases necessary to make his point clear. He should avoid using words that add nothing to the meaning of his passage. Listed below; you will find examples of different kinds of wordiness, followed by sentences that correct the wordiness.

1. Sometimes, extra words can be replaced by appropriate punctuation.

    Wordy: Swimming and sailing and bicycling and tennis are summer sports.
    Concise: Swimming, sailing, bicycling, and tennis are summer sports.

2. Wordiness can be avoided by combining two sentences into one sentence.

    Wordy: We were hot and tired. We wanted to go home.
    Concise: Hot and tired, we wanted to go home.

Wordiness often stems from the careless or needless repetition of words or ideas. Such repetition may involve an entire sentence that needlessly repeats an idea already expressed in some other part of the passage. Unless words are used for emphasis or clarity, repetition is to be avoided. A good writer should practice economy with words as all of us practice economy with money.

In the Improving Paragraphs question-type, a passage may include words, phrases, or entire sentences that violate the *economy* of writing. When a question directs you to a certain sentence in the passage and asks you how that sentence would be best written, see whether part or all of that sentence could be omitted without changing the meaning of the passage. If such an omission is possible, you will know that the correct choice is the one which omits the unnecessary words. In this way, you will be correcting the lack of economy in the passage.

In the following passage, you will be given an opportunity to see how *economy* in writing works.

----

[1]They are in their thirties now, many of them married, the fathers of young children. [2]They have been home for ten or eleven years, having slipped back quietly into society without victory parades to welcome them, without brass bands or cheering crowds or even recognition. [3]They are, in many ways, a perplexed and splintered generation. [4]They are a group of men, mostly blue-collar, who have, until recently, buried their experiences of the Vietnam War. [5]What has dominated the mood of Vietnam veterans has been a passion for isolation and anonymity. [6]What Vietnam veterans have felt most has been a desire to be left alone and unrecognized. [7]Only recently have the veterans begun to struggle to organize, to assert themselves, and to come to terms with an experience many of them sought to erase.

QUESTION

Sentence 6 should be

(1) left as it is
(2) moved to follow sentence 1
(3) moved to follow sentence 2
(4) moved to follow sentence 3
(5) omitted

ANSWER

Consider Choice A. Read sentence 5—then read sentence 6—then read sentence 7 (if necessary). Sentence 6 needlessly repeats the information which is already clearly stated in sentence 5. Accordingly, sentence 6 *violates the economy of writing*. Therefore, Choice A is incorrect. Since Choices B, C, and D would require the inclusion of sentence 6 in the passage, we know immediately that Choices B, C, and D are incorrect we must not include sentence 6 in the passage because it violates the economy principle. It follows that Choice E which tells us to omit sentence 6 from the passage is the correct choice.

Clarity

Every sentence in a passage must be clear in its meaning. The writer should allow no doubt about what he wishes to convey in that sentence. Moreover, the entire passage must be clear as a whole to the reader. Lack of clarity in writing may be caused by any of the following weaknesses:

1. **Indefinite antecedent of a pronoun.** Ambiguity arises when the writer does not make clear just what the pronoun refers to.

NOT CLEAR: She took the delicious nuts out of the containers and hid them in the closet.

[Did she hide the nuts or the containers?]

CLEAR: She took the delicious nuts out of the containers and hid the nuts in the closet.

2. **Lack of parallelism.** The same grammatical construction should be used for ideas of equal importance.

NOT CLEAR: Jane helps her mother by cooking and making her own clothes.

[Does Jane cook her own clothes?]

CLEAR: Jane helps her mother by cooking and by making her own clothes.

3. **Incomplete comparison.** If a comparison is not complete, the sentence may have an ambiguous meaning.

NOT CLEAR: Ann loves Tony more than Dick.

[Does Ann love Tony more than Dick loves Tony?

or

Does Ann love Tony more than Ann loves Dick?]

CLEAR: Ann loves Tony more than she loves Dick.

4. **Misplaced modifier.** A modifier should be placed as close as possible to the word it modifies.

Example 1

NOT CLEAR: The restaurant only has fish on Wednesdays.

[Some restaurant! It serves only fish on Wednesdays?

No other food whatsoever on Wednesdays?]

CLEAR: The restaurant has fish only on Wednesdays.

Example 2

NOT CLEAR: Does a man live here with one eye named Smith?

[What's the name of his other eye—Jones?]

CLEAR: Does a one-eyed man named Smith live here?

Example 3

NOT CLEAR: The jeweler sold the watch to that attractive woman with the Swiss movement.

[The jeweler must have given her a bargain.]

CLEAR: The jeweler sold the watch with the Swiss movement to that attractive woman.

5. **Dangling construction.** A phrase or clause should be placed in the right position in order to avoid misunderstanding.

NOT CLEAR: While enjoying lunch, the fire alarm sounded.

[The fire alarm must have been hungry.]

CLEAR: While I was enjoying lunch, the fire alarm sounded.

6. **Omission of necessary words.** A word or phrase that is necessary for the full meaning of a sentence must not be omitted. Sometimes the addition of another sentence may be necessary to make the passage clear.

NOT CLEAR: Winning at Las Vegas is something I never thought would happen.

[Someone must win once in a while at Las Vegas.]

CLEAR: Winning at Las Vegas is something I never thought would happen to me.

7. **Awkwardness.** An awkward sentence stands in the way of clarity.

NOT CLEAR: A higher salary will provide me with a college degree with the money that I will get to take evening courses.

[Confusing!]

CLEAR: A higher salary will provide me with the money to take evening courses so that I can eventually get a college degree.

Now let us consider the following selection in which one of the sentences has a clarity problem.

————————————————

[1]Outbreaks of recent deer killing have angered two Pennsylvania communities. [2]In both incidents, the deer were in captivity. [3]In Norristown, near Philadelphia, a 20-year-old man fatally shot a pregnant doe and a second deer in the Elmwood Park Zoo. [4]In William sport, a

20-year-old man stabbed a deer to death in a display pen. [5]The deer slayers were brought to trial on misdemeanor charges. [6]Each defendant told the judge that he had been drinking.

QUESTION

Sentence 6 should be

(A) left as it is
(B) changed to <u>Appearing before the judge, both defendants said that they had been drinking.</u>
(C) omitted as of no importance
(D) changed to <u>Each defendant told the judge that they had been drinking.</u>
(E) changed to <u>Both defendants told the judge that drinking was what they had been doing.</u>

ANSWER

Choice A is wrong because it lacks clarity. Who was drinking? Each defendant or the judge? Choice B is correct because it makes clear just who had been drinking. Choice C is incorrect because the sentence is quite relevant as it stands. Choice D is incorrect because there should be no switch from the singular subject (<u>Each</u>) of the main clause to the plural subject (<u>they</u>) of the dependent clause. Choice E is incorrect because it is awkward and verbose.

Paragraphing

There are four important characteristics of a paragraph:

1. Every piece of prose of any length is divided into sections called paragraphs.

2. A paragraph may consist of a single sentence, but it usually consists of several sentences.

3. Each paragraph is a **complete unit**—that is, it deals with a particular thing, or idea, or division of the subject.

4. Each paragraph must be **well-arranged**. The sentences must come in the right order and fit together properly, so that the whole paragraph is easy to understand.

Occasionally, a Logic and Organization question may ask you to determine where a passage should be divided into two paragraphs. The four important characteristics of a paragraph listed above should be a helpful guide for you to answer a paragraph-type question correctly.

Following is a passage and then a question which asks you about paragraphing.

------

[1]Stuart Gibbs was a 33-year-old history teacher at the high school in Mathews, Virginia. [2]He asked his 11th-grade students to write reports on Aldous Huxley's *Brave New World.* [3]This is a novel that depicts a world in which people are without traditional moral values. [4]The school administration warned him that he would be fired if he went ahead with this assignment. [5]He ignored the warning. [6]Mr. Gibbs is out of a school job today. [7]He has sued in Federal District Court for reinstatement. [8]The principal of the high school gives no reason for the discharge except that of insubordination. [9]The principal goes on to explain that, under the State of Virginia statute, a supervisor does not have to give a specific reason for discharging a teacher.

QUESTION

If the passage were divided into two paragraphs, the second paragraph would best begin with which of the following?

(A) Sentence 2
(B) Sentence 3
(C) Sentence 6
(D) Sentence 7
(E) Sentence 9

ANSWER

Consider Choice A. Sentence 2 cannot logically be separated from sentence 1. Therefore, Choice A is wrong.

Consider Choice B. Since sentence 3 explains sentence 2, Choice B is wrong.

Consider Choice C. Sentence 6 is a logical place for a new paragraph to start. The reason for this is that there is a definite time change between what has preceded sentence 6 and what begins with sentence 6. Therefore, Choice C is correct.

Consider Choice D. Sentence 7 indicates a direct follow-up of sentence 6: Mr. Gibbs was discharged so he sued. Therefore, Choice D is wrong.

Consider Choice E. The last sentence of the passage—sentence 9—"goes on to explain" what has been said in sentence 8. Therefore, Choice E is wrong.

Improving Paragraphs
Practice Tests

Directions: A paragraph with superscript numerals to indicate the order of each sentence in the paragraph, is presented. You are to answer the questions which follow the paragraph.

Test 1

[1]It would be easier to defend capital punishment if at least it were applied consistently—if the rich or notable went to the chair. [2]But that rarely happens. [3]Drifters, even those who get religion, get fried; former county officials, "filled with remorse," get short terms. [4]One reason is that all its faces are hooded. [5]There is a division of labor and no person or agency—be it prosecutor or jury or judge or governor or state or nation or hangman—need accept responsibility. [6]And from all this diversity of laws, juries, and defendants emerges a pattern of who among guilty murderers is condemned. [7]They are all poor.

1. In sentence 5, <u>be it prosecutor or jury or judge or governor or state or nation or hangman</u> would be best if

    (A) it were left as is
    (B) it were changed to <u>be it prosecutor as well as jury as well as judge as well as governor as well as state as well as nation as well as hangman</u>
    (C) it were changed to <u>be it prosecutor and jury and judge and governor and state and nation and hangman.</u>
    (D) it were changed to <u>be it prosecutor, jury, judge, governor, state, nation or hangman.</u>
    (E) it were omitted

2. "Why is there not more remorse about this system of capital punishment?" Where should this sentence be placed in the passage?

    (A) after sentence 3
    (B) after sentence 4

    (C) after sentence 5
    (D) after sentence 6
    (E) not included in the passage at all

3. In sentence 4, <u>all its faces are hooded</u> means

    (A) if the rich or notable went to the chair
    (B) all this diversity of laws, juries, and defendants
    (C) they are all poor
    (D) that all criminals are anonymous
    (E) that all those involved with passing the death sentence are anonymous

4. To combine sentences 6 and 7, the words <u>condemned. They are all poor</u> should be changed to

    (A) <u>condemned because they are all poor.</u>
    (B) <u>condemned; they are all poor.</u>
    (C) <u>condemned except the poor.</u>
    (D) <u>condemned and they are all poor.</u>
    (E) <u>condemned which is they are all poor.</u>

Explanatory Answers

1. **(D)** The best sentence is one that is as clear as possible, with as few extra words as possible: Left as is, sentence 5 is unnecessarily long with all the <u>or's</u>. Choice A, therefore, is wrong. Choices B and C repeat the same error. Each is unnecessarily long. Choice D is clear and as short as possible so it is correct. The details included in the phrase are too important to omit so Choice E is wrong.

2. **(A)** A question needs an answer. The best answer to this question begins with sentence 4; therefore, Choice A is correct. Choices B, C, and D are wrong. Sentences 5, 6, and 7 are part of the answer but they do not begin the answer and cannot be separated by a question. This question should be included to make clear why <u>one reason</u> (sentence 4) is necessary. Therefore Choice E is wrong.

3. **(E)** <u>Hooded</u> means <u>covered by a hood</u>. A hooded face would be anonymous. The correct choice must refer to this definition of <u>hooded</u>. Choices A, B, and C do not. Choice D names the wrong people as anonymous. Sentence 5 names the right <u>hooded</u> faces. Choice E is correct, as it names the same people that sentence 5 names.

4. **(B)** The subject of sentence 6 is a <u>pattern</u>. The pattern does not emerge because condemned murderers are poor; hence, Choice A is incorrect. Choice B is correct; it sets off and names the <u>pattern</u>. Choice C changes the meaning of the sentence and is, therefore, wrong. Choice D changes the meaning intended: "...a pattern of who among the guilty murderers is condemned—namely, the poor." Choice E is both awkward and ungrammatical.

Test 2

[1]Hypertension, or high blood pressure as it is commonly known, is the "silent killer" that affects the lives of more than tens of millions of Americans each year. [2]A famous doctor, whose work has done much to uncover an understanding of high blood pressure, says that hypertension means that there is too much pressure in the bloodstream. [3]It is like a garden hose with a too-tight nozzle. [4]Either the nozzle or the hose bursts, which is exactly what happen s to blood vessels when the pressure is too great. [5]If it is in the brain, you have a stroke. [6]If the vessel bursts in the heart, you have a heart attack. [7]Preventing these problems is easier than curing them.

1. What should be done with sentence 6?

   (A) It should follow sentence 4
   (B) It should follow sentence 1
   (C) It should be joined to sentence 5 with and
   (D) It should follow sentence 3
   (E) It should remain as it is

2. Sentence 4 should begin

   (A) with Once
   (B) with Eventually
   (C) with Someday
   (D) as it does now
   (E) with Without a doubt

3. Sentence 7 should

   (A) introduce the selection
   (B) remain as it is
   (C) be omitted
   (D) be joined to sentence 2 with and
   (E) follow sentence 1

4. In sentence 2, uncover should be

   (A) changed to accrue
   (B) left as it is
   (C) changed to determine
   (D) changed to pioneer
   (E) changed to refute

Explanatory Answers

1. **(A)** Choice A is correct. Sentence 6, which is closely allied to sentence 5 in meaning and structure, should go before sentence 5 because sentence 6 contains the antecedent idea referred to in sentence 5. Choice B is incorrect because sentence 6 would be out of order so early in the selection. Choices C and E are incorrect because sentence 6 should precede sentence 5, not follow it, even in a compound sentence. Choice D is incorrect because placing sentence 6 after sentence 3 would interrupt the process of logical development from sentence 3 to sentence 4.

2. **(B)** Choice A is incorrect. The conjunction once introduces a dependent clause. The other two clauses, beginning with which and when, are also dependent. Thus there is an incomplete sentence containing three dependent clauses and no main clause. Choice B is correct. Eventually is an appropriate transitional adverb. Choice C is incorrect because the adverbial phrase Some day requires the future tense and thus conflicts with the present tense of the verb bursts. Choice D is incorrect because the sentence requires an introductory word or phrase for smoothness and clarity. Choice E is incorrect because it is an inappropriate expression, which also calls for the future tense.

3. **(C)** Choice A is incorrect because sentence 7 is clearly not an introductory sentence. The phrase these problems refers to ideas expressed in preceding sentences. Choices B, D, and E are incorrect because sentence 7 introduces the new concept of prevention and does not belong in a paragraph which defines high blood pressure. Choice C is correct.

4. **(D)** Choices A, B, C, and E are incorrect because we are looking for a word which means to make fresh inroads or to increase our knowledge. Choice D, pioneer, conveys that meaning. Choice A, accrue, means to gather; Choice B, uncover, means to reveal or find, as a hidden secret ; Choice C, determine, means to make a decision; Choice E, refute, means to deny.

Test 3

[1]Tomorrow will be more than just a routine day for Samuel Byrnes, Jr. [2]He is a 42-year-old inmate serving a 28-to-30 year sentence for armed robbery and a life term for murder at Trenton State Prison in New Jersey. [3]Byrnes will take off his prison garb and don academic cap and gown to receive, at Rutgers University, a master's degree in, yes, criminal justice. [4]Then he'll head back to his cell. [5]He shares a cell with two other inmates. [6]It was after he received his bachelor's degree in criminal science there that he was able to sign up for the Rutgers program five years ago. [7]The convict completed high school in prison, then took college courses until he was able to get officials to trust him enough to let him out to study at Trenton State College.

1. Sentence 5 should

   (A) be placed before sentence 2
   (B) be placed at the end of the passage
   (C) be left as it is
   (D) be omitted
   (E) be placed before sentence 7

2. The word yes in sentence 3 should

   (A) be changed to nevertheless
   (B) be changed to moreover
   (C) be changed to get this
   (D) be left as it is
   (E) be omitted

3. Sentence 6 should

   (A) be placed after sentence 7
   (B) be placed after sentence 2
   (C) be omitted
   (D) be left as it is
   (E) be divided into two sentences with the first sentence ending after there

4. In sentence 7, then should be

   (A) changed to than
   (B) changed to he then
   (C) changed to then again
   (D) omitted
   (E) left as it is

Explanatory Answers

1. **(D)** Choice D is correct: Sentence 5 is irrelevant to the passage which is devoted solely to Byrnes' education while he is a prisoner. Accordingly, Choices A, B, C, and E are incorrect.

2. **(D)** Choices A and B are both grammatically and logically incorrect. Moreover and nevertheless are conjunctive adverbs. When used in the middle of sentences they link two main clauses. In addition, their meanings are not appropriate in this context. Choice C is incorrect. "Get this" is a slang term which, in spite of the fact that it conveys the situation's irony, is not acceptable in standard written English. Choice D is correct. The function of the word yes is (parenthetically) to emphasize the irony of the situation. A criminal's earning an advanced degree is ironic; the fact that the degree is in criminal justice intensifies the irony. Choice E is incorrect because, as discussed above, the word yes serves to emphasize the irony in this sentence.

3. **(A)** Choice A is correct. Sentences 6 and 7 are not in logical order. Byrnes' high school and college education should be mentioned prior to his acceptance in graduate school. In addition, sentence 6 contains the adverb there without an antecedent. By placing sentence 7 before sentence 6, the pronoun would have an antecedent: Trenton State College. Choice B is incorrect: Separating sentence 3 from sentences 1 and 2 would interrupt the flow of the writer's presentation. Choice C is incorrect: Sentence 6 contains important information about Byrnes' education and should not be omitted. Choice D is incorrect because, as explained above, the sentence is not in logical or grammatical order as it is now. Choice E is incorrect. The new second sentence beginning with That would be an incomplete sentence.

4. **(E)** Choice A is incorrect: The word than is used for comparative purposes, and is not appropriate in this context. Choice E is correct : The word then really means after which time and is properly used in the sentence. Choice B is incorrect because it creates a run-on sentence. Choice C is incorrect because Byrnes is not repeating a college course. Choice D is incorrect because it also would create a run-on sentence.

Test 4

[1]Charlie and Josephine were so devoted that they had been inseparable for nearly ten years. [2]Then one midwinter day, in a senseless act of violence so typical of our times, Charlie was fatally shot. [3]Fifteen minutes later, she, too, died. [4]Josephine saw it all and, horror-stricken, sank to her knees beside Charlie's still body, placing her head at the site of his mortal wound, [5]Charlie and Josephine were llamas. [6]They lived at the Lollipop Farm Zoo. [7]Josephine, who had been healthy until Charlie's sudden death, apparently died of a cracked heart, a phenomenon well known in poetry and folklore, but rarely acknowledged by modern medicine.

1. Sentence 4 is best placed

   (A) where it is now
   (B) before sentence 2
   (C) before sentence 3
   (D) after sentence 5
   (E) after sentence 6

2. To combine sentences 5 and 6, llamas. They lived should be changed to

   (A) llamas because they lived
   (B) llamas who lived
   (C) llamas when they lived
   (D) llamas but lived
   (E) llamas since they lived

3. If this passage were divided into two paragraphs, the new paragraph would best begin with which of the following?

   (A) sentence 1
   (B) sentence 2
   (C) sentence 3
   (D) sentence 4
   (E) sentence 5

4. In sentence 7, cracked is best replaced with

   (A) split
   (B) cut
   (C) fractured
   (D) broken
   (E) flawed

Explanatory Answers

1. **(C)** Choices A and B are wrong because they would put Josephine saw it all before anything had happened for her to see. Choice C is correct. Choices D and E are incorrect because they would move sentence 4 which describes Josephine's reaction to Charlie's death, too far away from sentence 2, the description of the senseless act of violence.

2. **(B)** Choices A and E are incorrect because they indicate, incorrectly, that the reason Josephine and Charlie are llamas is they live in a zoo. Choice B is correct since who is the correct subject of the subordinate clause: who lived at the Lollipop Farm Zoo. Choice C is wrong, making the ridiculous statement that the pair were llamas when they lived at the zoo, as if they could be another sort of animal when they lived elsewhere. Choice D is wrong since it indicates with the word but that it is exceptional to find llamas in a zoo.

3. **(E)** Sentences 1, 2, 3, and 4 all describe the circumstances that led to the deaths of the llamas. These sentences should not be separated; accordingly, Choices A, B, C, and D are incorrect. Choice E is correct. A new paragraph would best begin with sentence 5 which switches from the storytelling quality of the opening sentence s to a more factual account.

4. **(D)** The best choice is Choice D which expresses the unhappiness of someone who has lost a beloved. The other four choices, A, B, C, and E, bring to mind a physical break rather than an emotional one.

Test 5

[1]It now appears that pollution seeping into the earth itself has gone largely unnoticed. [2]In some cases it may be dangerous as a direct cause of cancer and other severe illnesses. [3]In recent years a great national concern has arisen over air and water pollution. [4]Each year, several hundred new chemical compounds are added to the 70,000 that already exist in America. [5]The wastes are often toxic from their production. [6]Nearly 92 billion pounds a year of wastes are produced. [7]Many of these wastes are placed in makeshift underground storage sites. [8]Federal officials now suspect that more than 800 such sites have the potential of becoming dangerous.

1. In sentence 1, <u>largely unnoticed</u> should be

   (A) changed to <u>somewhat unnoticed</u>
   (B) changed to <u>completely unnoticed</u>
   (C) changed to <u>dangerously unnoticed</u>
   (D) changed to <u>hardly unnoticed</u>
   (E) left as it is

2. Sentence 3 should be

   (A) placed at the beginning of the passage
   (B) placed at the end of the passage
   (C) placed after sentence 1
   (D) left where it is
   (E) omitted

3. If the passage were to be divided into two paragraphs, the second should begin with

   (A) sentence 5
   (B) sentence 4
   (C) sentence 8
   (D) sentence 6
   (E) sentence 7

4. Sentences 5 and 6 should be combined to read

   (A) The wastes from their production are often toxic, nearly 92 billion pounds a year.
   (B) Nearly 92 billion pounds of toxic waste a year are produced.
   (C) Nearly 92 billion pounds of waste produced a year are toxic.
   (D) The waste, nearly 92 billion pounds a year, are often toxic from their production.
   (E) The wastes from their production, nearly 92 billion pounds a year, are often toxic.

Explanatory Answers

1. **(E)** Choices A, B, C, and D are incorrect because they change the meaning intended. Choice E is correct because the sentence is correct as it stands.

2. **(A)** Choice A is correct: The passage is telling us that air and water pollution <u>has</u> been noticed, but that pollution of the <u>earth itself</u> has <u>not</u> been noticed; therefore the sentence about air and water pollution should be placed <u>before</u> sentences about earth pollution. Choice B is incorrect: It would not make sense to introduce the subject of air and water pollution at the end of the passage. Choice C is incorrect because placing the sentence after sentence 1 would interrupt the discussion of earth pollution; furthermore, the word <u>it</u> in sentence 2 would no longer refer to earth pollution but to air and water pollution. Choice D is wrong because sentence 3 interrupts the passage in its present position, and therefore should not be left where it is. Since the beginning of the passage is the best place for sentence 3, it should not be omitted, and so Choice E is wrong.

3. **(B)** Sentences 4, 5, 6, 7, and 8 are all related. They give information about the wastes that are produced, what is done with these wastes, etc. Sentences 1, 2, and 3 are about air, water, and earth pollution in general. Since sentence 4 begins the specific discussion of earth pollution, it is the logical sentence to begin a second paragraph. Therefore, Choice 2 is correct and all other choices are incorrect.

4. **(E)** Choice A is incorrect because the second phrase (<u>nearly 92 billion pounds a year</u>) is incomplete; also, it is unclear whether 92 billion pounds are produced in total or 92 billion pounds are toxic. Choice B is wrong because it states that 92 billion pounds are toxic, whereas the original sentence 6 states that 92 billion pounds are produced. (This does not mean that <u>all</u> 92 billion pounds are toxic.) Choice C is wrong for the same reason. Choice D is incorrect: The word <u>their</u> refers to <u>The wastes</u>, and so the sentence seems to say that the wastes are toxic from <u>their own</u> production. Choice E is correct: Here the word <u>their</u> refers back to <u>chemical compounds</u> in the previous sentence. Choice E also makes it clear that 92 billion pounds of waste are produced and that these are often toxic.

Test 6

[1]Arthur Ellis has a job few people envy when the spring rains come and the mosquitoes begin to swarm in southern Florida. [2]Five days a week, eight hours a day, Mr. Ellis Rolls up his sleeves and tempts mosquitoes to bite him. [3]His job is counting the pesky insects. [4]If more than 20 alight on his arms, which he holds outstretched, in 60 seconds, it means it is a "hot spot" and the inspector for the County Mosquito Control office puts in an order for a spray plane or truck. [5]Trucks are used in grassy or wooded areas; planes are needed for marsh and swamp regions where the mosquitos are found to be most highly concentrated.

[6]After 15 years as a mosquito scout, the 62-year-old Mr. Ellis says he doesn't mind the bites from the bloodthirsty insects. [7]"The Indians live out here but you never hear them complaining because they've built up a resistance," he says. [8]"I guess I'm like that."

1. Sentence 1 would be more clear if

   (A) a comma were placed after envy
   (B) it read "In southern Florida, Arthur Ellis has a job few people envy when the spring rains come and the mosquitoes begin to swarm."
   (C) a comma were placed after come
   (D) it read "When the spring rains come to southern Florida and the mosquitoes begin to swarm, Arthur Ellis has a job few people envy."
   (E) it read "Arthur Ellis has a job in southern Florida that few people envy when the spring rains come and the mosquitoes begin to swarm."

2. In sentence 4, his arms, which he holds outstretched would be best

   (A) changed to just his arms
   (B) left as it is
   (C) changed to his arms, held outstretched,
   (D) changed to Mr. Ellis's arms, which he holds outstretched
   (E) changed to his outstretched arms

3. What should be done with the rest of sentence 4 (after 60 seconds)?

   (A) The words it means it is a "hot spot" should be left out.
   (B) It should read it means Mr. Ellis has discovered a "hot spot" (etc.)
   (C) It should read Mr. Ellis smells a "hot spot" (etc.)
   (D) There should be a period after "hot spot" and a new sentence should begin with the words the inspector.
   (E) It should be left as it is.

4. What should be done with sentence 5?

   (A) It should be left as it is.
   (B) It should be made into two sentences, the second one beginning with the word planes.
   (C) It should be omitted.
   (D) The order of the two clauses should be reversed.
   (E) It should give more information as to why mosquitoes are more highly concentrated in marshes and swamps.

Explanatory Answers

1. **(D)** Choice A is incorrect: The Sentence as it stands is one complete thought, and placing a comma after envy would separate it into two clauses, the second of which (when the spring rains come and the mosquitoes begin to swarm in southern Florida) would be meaningless. Choice B does not make the sentence more clear because it implies that people do not envy Mr. Ellis's job during the time of the spring rains (which could mean they do envy it at other times). Choice C is incorrect for the same reason as for Choice A: a comma after come would separate the sentence into two incomplete clauses. A comma here would also destroy the important relationship between the spring rains and the mosquitoes. Choice D is correct because it makes it quite clear that (1) the appearance of the mosquitoes coincides with the spring rains, and (2) it is at this time that Mr. Ellis has a job and that few people envy his job. Choice E is wrong for the same reason as Choice B: It implies that people do not envy Mr. Ellis's job during the time of the spring rains, rather than clearly stating that Mr. Ellis has a job during the spring rains.

2. **(E)** As it stands, the sentence uses more words than necessary. Choice A is certainly less wordy but leaves out information that helps the reader to understand how Mr. Ellis performs his job. What is needed is to find a way of including this information in as few words as possible. Therefore choice B, leaving the clause as it is, is incorrect. Choice C is better but still uses more words than necessary. Choice D is wrong. It is not necessary to repeat Mr. Ellis's name because the word his could refer to none other than Mr. Ellis. Choice D

also increases the number of words. Choice E is correct because it gives us the necessary information in one word (<u>outstretched</u>) without interrupting the flow of the sentence.

3. **(B)** As it stands the sentence is unclear because the first <u>it</u> does not refer to any noun previously stated. The information that an area where a certain number of mosquitoes alight on Mr. Ellis is considered to have a high concentration of mosquitoes is important, however, and should not be left out as Choice A suggests. Choice B is correct because instead of the ambiguous <u>it</u> we now have <u>Mr. Ellis has discovered</u>. Choice C is wrong because Mr. Ellis does not "smell" a "hot spot." Choice D does not correct the ambiguous <u>it</u>; furthermore, dividing the clause into two sentences destroys the relationship between the discovery of a "hot spot" and the subsequent order for a spray plane or truck. Choice E is obviously wrong since Choice B so clearly improves the sentence.

4. **(C)** Sentence 5 is irrelevant to the passage, which is about Mr. Ellis's job, not about how the mosquitoes are controlled. Therefore leaving it as it is, as Choice A suggests, is wrong. Choice B is equally wrong: whether one sentence or two, the information is irrelevant here. Choice C is correct: Sentence 5 should be omitted entirely since it is irrelevant. Since the whole sentence should be omitted, Choice D is incorrect. Choice E, giving more information on an aspect which is not central to the theme of the passage, is incorrect.

Test 7

[1]In Kenya, a drive against rhinoceros hunting is being stepped up. [2]Demanding its horns to make knife handles and love potions, the animal faces extinction. [3]The President of Kenya directed the Ministry of Tourism and wildlife and the police to end the killing of the animal. [4]Conservationists have warned that the rhinoceros faces extinction within three years if hunters are not stopped. [5]A subsequent ban on the sale of wildlife trophies and curios has slowed the decrease in the rhino population, but poaching continues. [6]A ban on professional big game hunting, introduced in February in 1978, began the government's effort to protect the animal. [7]Urging international wildlife agencies and other governments to join Kenya in its campaign to save the animal, he said every effort should be made to dry up the market for rhino horn.

1. In sentence 3, the Ministry of Tourism and wildlife and the police should be

   (A) the Ministry of Tourism and Wildlife and the Police
   (B) the Ministry of Tourism and Wildlife and the police
   (C) the ministry of tourism and wildlife and the police
   (D) the Ministry of tourism and wildlife and the police
   (E) the ministry of Tourism and Wildlife and the police

2. What should be done with sentence 7?

   (A) It should be left where it is.
   (B) It should be moved to follow sentence 1.
   (C) It should be moved to follow sentence 2.
   (D) It should be moved to follow sentence 3.
   (E) It should be moved to follow sentence 4.

3. What should be done with sentence 5?

   (A) It should be left as is.

   (B) It should be made into two sentences, the new one beginning with But.
   (C) It should be moved to follow sentence 6.
   (D) It should be omitted
   (E) It should end after population, ommitting but poaching continues.

4. Sentence 2 would be best if it were

   (A) shortened into two sentences, the second beginning after potions
   (B) changed to The animal, demanding its horns to make knife handles and love potions, faces extinction
   (C) changed to The hunters, demanding its horns to make knife handles and love potions, faces extinction
   (D) changed to The animal faces extinction despite demand for its horns to make knife handles and love potions
   (E) changed to The animal faces extinction because of the demand for its horns to make knife handles and love potions

Explanatory Answers

1. **(B)** The Ministry of Tourism and Wildlife is the name of a government agency. All words in the name of a particular organization should be capitalized except articles (a, an, the), and short prepositions (to, in, at, for, etc.). Choice B is correct because it capitalizes Wildlife.

2. **(D)** Choices A, B, and C are incorrect because none of the sentences mentioned in these choices inform the reader who the he, in sentence 7, is. Choice D is correct. Only sentence 3 provides a noun, the President, which can be identified with the pronoun, he. Choice E provides a noun, conservationists, but it names a plural noun which would need to be followed by the pronoun they, not he.

3. **(C)** Choice A is incorrect because if sentence 5 were left as is, subsequent would make no sense. Choice B is wrong. There's no need to make two sentences. Choice C is correct. Sentence 6 provides a detail about the first legal action taken to protect the rhinoceros. Sentences 5 should follow it, describing the second of subsequent legal action taken. Both Choices D and E are wrong because they omit essential details.

4. **(E)** Sentence 2 makes no sense as it is. The animal is not demanding its own horn for anything. Choices A and B are wrong by not correcting this confusion. Choice C states, incorrectly, that the poachers face extinction. Choice D is wrong because the word despite conveys the wrong meaning. The correct choice is Choice E which makes good sense.

Test 8

[1]In the catalog of earth's more curious creatures, few are as wondrous as the kangaroos. [2]Many zoos around the world have kangaroos. [3]Kindly of face and bottom heavy of build; they outclass most of the animal kingdom in the long and high jump, boxing, and karate. [4]Born the size of a large lima bean, they can grow taller than a man. [5]Fully grown males—called boomers—may stand seven feet tall when fully erect and weigh close to two hundred pounds. [6]Loping across the countryside on highly developed hind legs, these superb animals average 12 to 15 miles an hour. [7]While gray kangaroos are excellent high jumpers, red kangaroos take long jump honors. [8]If need arises, they can accelerate to more than twice that speed. [9]I have seen young grays easily clear a six-foot fence and have measured a red kangaroo jump of 20 feet across flat ground.

1. Sentence 2 should

   (A) introduce the paragraph
   (B) be placed after sentence 3
   (C) be placed after sentence 4
   (D) be the concluding sentence of the passage
   (E) be omitted as irrelevant to the passage

2. Sentence 6 should begin with

   (A) Consequently
   (B) It is true that
   (C) Yet
   (D) Kangaroos are often seen
   (E) As a matter of fact

3. In sentence 3, build; they should be changed to

   (A) build, kangaroos in general
   (B) build, they
   (C) build, so that they
   (D) build. They
   (E) build; many of them

4. In sentence 3, outclass should be

   (A) changed to are much more outstanding than
   (B) changed to are superior to
   (C) changed to beat out
   (D) changed to defeat
   (E) left as it is

5. Sentence 7 should

   (A) follow sentence 4
   (B) follow sentence 5
   (C) be left where it is now
   (D) follow sentence 8
   (E) conclude the passage

Explanatory Answers

1. **(E)** Choice E is correct. Sentence 2 is irrelevant and therefore does not belong anywhere in the passage.

2. **(C)** Choice A is incorrect because it conveys the mistaken idea that the information given in sentence 6 is a result of that given in sentence 5. Choices B and E are incorrect because they fail to establish the contrasting relationship between sentences 5 and 6. Choice C is correct because it provides transition that shows that even though kangaroos are large (sentence 5), they can still run fast (sentence 6). Choice D is incorrect because it creates a run-on sentence.

3. **(B)** Choice A is grammatically correct, but unnecessarily wordy. Choice B is correct because it results in a concise, clear sentence. Choices C, D, and E are incorrect because kindly of face and bottom heavy of build, is not a complete sentence; therefore, it cannot be followed by a dependent clause (choice C), a period (choice D), or a semicolon (choice E).

4. **(E)** Choices A and B are in correct because they are too wordy. Choice C is incorrect because it is slang, and, therefore, unsuited to the overall tone of the passage. Choice D is incorrect because it conveys the idea of a direct confrontation between kangaroos and other animals in these skills. Choice E is correct.

5. **(D)** Choice A is incorrect because the logical flow of thought from sentence 4 to sentence 5 would be interrupted. Choice B is incorrect because the thought in sentence 5 obviously flows into that in sentence 6. Choice C is incorrect because in its present position sentence 7 interrupts the logical connection in thought between sentences 6 and 8. Choice D is correct because sentence 7 makes generalizations which are supported by specific facts in sentence 9; therefore, sentence 7 should immediately precede sentence 9, and not follow it, as suggested in choice D.

Test 9

[1]The poison arrow frog found in the Andes of northern Peru and Ecuador in most circumstances is very colorful and harmless. [2]Peru and Ecuador are South American countries. [3]The frog's skin, however, is very toxic and there is great danger if the person handling the frog has an open wound. [4]Indians in the region dip their arrows with the frog's venom, which is far more potent than curare. [5]Scientists are interested in the frog and use specimens for research into such diseases as, for example, spinal meningitis.

1. Sentence 2 should be

(A) left as it is
(B) placed at the end of the selection
(C) omitted
(D) placed at the beginning, before sentence 1
(E) added to sentence 1 with the word and

2. In sentence 1, the phrase in most circumstances should be

(A) placed at the end of the sentence after harmless
(B) omitted

(C) left as it is
(D) placed after the subject of the sentence frog
(E) changed to sometimes and placed at the beginning of the sentence

3. In sentence 5, the phrase for example should be

(A) omitted
(B) left as it is
(C) changed to you know
(D) changed to an example of
(E) changed to incidentally

Explanatory Answers

1. **(C)** Choice A is incorrect because sentence 2 has no relationship to sentence 1 or sentence 3. Choice B is incorrect because adding sentence 2 at the end of the selection would destroy unity of thought. Choice C is correct because the fact that the countries are in South America has nothing to do with the topic—the poison arrow frog. The sentence should be left out completely. Choice D is incorrect because sentence 2 is not the main idea of the selection and should not be placed as the introductory sentence. Choice E is incorrect because sentence 2 has no relationship to sentence 1 and should not be used with it in a compound sentence.

2. **(A)** Choice A is correct. When the phrase is placed at the end of the sentence after the adjective harmless, which it modifies, the meaning is clear. Choice B is incorrect because omitting the phrase would eliminate a very import ant qualification which the writer makes to his general statement about the frog being colorful and harmless. The phrase in most circumstances prepared the reader for the information revealed in sentence 3 about the frog's poisonous skin. Choice C is incorrect because in its present location the phrase is ambiguous. It is not clear whether the frog is found in the Andes Mountains in most circumstances or whether the frog is colorful and harmless in most circumstances. Choice D is incorrect because placing the phrase after frog would not only be awkward, but would change the meaning of the sentence by having the phrase modify found instead of harmless. Choice E is incorrect because using the adverb sometimes changes the meaning so that the reader feels the frog is dangerous most of the time, which is not the case.

3. **(A)** Choice A is correct. There is no need for the phrase in the sentence. It interrupts the smooth flow of thought. Choice B is incorrect for the same reason. Choice C is incorrect and would serve as nothing but a meaningless expression were it to be included in the sentence. Choice D is incorrect and would make the meaning of the sentence unclear. Choice E is incorrect because the adverb incidentally is often used to introduce information which is helpful, but not necessary. The use of incidentally would detract from the positive statement being made.

Test 10

[1]The symptoms of spring fever are vague, but persistent. [2]The days seem to have a softness that makes us feel as if our bones have turned to liquid, our minds to floating clouds. [3]We want to move to the country, to go to the South Seas. [4]A train whistle excites and love buds. [5]We want to follow the birds. [6]There's often a certain element of lust, some of it for life in general. [7]Sufferers often report an itch that can't be tickled and a wild desire to start new projects; winter doldrums rapidly become spring whirlwinds. [8]"The world's favorite season," wrote naturalist Edwin Teale, "is the spring. [9]All things seem possible..."

1. Sentence 5 should be placed

   (A) where it is
   (B) after sentence 1
   (C) after sentence 2
   (D) after sentence 3
   (E) after sentence 6

2. In sentence 7, the word tickled is best replaced by

   (A) scratched
   (B) bandaged
   (C) cured
   (D) pinched
   (E) cuddled

3. To combine sentences 2 and 3, the words to liquid. Our minds should be changed to

   (A) to liquid because our minds
   (B) to liquid while our minds
   (C) to liquid unless our minds
   (D) to liquid, our minds
   (E) to liquid except our minds

4. In sentence 8, the word world's should be

   (A) left as is
   (B) changed to satellite's
   (C) changed to earth' s
   (D) changed to globe's
   (E) changed to planet's

Explanatory Answers

1. **(D)** Sentence 5 is about a desire to follow. It is best placed after the other sentence which discusses this desire. That other sentence is Choice D. Choices A, B, C, and E are wrong.

2. **(A)** Choice A is correct. An itch should be scratched, not tickled or bandaged or cured or pinched or cuddled. Accordingly, Choices B, C, D and E are wrong.

3. **(D)** Choices A, B, and C are wrong for two reasons. First, they distort the meaning of the sentence. Second, the words used to join sentences 2 and 3 are subordinating conjunctions which should be followed by clauses. A clause is a related group of words that contains both a subject and a predicate. Our minds to floating clouds is not such a group of words. Using the conjunctions, because, while, and unless, with this phrase is incorrect. Choice D is correct, simply connecting two related phrases. Choice E is incorrect; it posits our minds to floating as an exception to our bones have turned to liquid. Such an exception is illogical.

4. **(A)** The only correct choice is Choice A. First, a quotation should not be altered. The quotation marks indicate that the words within the marks are taken verbatim from the speaker or author. In addition, the choices offered are more appropriate for a discussion of geography or astronomy than for a discussion of the favorite season of all people, all over the world.

Test 11

[1]I know plenty of pet owners who suffer frustration every spring from fleas. [2]It is infuriating to be beaten by enemies so tiny, but in this eternal war the humans are often the losers. [3]Even our most powerful weapons can either prove ineffective or backfire, hurting the animals we try to protect. [4]Many people do not realize how harmful they can be. [5]They can kill baby kittens or even puppies by causing anemia, they can strip an animal of its hair, and they make life unbearable for infested animals, particularly those allergic to their bites. [6]Kittens and puppies under two months can get sick or die if treated with a flea dust or spray, or by nursing from a mother exposed to any kind of flea repellent, including collars. [7]Long-haired cats can't wear flea collars, because they usually develop severe irritations around their necks. [8]A surprising number of animals are allergic to flea deterrents. [9]One of the big problems with flea control is that the control can be more dangerous than the fleas.

1. In sentence 2, but should be

   (A) left as it is
   (B) changed to so
   (C) omitted
   (D) changed to and
   (E) changed to but often

2. Sentence 9 should be

   (A) left as it is
   (B) placed after sentence 5
   (C) omitted
   (D) placed after sentence 7
   (E) joined to sentence 8 with and

3. In sentence 7, usually should be

   (A) left as it is
   (B) changed to infrequently
   (C) changed to every once in a while
   (D) placed at the end of the sentence, after the word necks
   (E) changed to most usually

4. In sentence 4, they should be

   (A) left as it is
   (B) changed to people
   (C) changed to weapons
   (D) changed to fleas
   (E) changed to animals

5. Sentence 5 should be

   (A) made into two sentences by placing a period after hair
   (B) changed by placing the conjunction and before the second clause, which would then begin "and they can strip an animal…"
   (C) shortened by eliminating the last section beginning with particularly
   (D) changed by adding the words which are after the pronoun those in the last part
   (E) left as it is

Explanatory Answers

1. **(A)** Choice A is correct. The conjunction but is correctly used to introduce a fact which is the opposite of what one would want. Choice B is incorrect because so would mean that a conclusion follows, which is not the case in this sentence. Choice C is incorrect because leaving out but would result in a run-on sentence, clearly lacking a joining word like but. Choice D is incorrect because the sentence would lack the ironic force of showing that a human being can be outclassed by a flea. Choice E is incorrect because of the unnecessary repetition of the adverb often.

2. **(B)** Choice A is incorrect because sentence 9 contains a general idea which should clearly precede sentences 6, 7, and 8. Choice B is the correct placement for sentence 9, which is a broad statement and should appear before the examples listed in sentences 6, 7, and 8. Choice C is incorrect because the idea in sentence 9 is necessary as a bridge between sentences 4 and 5 which talk about the dangerous nature of fleas, and sentences 6, 7, and 8, which deal with the effects of flea control on dogs and cats. Choice D is incorrect because placing sentence 9 here would destroy the logical nature of the selection since the idea, expressed in sentence 9 has already been elaborated on in sentences 6 and 7. Choice E is incorrect because sentence 9 clearly introduces the ideas in sentences 6, 7, and 8. It could not serve as the second half of a concluding sentence.

3. **(A)** Choice A is correct. Choice B is incorrect because infrequently means seldom, which is not

the meaning of the sentence. Choice C is incorrect because it, too, is opposite in meaning to the idea of the sentence. It is also an awkward phrase as used in this sentence. Choice D is incorrect because the adverb usually should be placed as close as possible to the word it describes, which is develop. Otherwise, the meaning is not clear. Choice E is incorrect because there is no comparison in the sentence and, therefore, no need to use the form most usually.

4. **(D)** Choice A is incorrect because the pronoun they is unclear regarding the word it represents. It could refer to people, weapons, animals, or fleas. Choices B, C, and E are incorrect because the intention of the passage is to show that fleas are harmful, not people, weapons, or animals. Choice D is correct and avoids ambiguity (an unclear meaning).

5. **(E)** Choice A is incorrect because placing a period after hair would transform the first two clauses into a run-on sentence. Choice B is incorrect because adding and ruins the rhythm of the original sentence. Whenever a series of words, phrases, or clauses is used, the conjunction is usually placed only before the last item or section of the series, not before each part of the series. Choice C is incorrect because leaving out the last phrase would omit a piece of information which is important in understanding the damaging effect that fleas can have on animals allergic to their bite. Choice D is incorrect because adding the words which are is not necessary to improve the meaning of the sentence. The words allergic to their bites constitute an elliptical clause, and the words which are not required. It is not advisable to make sentences longer than they have to be. Choice E is correct.

Test 12

[1]To enter the perceptual world of whales and dolphins, you would have to change your primary sense from sight to sound. [2]Your brain would process and store sound pictures rather than visual images. [3]Individuals and other creatures would be recognized either by the sounds they made or by the echoes they returned from the sounds you made. [4]Your sense of neighborhood, of where you are, and whom you are with, would be a sound sense. [5]Sound is the primary sense in the life of whales and dolphins. [6]Vision is often difficult or impossible in the dark and murky seas. [7]Many whales and dolphins navigate and hunt at night or below the zone of illuminated water. [8]Vision depends on the presence of light, sounds can be made and used at any time of the day or night, and at all depths. [9]Sounds are infinitely variable: loud to soft, high notes to low notes, short silences to long silences, and many other combinations. [10]Sounds can be stopped abruptly in order to listen to a neighbor in the silence. [11]They can be finitely directed and pinpointed by the listener. [12]And communicating and locating by sound does not require a disrupt ion of daily routines. [13]Whales and dolphins can keep in sound contact simply by blowing bubbles as they exhale.

1. If the passage were split into two paragraphs, the second paragraph should begin with the sentence

   (A) Many whales and dolphins navigate and hunt at night or below the zone of illuminated water.
   (B) Sounds are infinitely variable (etc.).
   (C) Sound is the primary sense in the life of whales and dolphins.
   (D) Your sense of neighborhood, of where you are, and whom you are with, would be a sound sense.
   (E) Vision is often difficult or impossible in the dark and murky seas.

2. What should be done with sentence 8?

   (A) The comma after the word light should be omitted and the word and inserted.
   (B) A semicolon should be substituted for the comma after light.
   (C) After the, word sounds there should be a comma, then the word however; and then another comma.
   (D) The sentence should begin with the words for instance.
   (E) The sentence should begin with the word whereas.

3. Sentence 11 would be more clear if

   (A) The words by the speaker were added after the word directed.
   (B) The sentence began with Sounds rather than They.
   (C) The word finitely were used again before pinpointed.
   (D) The words by whales or dolphins were inserted after directed.
   (E) The word always followed the word can.

4. The last sentence, sentence 13, should be

   (A) omitted
   (B) left as it is
   (C) placed before sentence 12
   (D) expanded to explain that whales and dolphins are mammals and therefore exhale through lungs
   (E) changed to read: Whales and dolphins can keep in contact with each other through sound simply by blowing bubbles as they exhale.

Explanatory Answers

1. **(C)** Choice A is incorrect because the sentence is dealing with the limitations in the use of vision in whales and dolphins, and the subject of vision has already been introduced in the previous sentence, sentence 6. Choice B is incorrect for similar reasons: The subject of sound has just been discussed in the previous sentence and it is logical that this discussion continue. Choice C is correct. All the sentences before this address themselves to the reader and explain what changes would have to occur in order for us to perceive the world as whales and dolphins do. Sentence 5 turns the discussion to whales and dolphins themselves and their use of sound. (Notice that sentence 1 says "...you would have to change your primary sense..." and sentence 5 says "Sound is the primary sense in the life of whales and dolphins.") This is the only logical place to begin a second

paragraph. Choice D is incorrect because, as it has been stated, sentences 1 through 4 address the reader and there fore belong in one paragraph. Choice E is wrong because, although it is introducing the subject of vision in whales and dolphins for the first time, it is necessary that it follow directly after sentence 5 in order to show that sound is the primary sense <u>because</u> vision is restricted in the dark and murky seas.

2. **(E)** As it stands, sentence 8 contain s two complete thoughts—one about vision and one about sound, separated only by a comma, which is grammatically incorrect. Although Choice A remedies this situation, it does not make clear that a <u>comparison</u> is being made between the uses of vision and hearing. This is also true of Choice B. Choice C makes the comparison clear by the use of the word <u>however</u>, but leaves the two thoughts separated only by a comma, and is therefore wrong. Choice D is wrong for two reasons: The sentence is not really giving an example of something which was stated previously, and therefore the words <u>for instance</u> do not make sense here; furthermore, the words <u>for instance</u> do not make the comparison clear, and so the sentence remains as two separate thoughts with only a comma between them. Choice E remedies the situation completely: The word <u>whereas</u> tells us immediately that a comparison is about to be made, and the first part of the sentence ("Whereas vision depends on the presence of light") is now an <u>incomplete</u> thought which must be followed by a comma and then the rest of the sentence.

3. **(A)** The sentence as it stands is unclear because it would make it seem that the listener directs as well as pinpoints the sounds, whereas it is the <u>speaker</u> who directs them. Therefore Choice A is correct. There is no need for the sentence to begin with the word <u>sounds</u>; since sentence 10 began with it, the word <u>they</u> in sentence 11 clearly refers to <u>sounds</u>. Therefore Choice B does nothing to improve the sentence. Choice C is incorrect because to pinpoint means to locate precisely or exactly, and therefore it would be redundant to insert the word <u>finitely</u>. Although Choice D improves the sentence by telling us <u>who</u> directs the sounds, Choice A is better because it is the <u>speaker</u> who directs the sounds and the listener who pinpoints them, whether whale or dolphin. Choice E is wrong because it would be assumed by the reader that if sounds <u>can</u> be finitely directed and pinpointed, they would be in most cases; to say <u>always can</u> would be too extreme.

4. **(B)** Sentence 13 is necessary to show that emitting and listening to sounds do not disrupt the routines of whales and dolphins, stated in sentence 12. To omit the sentence, as Choice A suggests , is incorrect. Choice B is correct; it should be left as it is. Choice C is wrong; sentence 13 explains sentence 12, and therefore needs to follow it, not precede it. Choice D is incorrect because the passage is about the use of sound by whales and dolphins, not about the fact that they are mammals. To go in to an explanation of this would be to go into disproportionate detail on this one topic. Choice E is wrong for two reasons: (1) The <u>with each other</u> is understood (one has contact <u>with</u> something; otherwise it is not <u>contact</u>). (2) It also implies that whales keep in contact with dolphins and dolphins with whales, whereas what the author means is that whales and dolphins each keep in contact with their own kind. To insert <u>with each other</u>, therefore, makes the sentence quite confusing.

Test 13

[1]Most doctors across the country are probably not yet questioning patients about what kind of light they live under every day, some doctors are coming to believe that this query may be an entirely relevant one. [2]Unfortunately, the artificial light most of us live under is vastly inferior to the natural variety, so the theory goes, and we may be as starved for certain constituents of full-spectrum light as we are for the nutrients and vitamins taken out of refined foods. [3]Light, they contend, is a nutrient just as much as water or food, and is absorbed by our bodies and used in a variety of metabolic processes. [4]Studies done in schools around the country showed that children who spent a year in classrooms that had full-spectrum rather than cool-white fluorescent light were less hyperactive, had better grades, and grew faster. [5]In another study it was found that children who spent their days under cool-white light developed significantly more cavities than those working under light that had low levels of ultraviolet added to it. [6]Zoos have been finding that pit vipers, which have long preferred to starve rather than eat in captivity, were accepting food within a few number of days after sunlight-simulating lamps containing ultraviolet were installed.

1. Sentence 1 would be correct if it were to begin with

   (A) Because
   (B) In general,
   (C) Considering
   (D) Though
   (E) It is safe to say that

2. Sentence 3 is best placed

   (A) at the beginning of the passage
   (B) after sentence 1
   (C) where it is now
   (D) after sentence 4
   (E) after sentence 5

3. Were the passage to be divided into three paragraphs, the second paragraph should begin with

   (A) sentence 2
   (B) sentence 3
   (C) sentence 4
   (D) sentence 5
   (E) sentence 6

4. In sentence 6 the phrase within a few number of days should

   (A) remain the same
   (B) have within changed to after
   (C) be reduced to a few days
   (D) be replaced by shortly
   (E) be replaced by not long

Explanatory Answers

1. **(D)** Choices A and C are in correct because they imply a cause/effect relationship not indicated by the remainder of the sentence. Choices B and E create run-on sentences. Choice D is correct because it establishes the correct relationship in both structure and meaning.

2. **(B)** Choice A leaves the meaning of the sentence unclear because there is no preceding noun to which they can refer. Choice B is correct because they clearly refers to the doctors who think sunlight is important for health, and because the sentence provides a transition to sentence 2. Choice C in incorrect because the referent of they is unclear. Choice D is in correct because the logical flow from sentence 4 to sentence 5 is interrupted. Choice E is incorrect because they grammatically would refer to children in sentence 5; the meaning of the sentences, however, makes this reference impossible.

3. **(C)** Choices A and B are incorrect because sentences 2 and 3 are part of the general introduction. Choice C is correct because sentence 4 is the beginning of a separate topic giving specific information about how some artificial light is harmful. Choice D is incorrect because sentence 5 gives information similar to that of sentence 4 and, therefore, belongs in the same paragraph. Choice E is incorrect because sentence 6 is the second break in the passage; consequently, it could be the beginning of the third paragraph.

4. **(C)** Choice A is incorrect because a few number of days is needlessly wordy. Choice B is in correct because the phrase still remains unwieldy. Choice C is correct because the meaning is conveyed clearly and concisely. Choices D and E are incorrect because they are too vague: They could refer to several minutes, several hours, or several days.

Test 14

[1]The Aztecs taught the Spanish, the ones who conquered them, about cocoa. [2]The Spanish were the first to add sugar, and hot chocolate became the rage of the Spanish court. [3]The Aztecs enjoyed cocoa's naturally bitter taste. [4]Some health expert s now say that chocolate is a stimulant and should be avoided. [5]Louis XIV of France became interested in chocolate when he married Maria Teresa of Spain. [6]She is remarked to have presented him with chocolate as an engagement gift.

1. Sentence 1 should be changed to read

   (A) The Aztecs taught the Spanish who conquered them about cocoa.
   (B) The Aztecs taught the Spanish about cocoa when they conquered them.
   (C) The Aztecs taught the Spanish about cocoa when they were conquered.
   (D) The Aztecs taught the Spanish about cocoa.
   (E) The Aztecs t aught the Spanish conquerors about cocoa.

2. Sentence 3 should be

   (A) placed at the beginning of the paragraph
   (B) placed after sentence 1
   (C) placed after sentence 4
   (D) placed after sentence 6
   (E) left where it is

3. What should be done with sentence 4?

   (A) The word now should be omitted.
   (B) The word Some should be omitted.
   (C) The whole sentence should be omitted.
   (D) It should be placed at the end of the paragraph.
   (E) It should be placed at the beginning of the paragraph.

4. In sentence 6, remarked should be changed to

   (A) said
   (B) purportedly
   (C) reporting
   (D) recorded
   (E) supposedly

Explanatory Answers

1. **(E)** As it stands, the sentence is wordy and awkward. Choice A improves it somewhat but still uses more words than necessary. Choice B is ambiguous as to who conquered whom. Choice C is also ambiguous because it is not clear whether they refers to the Aztecs or the Spanish. Choice D leaves out the information that it was the Spanish conquerors who learned about cocoa from the Aztecs; it implies that the Aztecs taught the Spanish people in general, and is therefore wrong. Choice E is correct because it gives the necessary information in one word, conquerors.

2. **(B)** The passage is essentially about the history of cocoa, and it would not be fitting to begin wit h sentence 3 which is about how the Aztecs enjoyed cocoa. Choice A is therefore incorrect. Choice B is correct: Once the subject of the passage has been stated (sentence 1), it is appropriate to state how the Aztecs used cocoa before going on to explain how the Spanish used it. Choices C and D are wrong : It is not appropriate to return to a sentence about the Aztecs after sentences about the use of cocoa in Spain and France. Choice E, leaving the sentence where it is, is wrong for reasons already stated. It is best if we know how the Aztecs enjoyed cocoa before finding out how the Spanish enjoyed it, not after.

3. **(C)** Sentence 4 is irrelevant to the passage. Choices A and B do not remedy the situation and are therefore incorrect. Choice C is right. The sentence should be omitted. The sentence would still be irrelevant placed somewhere else in the passage, and so Choices D and E are wrong.

4. **(A)** Choice A (said) gives the meaning intended. Choice B is incorrect because it would have to read purported to have presented to be correct. Choice C is incorrect: reporting would have to be replaced by reported to be correct. Choice D is wrong because it would have to read recorded as having presented. Choice E incorrect because it would have to read supposed to have presented.

More Questions with Explanatory Answers

Take these tests and see how you do. Refer to Explanatory Answers for questions you missed.

IDENTIFYING ERRORS

Directions: The following sentences test your knowledge of grammar, usage, diction (choice of words), and idiom.

Some sentences are correct.
No sentence contains more than one error.

You will find that the error, if there is one, is underlined and lettered. Elements of the sentence that are not underlined will not be changed. In choosing answers, follow the requirements of standard written English.

If there is an error, select the <u>one underlined part</u> that must be changed to make the sentence correct and fill in the corresponding oval on your answer sheet.

If there is no error, fill in answer oval E.

EXAMPLE:

The <u>other</u> delegates and <u>him</u> <u>immediately</u>
    A   B   C
accepted the resolution <u>drafted by</u> the
                         D
neutral states. <u>No error.</u>
            E

SAMPLE ANSWER
Ⓐ ● Ⓒ Ⓓ Ⓔ

---

1. The Chairman <u>of the Board</u> of Directors made it <u>clear</u> at the meeting that he <u>will not</u> step
           A   B   C
down from his position <u>as chairman.</u> <u>No error.</u>
                   D   E

2. Although Hank was the captain of our high school track team, and <u>was hailed</u> as the
                                                A
fastest man on the team, I have <u>no doubt about</u> <u>my being able</u> to run faster than <u>him</u>
                           B   C   D
today. <u>No error.</u>
      E

3. <u>These kind</u> of people who have little education, who have no desire for cultural pursuits,
     A
and whose sole purpose <u>is acquiring</u> wealth, are not the <u>type</u> I wish to <u>associate with</u>.
                      B   C   D
<u>No error.</u>
 E

4. <u>Whether</u> the sales campaign <u>succeeds</u> <u>will probably not be known</u> for at least a year, but
   A   B   C

it is clear now that the stakes <u>are</u> high. <u>No error.</u>
                    D   E

5. Neither Sam Atkins <u>nor</u> Henry Miller, sales representatives for the company, presented
               A

<u>their</u> summaries of sales <u>before</u> the deadline <u>for doing so.</u> <u>No error.</u>
 B   C   D   E

6. A recent poll <u>has indicated</u> that Harold, who is a senior at South Palmetto High School, is
           A

considered <u>brighter</u> than <u>any student</u> in the <u>senior class</u> at that school. <u>No error.</u>
         B   C   D   E

7. When one <u>leaves</u> his car <u>to be repaired</u>, <u>he assumes</u> that the mechanic will repair the car
        A   B   C

<u>good</u>. <u>No error.</u>
 D   E

8. Bob could easily <u>have gotten</u> a higher score <u>on</u> his college entrance test if he
          A   B

<u>would have read</u> more <u>in his school career.</u> <u>No error.</u>
   C   D   E

9. <u>Any</u> modern novelist <u>would be thrilled</u> to have <u>his</u> stories compared <u>with Dickens.</u>
 A   B   C   D
<u>No error.</u>
 E

10. When my <u>Uncle Pancho's</u> plane <u>arrives</u> at the airport <u>in San Diego</u>, <u>I shall have already left</u>
           A   B   C   D
San Diego for Mexico City. <u>No error.</u>
                    E

11. Many people in the United States <u>don't</u> scarcely know <u>about</u> the terrible hardships that
                         A   B

the Vietnamese <u>are experiencing</u> in their <u>war-ravaged</u> country. <u>No error.</u>
          C   D   E

12. Cesar Chavez, president of the United Farm Workers Union, <u>called for</u> a Congressional
                                        A

investigation of certain California lettuce growers, <u>whom</u>, he said, <u>were giving</u> bribes to a
                                      B   C

<u>rival union.</u> <u>No error.</u>
  D   E

13. The automobile industry <u>is experimenting</u> with a new <u>type of a</u> motor that will consume
                    A   B

<u>less</u> gasoline and <u>cause</u> much less pollution. <u>No error.</u>
 C   D   E

14. The girl <u>who won</u> the beauty contest is <u>nowhere near</u> as beautiful <u>as</u> my mother was
        A   B   C

when she <u>was</u> a bride. <u>No error.</u>
       D   E

15. Sitting <u>opposite</u> my sister and <u>me</u> in the subway were <u>them</u> same men who walked
             A   B   C

    <u>alongside</u> us and tried to pinch us on Fifth Avenue. <u>No error.</u>
      D   E

16. <u>Even if</u> Detroit could provide <u>nonpolluting</u> cars by the original deadline to meet
     A   B

    <u>prescribed</u> federal standards for clean air, the effect in big cities would be slight because
    C

    <u>only</u> new cars would be properly equipped. <u>No error.</u>
    D   E

17. None of the crew members who <u>flew</u> with me <u>over</u> Hanoi is happy today <u>about</u> the
                                 A   B   C

    destruction <u>caused</u> in that bombing mission. <u>No error.</u>
              D   E

18. It was our <u>neighbor's</u> opinion that if Kennedy <u>was</u> alive today, the country <u>would have</u>
              A   B   C

    fewer problems <u>than</u> it has now. <u>No error.</u>
                  D   E

19. We, <u>as</u> parents who are interested in the welfare of our son, are <u>strongly</u> opposed to <u>him</u>
        A   B   C

    associating with individuals who <u>do not seem</u> to have moral scruples. <u>No error.</u>
                                  D   E

20. If anyone in the audience <u>has</u> anything <u>to add</u> to <u>what</u> the speaker has already said, let
                            A   B   C

    <u>them</u> speak up. <u>No error.</u>
    D   E

21. <u>It</u> was very nice of the <u>Rodriguezes</u> to invite my husband, my mother, and <u>I</u> to their New
    A   B   C

    <u>Year's</u> Eve party. <u>No error.</u>
    D   E

22. Neither rain nor snow <u>nor</u> sleet <u>keep</u> the postman <u>from</u> delivering our letters, which we
                         A   B   C

    so much <u>look forward</u> to receiving. <u>No error.</u>
             D   E

23. Namath played a <u>real</u> fine game <u>in spite of</u> the fact that the Jets lost <u>by</u> a touchdown
                    A   B   C

    <u>which</u> the opposing team scored in the last minute of play. <u>No error.</u>
    D   E

24. You <u>may not</u> realize <u>it</u> but the weather in Barbados <u>during Christmas</u> is <u>like New York</u> in
        A   B   C   D

    June. <u>No error.</u>
              E

IMPROVING SENTENCES

<u>**Directions:**</u> **The following sentences test correctness and effectiveness of expression. In choosing answers, follow the requirements of standard written English; that is, pay attention to grammar, choice of words, sentence construction, and punctuation.**

In each of the following sentences, part of the sentence or the entire sentence is underlined. Beneath each sentence you will find five ways of phrasing the underlined part. Choice A repeats the original; the other four are different.

Choose the answer that best expresses the meaning of the original sentence. If you think the original is better than any of the alternatives, choose it; otherwise choose one of the others. Your choice should produce the most effective sentence—clear and precise, without awkwardness or ambiguity.

EXAMPLE: SAMPLE ANSWER

Laura Ingalls Wilder published her first book
<u>and she was sixty-five years old then.</u>

(A) and she was sixty-five years old then
(B) when she was sixty-five
(C) being age sixty-five years old
(D) upon the reaching of sixty-five years
(E) at the time when she was sixty-five

25. There is great disagreement today about the need for vitamin supplements, <u>many doctors being on one side as opposed to nutritionists.</u>

(A) many doctors being on one side as opposed to nutritionists
(B) which finds many doctors on one side with nutritionists on the other
(C) putting many doctors on one side and nutritionists on the other
(D) with many doctors on one side and nutritionists on the other
(E) what with many doctors on one side and nutritionists on the other

26. Because of the size and weight of the stones that constitute Stonehenge, some people are convinced <u>how it was erected</u> by extraterrestrial beings.

(A) how it was erected
(B) that it was erected
(C) that they were erected
(D) that it was done
(E) that it has been erected

27. Even in apparently peaceful neighborhoods, one often finds conflict between parents and school officials over such issues as <u>wanting smaller classes, curriculum, and the importance of nonacademic subjects</u> like art, music, and physical education.

    (A) wanting smaller classes, curriculum, and the importance of nonacademic subjects
    (B) class size, curriculum, and that nonacademic subjects are not important
    (C) class size, curriculum, and the importance of nonacademic subjects
    (D) how many children are in a class, what they read, and the importance of nonacademic subjects
    (E) class size, curriculum, and nonacademic subjects

28. The presentation of Edwardian England as a period of romance lets the viewer forget the poverty and squalor in which the majority lived <u>and inspire</u> him to laugh at the foolish mores of the rich and fashionable.

    (A) and inspire
    (B) and inspires
    (C) which inspires
    (D) inspiring
    (E) and this inspires

29. <u>Deciding whether Shakespeare's plays or his sonnets are better poetry, that is a task</u> only for those prepared to examine the texts closely and able to distinguish subtle differences in the use of poetic devices.

    (A) Deciding whether Shakespeare's plays or his sonnets are better poetry, that is a task
    (B) In deciding whether Shakespeare's plays or his sonnets are better poetry is a task
    (C) In order to decide whether Shakespeare's plays or his sonnets are better poetry is a task
    (D) Deciding whether Shakespeare's plays or his sonnets are the best poetry is a task
    (E) Deciding whether Shakespeare's plays or his sonnets are better poetry is a task

30. While Cézanne, Seurat, and Gauguin were primarily concerned with objective or formal principles, other Post-Impressionists, like van Gogh, <u>were exploring</u> more subjective means of artistic expression.

    (A) were exploring
    (B) was exploring
    (C) exploring
    (D) who were exploring
    (E) who was exploring

31. Unlike "The Tell-Tale Heart" and "The Black Cat," <u>verisimilitude is achieved in "The Cask of Amontillado" by a clearly defined setting and time and by characters who are given names and realistic dialogue.</u>

    (A) verisimilitude is achieved in "The Cask of Amontillado" by a clearly defined setting and time and by characters who are given names and realistic dialogue
    (B) "The Cask of Amontillado" achieves verisimilitude by a clearly defined setting and time and by characters who are given names and realistic dialogue
    (C) a clearly defined setting and time and characters who have names and realistic dialogue give "The Cask of Amontillado" verisimilitude
    (D) in "The Cask of Amontillado" verisimilitude is achieved by a clearly defined setting and time and characters who are given names and realistic dialogue
    (E) verisimilitude is achieved by a clearly defined setting and time and by characters who are given names and realistic dialogue in "The Cask of Amontillado"

32. The poets of the 1920s tended to be difficult, introverted, and experimental; the poets of the 1930s, reacting to the urgent demands of the political situation, <u>and to a large extent having rejected</u> such an approach in favor of a more literal, realistic statement.

    (A) and to a large extent having rejected
    (B) and to a large extent rejecting
    (3) to a large extent rejected
    (D) and to a large extent rejected
    (E) they rejected to a large extent

33. One often hears the claim that communism, <u>despite its opposition to traditional forms of organized religion and professed atheism, is itself religious.</u>

    (A) despite its opposition to traditional forms of organized religion and professed atheism, is itself religious
    (B) despite its opposition to traditional forms of organized religion and its professed atheism, is itself religious
    (C) despite its opposition to traditional forms of organized religion and its professed atheism, are themselves religious
    (D) despite its opposition to traditional forms of organized religion and professed atheism, is itself a religion
    (E) despite its opposition to traditional forms of organized religion and its professed atheism, is itself a religion

34. Laws are made and enforced by human beings; as long as there are imperfect lawmakers, <u>imperfect laws are going to be a natural consequence.</u>

    (A) imperfect laws are going to be a natural consequence
    (B) they will be imperfect laws
    (C) imperfect laws are to be expected
    (D) there will be imperfect laws
    (E) it will mean imperfect laws

35. <u>With their noise and bad manners, the children angered the receptionist, which made her ask</u> their mother to take them outside to wait for the doctor.

(A) With their noise and bad manners, the children angered the receptionist, which made her ask
(B) The children were noisy and ill-mannered, which made the receptionist so angry that she asked
(C) The children were noisy and ill-mannered, thus angering the receptionist so that she asked
(D) The noisy and ill-mannered children so angered the receptionist that she asked
(E) Noisy and ill-mannered, the children made the receptionist so angry as to ask

36. <u>If the problem of pollution</u>—air, water, noise, etc.—is important, indeed vital, to every American is a fact that we all know but that many of us are choosing to ignore.

(A) If the problem of pollution
(B) That the problem of pollution
(C) How the problem of pollution
(D) When the problem of pollution
(E) Because the problem of pollution

37. He <u>has waited for her and been disappointed by her</u> so often that he was astonished when she arrived right on time.

(A) has waited for her and been disappointed by her
(B) had waited and been disappointed by her
(C) has waited and been disappointed by her
(D) had waited for her and been disappointed by her
(E) had waited, only to be disappointed, for her

38. <u>The main problem is to determine the feasibility of becoming, other considerations notwithstanding, "energy-independent"</u> within this century.

(A) The main problem is to determine the feasibility of becoming, other considerations notwithstanding, "energy-independent"
(B) The main problem is to determine, other considerations notwithstanding, the feasibility to become "energy-independent"
(C) To determine the feasibility, other considerations notwithstanding, of becoming "energy-independent" is the main problem
(D) Other considerations notwithstanding, the problem of determining the feasibility of becoming "energy-independent" is the main one
(E) The main problem, other considerations notwithstanding, is to determine the feasibility of becoming "energy-independent"

39. After the debate, <u>it was voted by the spectators</u> to be in favor of the resolution.

(A) it was voted by the spectators to be
(B) the spectators voted
(C) in a vote by the spectators they were
(D) the spectators by vote, turned out to be
(E) in their vote, the spectators were

40. It is difficult to say whether Newton or Einstein <u>was the most brilliant, because each made</u> <u>great strides forward in his field</u> of scientific inquiry.

(A) was the most brilliant, because each made great strides forward in his field
(B) was the most brilliant, because each made great strides forward in their fields
(C) were the more brilliant, because each made great strides forward in their fields
(D) was the more brilliant, because each made great strides forward in his field
(E) were the more brilliant, because each made great strides forward in his field

41. Russia's most celebrated composer, Peter Ilyich Tchaikovsky, once described himself as "Russian to the core" and <u>a devotee of</u> the Russian spirit.

(A) a devotee of
(B) that he was devoted to
(C) devoted to
(D) devoting himself to
(E) devoted himself to

42. Although James Fenimore Cooper was a recognized talent in Europe, <u>they did not read his</u> <u>works in the United States and looked down on him</u> as a frontier writer.

(A) they did not read his works in the United States and looked down on him
(B) he was unread in the United States and was looked down on
(C) they did not read him in the United States, looking down on him
(D) in the United States he was unread because they looked down on him
(E) in the United States they not only did not read his works but also looked down on him

43. Bill Bradley was not only athletic enough to be a basketball star <u>but also intelligent enough</u> to be a Rhodes scholar.

(A) but also intelligent enough
(B) but he was sufficiently intelligent
(C) but he also had the intelligence
(D) but that he was also intelligent enough
(E) but because of his intelligence he was also

44. When reading Iris Murdoch's novels, one often wonders <u>does she want the reader to</u> <u>believe that these or those characters are moral and virtuous</u>.

(A) does she want the reader to believe that these or those characters are moral and virtuous
(B) which characters does she want the reader to believe are moral and virtuous
(C) whether she wants us to see these or those characters as moral and virtuous
(D) which characters she wants the reader to believe are moral and virtuous
(E) which characters she wants for the reader to believe moral and virtuous

45. With Degas, a small drawing or monotype can reveal <u>as much or sometimes more than</u> a full-blown composition.

    (A) as much or sometimes more than
    (B) as much as or sometimes more than
    (C) so much as or sometimes more than
    (D) as much as or preferably more than
    (E) as much or more than

46. Having inherited great wealth, <u>his pursuit of a literary career would not be hampered by worries</u> about earning a living.

    (A) his pursuit of a literary career would not be hampered by worries
    (B) a literary career was open to him without having to worry
    (C) his desire to pursue a literary career could be satisfied without worrying
    (D) he was free to pursue a literary career without worrying
    (E) the opportunity to pursue a literary career would be unimpeded by worries

47. <u>Great devastation was experienced by the town, which was caused by the tornado.</u>

    (A) Great devastation was experienced by the town, which was caused by the tornado.
    (B) Great devastation, caused by the tornado, was visited upon the town.
    (C) The town was devastated by the tornado.
    (D) The tornado brought great devastation to the town.
    (E) The tornado's devastation destroyed the town.

48. At the end of the game, everybody rushed out of the stadium, <u>running to their cars, and then sat</u>, waiting for the traffic to move.

    (A) running to their cars, and then sat
    (B) ran to their cars, and then sat
    (C) running to his car, and then sat
    (D) ran to his car, and then sat
    (E) running to his car, and then sitting

Directions: The following passage is an early draft of an essay. Some parts of the passage need to be rewritten.

Read the passage and select the best answers for the questions that follow. Some questions are about particular sentences or parts of sentences and ask you to improve sentence structure or word choice. Other questions ask you to consider organization and development. In choosing answers, follow the requirements of standard written English.

Questions 49–52 refer to the following passage.

[1]There is no escaping it: dating and cars are inextricably linked up together. [2]In the suburbs of Los Angeles in 1950, a high school boy couldn't conduct his dating life without a car. [3]It was the fundamental tool of the courtship ritual. [4]Of course, you could borrow the family car to go on a date. [5]This was deeply humiliating. [6]It was "stock"—that is, not hopped-up, modified, or customized. [7]It bore no mark of personality. [8]It had no identity.

49. In sentence 4, you would be better if it were

(A) left as is
(B) changed to one
(C) changed to a high school student
(D) changed to he
(E) changed to someone

50. Sentence 6 would be best if

(A) it were left as is
(B) it were made into two sentences, the new one beginning with that is
(C) it were shortened to It was "stock"
(D) it were joined to sentence 7 with because
(E) it were rewritten without quotation marks around stock

51. Sentence 5 should begin with

(A) So
(B) Since
(C) Unless
(D) Because
(E) But

52. The it in sentences 7 and 8 refers to

(A) the same noun that the it in sentence 3 refers to
(B) the "stock" car
(C) the hopped-up, modified, or customized car
(D) the boy's own car
(E) the car the boy would like to own

Questions 53–56 refer to the following passage.

[1]A loss of tradition has had devastating effects on American Indian communities. [2]"When we ceased to have a relationship with the world around us through our religion, we went berserk," says Victoria Santana, a lawyer with the American Indian Law Center in Albuquerque. [3]"Look at the studies of alcoholism and crime among Indians." [4]There is now some evidence that the once-dying Indian religions are being revived. [5]Forty years ago, Indians would deny their religion. [6]They didn't want to be persecuted. [7]Crow Indian grandparents are teaching their grandchildren the old ways. [8]Young Sioux in South Dakota are performing the once-forbidden Sun Dance, a vigorous four-day ritual in which the skin and muscle layers are crippled with bone slivers.

53. Sentence 6 could be joined to sentence 5 with the word(s)

(A) unless
(B) so that
(C) while
(D) because
(E) except that

54. The word crippled in sentence 8 would best be

(A) left as is
(B) changed to pierced
(C) changed to scratched
(D) changed to beset
(E) changed to beaten

55. Sentence 7 would be best if it began with

(A) However, while
(B) In the past, since
(C) But,
(D) Yes,
(E) But today,

56. Sentence 8 would be best if it were

(A) made into two sentences, the new one beginning with <u>A</u>
(B) made into two sentences, the new one beginning with <u>In</u>
(C) joined to sentence 7 with the word <u>and</u>
(D) left as is
(E) moved to follow sentence 2

Questions 57–60 refer to the following passage.

[1]At some moment in our lives most of us are called upon to make a speech—at a town meeting or community function, a graduation, or even a family gathering. [2]Yet, few of us do it well. [3]Either we talk unprepared, stumbling over words, or we overtalk, and we bore our audience. [4]Actually, however, the basics of effective speechmaking are simple. [5]Know your audience. [6]Get a theme. [7]Research it. [8]Make notes if you must. [9]But do it using key words that will bring entire sentences to mind. [10]Practice before a mirror. [11]Make the speech before your family or friends, and ask for their criticism. [12]Finally, when you're speaking in public remember: Have humor, be sincere, be brief, be seated.

57. In sentence 3, the phrase <u>and we bore our audience</u> should

(A) be changed to <u>boring our audience</u>
(B) remain as it is
(C) be omitted entirely
(D) be changed to <u>boring our audience with our longwindedness</u>
(E) be shortened to <u>and bore our audience</u>

58. Were the passage to be divided into two paragraphs, the second paragraph should begin with

(A) sentence 2
(B) sentence 3
(C) sentence 4
(D) sentence 5
(E) sentence 12

59. Sentence 2 should

(A) remain as it is
(B) be omitted
(C) begin with <u>Although</u> instead of <u>Yet</u>
(D) begin with <u>Therefore</u> instead of <u>Yet</u>
(E) begin with <u>While</u> instead of <u>Yet</u>

60. Sentences 10 and 11 should

(A) be combined to form one sentence with a semi-colon after <u>mirror</u>
(B) be combined to form one sentence by using the conjunction <u>and</u>
(C) be combined to form one sentence, adding <u>although you should</u> after <u>mirror</u>
(D) be combined to form one sentence beginning with <u>After you</u>
(E) be left as they are

ANSWER KEY FOR WRITING SKILLS TEST

1. C	21. C	41. C
2. D	22. B	42. B
3. A	23. A	43. A
4. E	24. D	44. D
5. B	25. D	45. B
6. C	26. B	46. D
7. D	27. C	47. C
8. C	28. B	48. D
9. D	29. E	49. D
10. E	30. A	50. A
11. A	31. B	51. E
12. B	32. C	52. B
13. B	33. E	53. D
14. B	34. D	54. B
15. C	35. D	55. E
16. E	36. B	56. D
17. E	37. D	57. A
18. B	38. E	58. C
19. C	39. B	59. A
20. D	40. D	60. E

EXPLANATORY ANSWERS FOR
WRITING SKILLS TEST

Identifying Errors

1. **(C)** "…that he *would* not step down…" Since the verb of the main clause (*made*) is in the past tense, the verb of the subordinate clause must also be in the past tense (*would speak*). Incidentally, *would speak* is a past subjunctive.

2. **(D)** "…no doubt about my being able to run faster than *he* today." The nominative case (*he*—not *him*) must be used after the conjunction *than* when the pronoun is the subject of an elliptical clause ("than he can run today").

3. **(A)** "*These kinds* of people…" A plural pronoun-adjective (*These*—not *this*) must be used to modify a plural noun (*kinds*).

4. **(E)** All underlined parts are correct.

5. **(B)** "…presented *his* summaries of sales…" Singular antecedents (*Atkins* and *Miller*) which are joined by *or* or *nor* are referred to by singular pronouns (*his*, in this case—not *their*).

6. **(C)** "…brighter than *any other* student…" As the original sentence stands, Harold is brighter than himself. In a comparative construction, we must be sure that, if A and B are compared, A is not included as part of B.

7. **(D)** "…will repair the car *well*." The adverb (*well*)—not the adjective (*good*)—is used to modify the verb (*will repair*).

8. **(C)** "…if he *had read* more…" The "if" clause of a contrary-to-fact past tense requires the verb *had read*—not *would have read*.

9. **(D)** "…to have his stories *compared with those of Dickens*." We have an improper ellipsis in the original sentence. The additional words (*those of*) are necessary to complete the meaning of the sentence.

10. **(E)** All underlined parts are correct.

11. **(A)** "Many people in the United States *scarcely know*…" Omit the word *don't*. The word *scarcely* is sufficiently negative to express the meaning intended.

12. **(B)** "…*who*, he said, were giving bribes…" The subject of the dependent clause must have a nominative case form (*who*) not an objective case form (*whom*)

13. **(B)** "…with a new *type of* motor…" Do not use the article *a* or *an* after *kind of, type of, sort of*, etc.

14. **(B)** "…is not *nearly* as beautiful…" Do not use the expression *nowhere near for not nearly*.

15. **(C)** "…were those same men…" The demonstrative pronoun-adjective form (*those*)—not the personal pronoun form (*them*)—must be used to modify the noun *men*.

16. **(E)** All underlined parts are correct.

17. **(E)** All underlined parts are correct.

18. **(B)** "…that if Kennedy *were* alive today…" The verb in a condition contrary to fact is *were* for all persons—never *was*.

19. **(C)** "…are strongly opposed to *his* associating with…" A pronoun in the possessive case (*his*) not in the objective case (*him*)—should be used to modify a gerund (*associating*) when that pronoun indicates the person who is performing the action of the gerund.

20. **(D)** "…let *him* speak up." An indefinite antecedent (*anyone*) must be referred to by a singular pronoun (*him*—not *them*).

21. **(C)** "…to invite my husband, my mother and *me*…" All of the words of a

compound object must be in the objective case. Note that the words *husband*, *mother*, and *me* are all direct object s of the infinitive *to invite*.

22. **(B)** "Neither rain nor snow nor sleet *keeps* the postman..." When subjects are connected by *neither...nor*, the verb must agree with the subject which is closest to the verb—*sleet* is the closest subject to the verb (*keeps*) in the sentence. Since *sleet* is singular, the verb (*keeps*) must be singular.

23. **(A)** "Namath played a *really* fine game..." An adverb (*really*)—not an adjective (*real*)—is used to modify the adjective *fine*.

24. **(D)** "...is like *that* of New York in June." We have an improper ellipsis here. We must include the words *that of*, meaning *the weather of*.

Improving Sentences

25. **(D)** Choice A is incorrect because it omits "on the other" after "nutritionists," thus leaving the thought incomplete. Choice B is incorrect because "which" has no definite antecedent. Choice C is incorrect because it is awkward. Choice E is incorrect because "what with" is too informal.

26. **(B)** Choice A is incorrect because "how" is substituted for "that." Choice C is incorrect because "they" could refer to either "people" or "stones." Choice D is incorrect because "done" is an inexact word in this sentence. Choice E is incorrect because the present perfect tense ("has been") indicates action that began in the past and continues in the present; in this case, the present perfect tense is illogical.

27. **(C)** Choices A, B, and D lack parallel construction and are therefore incorrect. Choice E is incorrect because "non-academic subjects" are not an issue—"the importance" of them is the issue.

28. **(B)** The subject of the sentence is "presentation," which is singular. Choice A is incorrect and Choice B correct because the singular verb is correct ("inspires"). Choice C is incorrect because "which" has no logical antecedent. Choice D is incorrect because "inspiring," a participle, does not modify anything. Choice E is incorrect because there is no logical antecedent for "this."

29. **(E)** Choice A is incorrect because "that" is redundant: "deciding" is the subject and "that" merely repeats it. Choices B and C are incorrect because they have no subject. Prepositional phrases cannot act as subjects of sentences. Choice D is incorrect because only two items are being compared, so the comparative ("better"), not the superlative ("best"), is needed. Choice E is correct because a gerund ("deciding") can act as the subject of a sentence.

30. **(A)** The subject of the verb is "other Post-Impressionists," which is plural; therefore, Choice A is correct and Choice B is incorrect. Choices C, D, and E deprive the sentence of a main clause verb, Choice C by supplying only a participle, Choices D and E by making a subordinate clause out of the main verb.

31. **(B)** In Choices A, C, D, and E, faulty comparisons are made. Only the story, "The Cask of Amontillado," can logically be compared to the two stories in the introductory phrase.

32. **(C)** Choices A and B are incorrect because they deprive the second clause of the sentence of a main verb; a participle ("having rejected," "rejecting,") cannot serve as the main verb of an independent clause. Choice D is incorrect because "and," which is a coordinating conjunction, is used to join a participle ("reacting") and a main verb

("rejected"). A coordinating conjunction is used to connect only equal grammatical elements. Choice E is incorrect because "they" is redundant; "poets" is the subject and "they" simply repeats it.

33. **(E)** Choices A, B, and C are incorrect because communism, a system of beliefs, cannot be "religious." Choice A is further incorrect because "its" before "professed atheism" is omitted; this omission makes the sentence say that communism is opposed to professed atheism. Choice C is further incorrect because "themselves" has no antecedent, and "are" should be the singular "is" (the subject is "communism"). Choice D is incorrect because it omits "its" before "professed atheism."

34. **(D)** Choices A and C are awkward. Choice B is incorrect because "they" refers to "lawmakers." Choice E is incorrect because "it" has no specific antecedent and because the choice is awkward.

35. **(D)** Choice D is the most straightforward of the choices and is correct. Choices A and B are incorrect because there is no antecedent for "which" in either sentence. Choice C is incorrect because "thus" is unidiomatic here. Choice E is incorrect because "as to ask" should be "that she asked."

36. **(B)** Choices A, D, and E are incorrect because "if," "when," and "because," do not introduce noun clauses. A noun clause is needed as the subject of the sentence since the verb is "is." "How the problem of pollution is important" does not make sense, so Choice C is incorrect. Choice B is correct because "that" does introduce noun clauses.

37. **(D)** Choices A and C are incorrect because "has waited" should be "had waited," the past perfect, not the present perfect. The past perfect tense indicates action that preceded another action in the past; since the second clause contains the past tense ("was astonished"), the past perfect is logical. Choices B and C are incorrect because they omit "for" after "waited"; "for" is needed because "waited by her" does not make sense. Choice E is

incorrect because "by" after "disappointed" is needed; "disappointed for her" does not make sense.

38. **(E)** "Other considerations notwithstanding" logically should be close to "the main problem," so Choices A, B, and C are incorrect. Choice B is also incorrect because "feasibility to become" is unidiomatic. Choice D is incorrect because "is the main one" sounds awkward here.

39. **(B)** Choices A, C, D, and E are too roundabout. Choices A and C use the passive voice unnecessarily and, therefore, in a weak manner. Choices C and E use prepositional phrases in a way that makes the sentence verbose—"the spectators they," in Choice C, and "their vote, the spectators," in Choice E. Choice D is awkward.

40. **(D)** One problem in this sentence is agreement—subject-verb agreement and pronoun-antecedent agreement. A second problem is the use of "most" or "more" when two items are being compared. "More" is used when only two items are being compared (the comparative degree), and "most" is used when three or more items are being compared (the superlative degree). Since only two items are being compared here, "more" is correct and Choices A and B are incorrect. Choices B and C are incorrect because "their" should be "his," agreeing with "each," which is singular. Choices C and E are incorrect because "were" should be "was." When a compound subject is joined by "or," the verb agrees in number with that element that is closer to the verb—i.e., "Einstein," which is singular.

41. **(C)** Choices A, B, D, and E all lack needed parallelism. "Russian to the core" is an adjectival phrase, so the phrase after "and" should also be adjectival. Choice A gives a noun. Choice B gives a dependent clause, Choice D gives a participial phrase with an object (*himself*), and Choice E gives a verb and its object. Choice C gives a participle (acting as an adjective) without an object.

42. **(B)** Choices A, C, D, and E are all incorrect because "they" has no antecedent.

The passive voice is preferable to an imprecise "they."

43. **(A)** Choices B, C, D, and E are incorrect because they are not in parallel construction with the first part of the sentence. "Not only" and "but also" should be followed by the same grammatical construction. In Choice A, "not only" is followed by an adjective ("athletic"), as is "but also" ("intelligent"). Choice B deviates from the previous "athletic enough" construction by placing the adverb "sufficiently" in front of the adjective "intelligent." In Choice C, "but also" is followed by the verb "had." In Choice D, "not only" is followed by a "that" clause. In Choice E, "not only" is followed by a prepositional phrase.

44. **(D)** Choices A and B are incorrect because they turn the entire sentence into a direct question—though awkwardly. Choice C is incorrect because "one" (the subject of the sentence) is the third person singular, while "us" is third person plural; "us" has no antecedent. Choice E is incorrect because "wants for" is poor diction and because "to believe moral and virtuous" omits the necessary verb *to be*.

45. **(B)** "As much as" and "more than" are complete expressions; neither one should have any of its parts left out. Choice A omits the second "as." Choice C is incorrect because the correlative "so…as" is used only in a negative statement. Choices D and E are incorrect because they change the meaning of the original sentence.

46. **(D)** Choices A, B, C, and E create a dangling participial phrase; "having inherited" modifies "he," so "he" must be the subject of the sentence.

47. **(C)** Choices A and B are incorrect because the passive voice is used in a round about manner. In addition, in Choice A "which" has no definite antecedent, and in Choice B "was visited" is pompous. In Choice C, "which" is correct; the passive voice is used to good advantage by making "the town" the subject of the sentence. Choice D is incorrect because "brought great devastation to" is wordy; "devastated" could correctly replace the four words. Choice E is incorrect because it is redundant: "devastation" is destruction.

48. **(D)** Choices A, C, and E are incorrect because "running" should be "ran," one of the three main verbs, "rushed," "ran," and "sat." Choice E is further incorrect because it gives "sitting" instead of "sat." Choices A and B are incorrect because "their" should be "his"; "everybody" is singular and therefore takes a singular pronoun.

Improving Paragraphs

49. **(D)** Choices A, B, and E all provide incorrect pronouns for the noun phrase, a <u>high school boy</u>. Choice C is wrong because it is repetitive. The best choice is Choice D.

50 **(A)** Choice A is right. Choice B is wrong because there is no need to divide the sentence. Choice C is wrong because it eliminates the essential details that define "<u>stock</u>." Choice D is incorrect because it would create a meaningless sentence. Choice E is wrong; the quotation marks around <u>stock</u> indicate that the author is using this word in a unique way.

51. **(E)** Choices A, B, and D are wrong because they all state that the boy borrows the family car <u>because</u> to do so is <u>deeply humiliating</u>. The following sentences make clear that this isn't true. Choice C is wrong because it says that he can borrow the car <u>unless</u> it is humiliating. This would suggest that, sometimes, to borrow the family car is not humiliating. The remainder of the passage indicates that it is always humiliating. Choice E is correct. The boy could borrow the family car <u>but</u> he doesn't want to because it is deeply humiliating.

52. **(B)** Choice A is incorrect because the "it" in sentence 3 refers to cars in general, while the "it" in sentences 7, 8, and 9 refers to the "<u>stock</u>" or family car. Therefore, Choice B is correct, while Choices C, D, and E are incorrect.

53. **(D)** Sentence 6 explains why American Indians used <u>to deny their religion</u>. To join sentence 5, sentence 6 must begin with a word that indicates explanation. Accordingly, Choice D is correct.

54. **(B)** Choices A, C, D, and E are incorrect because they are not fitting descriptions of the effect a bone splinter would have. Choice B is the best choice since it is the most vivid and precise.

55. **(E)** Sentence 7 begins a description of a change in the American Indian community. It should begin with a word or with words that indicate a shift from the past to the future, from one idea to a new one. Only Choice E achieves this.

56. **(D)** Choices A and B are incorrect because the new sentences they create are incomplete. Choice C is wrong because it would create an unnecessarily long compound complex sentence. Choice D is correct. Choice E is incorrect. It would break up a quotation that must remain connected.

57. **(A)** Choice A is correct because it balances the structure of the clauses following <u>either</u> and <u>or</u>. Choices B, C, and E are incorrect because they destroy this parallel structure. Choice D is' incorrect because the additional words are unnecessary: the idea of long-windedness has already been expressed in <u>overtalk</u>.

58. **(C)** Choices A and B are incorrect because they are clearly part of the introductory generalizations about speech-making. Choice C is correct because it begins a new topic—the basics of effective speechmaking. Choice D is incorrect because sentence 5 clarifies the statement made in sentence 4 and therefore must follow sentence 4 in the same paragraph. Choice E is incorrect because it is obviously the concluding sentence of the passage.

59. **(A)** Choice A is correct because sentence 2 establishes the relationship between sentences 1 and 3. Choice B is incorrect because without sentence 2 there would be no transition from sentence 1 to sentence 3. Choices C and E are incorrect because they would result in incomplete sentences. Choice D is incorrect because <u>Therefore</u> erroneously implies a cause/effect relationship between sentences 1 and 2.

60. **(E)** Choices A and D, while grammatically correct, alter the style of the paragraph, in which the author mainly uses short, forceful, declarative sentences. Choice B results in a loose, rambling sentence, which lessens the impact of the separate statements. Choice C is incorrect because the use of the conjunction <u>although</u> results in an illogical relationship between the two sentences. Choice E is correct because it is faithful to the author's style.

Part 4
Two SAT Writing
Practice Tests

Three Important Reasons for Taking These Practice Tests

Each of the two Practice SATs in the final part of this book is modeled very closely after the actual writing SAT Test. You will find that each of these Practice Tests has

a) the same level of difficulty as the actual SAT

and

b) the same question formats that the actual SAT questions have.

Accordingly, *taking each of the following tests is like taking the actual SAT.* There are five important reasons for taking each of these Practice SATs:

1. To find out in which areas of the writing SAT you are still weak.

2. To know just where to concentrate your efforts to eliminate these weaknesses.

3. To strengthen your grammar and writing skills, look at Part 3, The SAT Writing Test and Part 1 and 2, A Brief Review of English Grammar and The SAT Grammar and Usage Refresher.

These three reasons for taking the two Practice Tests in this section of the book tie up closely with a very important educational principle:

WE LEARN BY DOING!

Ten Tips for Taking the Practice Tests

1. Observe the time limits exactly as given.

2. Allow no interruptions.

3. Permit no talking by anyone in the "test area."

4. Use the Answer Sheets provided at the beginning of each Practice Test. Don't make extra marks. Two answers for one question constitute an omitted question.

5. Use scratch paper to figure things out. (On your actual SAT, you are permitted to use the testbook for scratchwork.)

6. Omit a question when you start "struggling" with it. Go back to that question later if you have time to do so.

7. Don't get upset if you can't answer several of the questions. You can still get a high score on the test. Even if only 40 to 60 percent of the questions you answer are correct, you will get an average or above-average score.

8. You get the same credit for answering an easy question correctly as you do for answering a tough question correctly.

9. It is advisable to guess if you are sure that at least one of the answer choices is wrong. If you are not sure whether one or more of the answer choices are wrong, statistically it will not make a difference to your total score if you guess or leave the answer blank.

10. *Your SAT score increases by approximately 10 points for every answer you get correct.*

SAT WRITING TEST 1

To See How You'd Do on an SAT and
What You Should Do to Improve

This SAT Writing Test is very much like the actual writing SAT. It follows the genuine SAT very closely. Taking this test is like taking the actual SAT. Following is the purpose of taking this test:

1. to find out what you are *weak* in and what you are *strong* in;
2. to know where to concentrate your efforts in order to be fully prepared for the actual test.

Taking this test will prove to be a very valuable time saver for you. Why waste time studying what you already know? Spend your time profitably by studying what you *don't* know. That is what this test will tell you.

In this book, we do not waste precious pages. We get right down to the business of helping you to increase your SAT scores.

Other SAT preparation books place their emphasis on "drill, drill, drill." We do not believe that drill work is of primary importance in preparing for the SAT exam. Drill work has its place. In fact, this book contains a great variety of drill material questions, practically all of which have explanatory answers. But drill work must be coordinated with learning the skills. These skills will help you to think clearly and critically so that you will be able to answer many more SAT questions correctly.

Ready? Start taking the test. It's just like the real thing.

Answer Sheet for Practice Test 1

SECTION 1

Begin your essay on this page. If you need more space, continue on the next page. Do not write outside of the essay box.

Continue on the next page if necessary.

Continuation of ESSAY Section 1 from previous page. Write below only if you need more space.

Start with number 1 for each new section. If a section has fewer questions than answer spaces, leave the extra answer spaces blank. Be sure to erase any errors or stray marks completely.

SECTION 2

1 Ⓐ Ⓑ Ⓒ Ⓓ Ⓔ   11 Ⓐ Ⓑ Ⓒ Ⓓ Ⓔ   21 Ⓐ Ⓑ Ⓒ Ⓓ Ⓔ   31 Ⓐ Ⓑ Ⓒ Ⓓ Ⓔ
2 Ⓐ Ⓑ Ⓒ Ⓓ Ⓔ   12 Ⓐ Ⓑ Ⓒ Ⓓ Ⓔ   22 Ⓐ Ⓑ Ⓒ Ⓓ Ⓔ   32 Ⓐ Ⓑ Ⓒ Ⓓ Ⓔ
3 Ⓐ Ⓑ Ⓒ Ⓓ Ⓔ   13 Ⓐ Ⓑ Ⓒ Ⓓ Ⓔ   23 Ⓐ Ⓑ Ⓒ Ⓓ Ⓔ   33 Ⓐ Ⓑ Ⓒ Ⓓ Ⓔ
4 Ⓐ Ⓑ Ⓒ Ⓓ Ⓔ   14 Ⓐ Ⓑ Ⓒ Ⓓ Ⓔ   24 Ⓐ Ⓑ Ⓒ Ⓓ Ⓔ   34 Ⓐ Ⓑ Ⓒ Ⓓ Ⓔ
5 Ⓐ Ⓑ Ⓒ Ⓓ Ⓔ   15 Ⓐ Ⓑ Ⓒ Ⓓ Ⓔ   25 Ⓐ Ⓑ Ⓒ Ⓓ Ⓔ   35 Ⓐ Ⓑ Ⓒ Ⓓ Ⓔ
6 Ⓐ Ⓑ Ⓒ Ⓓ Ⓔ   16 Ⓐ Ⓑ Ⓒ Ⓓ Ⓔ   26 Ⓐ Ⓑ Ⓒ Ⓓ Ⓔ   36 Ⓐ Ⓑ Ⓒ Ⓓ Ⓔ
7 Ⓐ Ⓑ Ⓒ Ⓓ Ⓔ   17 Ⓐ Ⓑ Ⓒ Ⓓ Ⓔ   27 Ⓐ Ⓑ Ⓒ Ⓓ Ⓔ   37 Ⓐ Ⓑ Ⓒ Ⓓ Ⓔ
8 Ⓐ Ⓑ Ⓒ Ⓓ Ⓔ   18 Ⓐ Ⓑ Ⓒ Ⓓ Ⓔ   28 Ⓐ Ⓑ Ⓒ Ⓓ Ⓔ   38 Ⓐ Ⓑ Ⓒ Ⓓ Ⓔ
9 Ⓐ Ⓑ Ⓒ Ⓓ Ⓔ   19 Ⓐ Ⓑ Ⓒ Ⓓ Ⓔ   29 Ⓐ Ⓑ Ⓒ Ⓓ Ⓔ   39 Ⓐ Ⓑ Ⓒ Ⓓ Ⓔ
10 Ⓐ Ⓑ Ⓒ Ⓓ Ⓔ   20 Ⓐ Ⓑ Ⓒ Ⓓ Ⓔ   30 Ⓐ Ⓑ Ⓒ Ⓓ Ⓔ   40 Ⓐ Ⓑ Ⓒ Ⓓ Ⓔ

SECTION 3

1 Ⓐ Ⓑ Ⓒ Ⓓ Ⓔ   11 Ⓐ Ⓑ Ⓒ Ⓓ Ⓔ   21 Ⓐ Ⓑ Ⓒ Ⓓ Ⓔ   31 Ⓐ Ⓑ Ⓒ Ⓓ Ⓔ
2 Ⓐ Ⓑ Ⓒ Ⓓ Ⓔ   12 Ⓐ Ⓑ Ⓒ Ⓓ Ⓔ   22 Ⓐ Ⓑ Ⓒ Ⓓ Ⓔ   32 Ⓐ Ⓑ Ⓒ Ⓓ Ⓔ
3 Ⓐ Ⓑ Ⓒ Ⓓ Ⓔ   13 Ⓐ Ⓑ Ⓒ Ⓓ Ⓔ   23 Ⓐ Ⓑ Ⓒ Ⓓ Ⓔ   33 Ⓐ Ⓑ Ⓒ Ⓓ Ⓔ
4 Ⓐ Ⓑ Ⓒ Ⓓ Ⓔ   14 Ⓐ Ⓑ Ⓒ Ⓓ Ⓔ   24 Ⓐ Ⓑ Ⓒ Ⓓ Ⓔ   34 Ⓐ Ⓑ Ⓒ Ⓓ Ⓔ
5 Ⓐ Ⓑ Ⓒ Ⓓ Ⓔ   15 Ⓐ Ⓑ Ⓒ Ⓓ Ⓔ   25 Ⓐ Ⓑ Ⓒ Ⓓ Ⓔ   35 Ⓐ Ⓑ Ⓒ Ⓓ Ⓔ
6 Ⓐ Ⓑ Ⓒ Ⓓ Ⓔ   16 Ⓐ Ⓑ Ⓒ Ⓓ Ⓔ   26 Ⓐ Ⓑ Ⓒ Ⓓ Ⓔ   36 Ⓐ Ⓑ Ⓒ Ⓓ Ⓔ
7 Ⓐ Ⓑ Ⓒ Ⓓ Ⓔ   17 Ⓐ Ⓑ Ⓒ Ⓓ Ⓔ   27 Ⓐ Ⓑ Ⓒ Ⓓ Ⓔ   37 Ⓐ Ⓑ Ⓒ Ⓓ Ⓔ
8 Ⓐ Ⓑ Ⓒ Ⓓ Ⓔ   18 Ⓐ Ⓑ Ⓒ Ⓓ Ⓔ   28 Ⓐ Ⓑ Ⓒ Ⓓ Ⓔ   38 Ⓐ Ⓑ Ⓒ Ⓓ Ⓔ
9 Ⓐ Ⓑ Ⓒ Ⓓ Ⓔ   19 Ⓐ Ⓑ Ⓒ Ⓓ Ⓔ   29 Ⓐ Ⓑ Ⓒ Ⓓ Ⓔ   39 Ⓐ Ⓑ Ⓒ Ⓓ Ⓔ
10 Ⓐ Ⓑ Ⓒ Ⓓ Ⓔ   20 Ⓐ Ⓑ Ⓒ Ⓓ Ⓔ   30 Ⓐ Ⓑ Ⓒ Ⓓ Ⓔ   40 Ⓐ Ⓑ Ⓒ Ⓓ Ⓔ

SECTION 1

Time: 25 Minutes—Turn to page 179 of your answer sheet to write your ESSAY.

The purpose of the essay is to have you show how well you can express and develop your ideas. You should develop your point of view, logically and clearly present your ideas, and use language accurately.

You should write your essay on the lines provided on your answer sheet. You should not write on any other paper. You will have enough space if you write on every line and if you keep your handwriting to a reasonable size. Make sure that your handwriting is legible to other readers.

You will have 25 minutes to write an essay on the assignment below. *Do not write on any other topic. If you do so, you will receive a score of 0.*

Think carefully about the issue presented in the following quotation and the assignment below.

"The most exciting thing we can experience is the mysterious. It is the fundamental emotion which stands at the cradle of true art and true science. He who does not know it and can no longer wonder, no longer feel amazement, is as good as dead, a snuffed-out candle."

—Adapted from Albert Einstein, "What I Believe."

Assignment: In which ways have you experienced "the mysterious," and how has that made you feel alive and excited about life? Based on your experience or experiences, discuss how the above quote rings true and how science or art illustrates the "mysterious."

DO NOT WRITE YOUR ESSAY IN YOUR TEST BOOK. You will receive credit only for what you write on your answer sheet.

BEGIN WRITING YOUR ESSAY ON PAGE 179 OF THE ANSWER SHEET.

If you finish before time is called, you may check your work on this section only.
Do not turn to any other section in the test.

SECTION 2

Time: 25 Minutes—Turn to Section 2 (page 181) of your answer sheet to answer the questions in this section.
35 Questions

Directions: For each question in this section, select the best answer from among the choices given and fill in the corresponding circle on the answer sheet.

The following sentences test correctness and effectiveness of expression. Part of each sentence or the entire sentence is underlined; beneath each sentence are five ways of phrasing the underlined material. Choice A repeats the original phrasing; the other four choices are different. If you think the original phrasing produces a better sentence than any of the alternatives, select choice A; if not, select one of the other choices.

In making your selection, follow the requirements of standard written English; that is, pay attention to grammar, choice of words, sentence construction, and punctuation. Your selection should result in the most effective sentence—clear and precise, without awkwardness or ambiguity.

EXAMPLE:

Laura Ingalls Wilder published her first book and she was sixty-five years old then.

(A) and she was sixty-five years old then
(B) when she was sixty-five
(C) at age sixty-five years old
(D) upon the reaching of sixty-five years
(E) at the time when she was sixty-five

1. After the defendant charged him with being prejudiced he judge withdrew from the case.

   (A) After the defendant charged him with being prejudiced
   (B) On account of the defendant charged him with being prejudiced
   (C) Charging the defendant with being prejudiced
   (D) Upon the defendant charging him with being prejudiced
   (E) The defendant charged him with being prejudiced

2. Although the mourners differed in color and in dress, they all sat silently together for an hour to honor Whitney M. Young, Jr.

   (A) Although the mourners differed in color and in dress
   (B) Because the mourners differed in color and in dress
   (C) The mourners having differed in color and in dress
   (D) When the mourners differed in color and in dress
   (E) The mourners differed in color and in dress

3. To avoid the hot sun, our plans were that we would travel at night.

   (A) To avoid the hot sun, our plans were that we would travel at night.
   (B) To try to avoid the hot sun, our plans were for travel at night.
   (C) Our plans were night travel so that we could avoid the hot sun.
   (D) We planned to travel at night, that's how we would avoid the hot sun.
   (E) To avoid the hot sun, we made plans to travel at night.

4. Whatever she had any thoughts about, they were interrupted as the hotel lobby door opened.

   (A) Whatever she had any thoughts about
   (B) Whatever her thoughts
   (C) Whatever be her thoughts
   (D) What her thoughts were
   (E) What thoughts

5. The use of radar, as well as the two-way radio, make it possible for state troopers to intercept most speeders.

   (A) make it possible
   (B) makes it possible
   (C) allows the possibility
   (D) makes possible
   (E) make it a possibility

6. <u>Irregardless what reasons or excuses are offered</u>, there is only one word for his behavior: cowardice.

    (A) Irregardless what reasons or excuses are offered
    (B) Regardless about what reasons or excuses he may offer
    (C) Since he offered reasons and excuses
    (D) Nevertheless he offered reasons and excuses
    (E) No matter what reasons and excuses are offered

7. <u>What a man cannot state, he does not perfectly know.</u>

    (A) What a man cannot state, he does not perfectly know.
    (B) A man cannot state if he does not perfectly know.
    (C) A man cannot perfectly know if he does not state.
    (D) That which a man cannot state is that which he cannot perfectly know.
    (E) What a man cannot state is the reason he does not perfectly know.

8. Professional writers realize that <u>they cannot hope to effect</u> the reader precisely as they wish without care and practice in the use of words.

    (A) they cannot hope to effect
    (B) they cannot hope to have an effect on
    (C) they cannot hope to affect
    (D) they cannot hope effecting
    (E) they cannot try to affect

9. I've met two men <u>whom, I believe</u>, were policemen.

    (A) whom, I believe
    (B) who, I believe
    (C) each, I believe
    (D) and I believe they
    (E) who

10. Such people <u>never have and never will be trusted</u>.

    (A) never have and never will be trusted
    (B) never have and will be trusted
    (C) never have trusted and never will trust
    (D) never have been trusted and never will be trusted
    (E) never have had anyone trust them and never will have anyone trust them

11. Your employer would have been inclined to favor your request <u>if you would have waited for an occasion</u> when he was less busy.

    (A) if you would have waited for an occasion
    (B) if you would only have waited for an occasion
    (C) if you were to have waited for an occasion
    (D) if you waited for an occasion
    (E) if you had waited for an occasion

The following sentences test your ability to recognize grammar and usage errors. Each sentence contains either a single error or no error at all. No sentence contains more than one error. The error, if there is one, is underlined and lettered. If the sentence contains an error, select the one underlined part that must be changed to make the sentence correct. If the sentence is correct, select choice E. In choosing answers, follow the requirements of standard written English.

EXAMPLE:

The other delegates and him immediately
   A   B   C

accepted the resolution drafted by the
                         D

neutral states. No error.
               E

12. Because of the bomb threat everyone was asked
    A   B

to evacuate the bank but a security guard,
                  C

a fireman, and I. No error.
           D   E

13. Having drank almost all the lemonade which his
    A   B

wife had made for the picnic, Dick could not face
      C   D

her. No error.
     E

14. The wealthy socialite decided that her fortune

would be left to whomever of her relatives
    A   B

could present her with the best plan for dispensing
    C

part of the money to deserving charities. No error.
                  D   E

15. Shortly after arriving at the amusement park with
           A

the eager third-graders, the parents realized that
                        B

they had brought nowhere near the number of
              C   D

chaperones required to control the children.

No error.
  E

16. The board members along with the chairman were
                 A   B

planning a series of speakers to lecture on different
  B   C

dividend plans for their employees. No error.
              D   E

17. Due to his not studying and not attending review
   A   B

sessions, Paul got a failing mark in his bar exam,
            C

resulting in a retraction of the job offer from the
        D

law firm. No error.
        E

18. When I was in high school, I worked hard to buy
      A   B

the kind of a car that most of my friends were
     C   D

also driving. No error.
         E

19. The literature professor has complained that many
                 A

student poets are so conceited that they compare
               B

their poems with Robert Frost. No error.
  C   D   E

20. I appreciate you offering to help me with my
           A   B

research project, but the honor system prevents
                        C

students from giving and receiving assistance.
                           D

No error.
  E

21. In the final heat of the mile race, only two runners
                          A

finished the race, but even the slowest of the
                  B

two was able to break the school record that
     C

had been set a decade earlier. No error.
  D   E

GO ON TO THE NEXT PAGE

22. Passing the <u>written</u> test <u>that</u> is required for a
              A   B
driver's license is usually <u>easier</u> than <u>to pass</u> the
                         C   D
driving test. <u>No error.</u>
              E

23. All the <u>aspiring</u> young writers submitted their
             A
<u>stories</u>, each <u>hoping</u> that <u>they</u> would win first prize.
        B   C   D
<u>No error.</u>
       E

24. Her answer <u>to</u> the essay question on the test was
               A
<u>all together</u> incorrect, but because it was very
       B
<u>well written</u> she received <u>partial</u> credit for her work.
       C   D
<u>No error.</u>
       E

25. When I introduced Scott and Wilma, <u>they</u> acted
                               A
<u>as if</u> they <u>never met</u> before <u>even though</u> they had
       B   C   D
gone to the same high school. <u>No error.</u>
                         E

26. The realtor felt <u>badly</u> about not <u>being able</u> to sell
                 A   B
<u>their</u> house, because they were in a big hurry
       C
<u>to move to</u> their condominium. <u>No error.</u>
       D   E

27. The president of the newly formed nation <u>took</u>
                                   A
steps <u>to encourage</u> <u>several thousands</u> of people to
            B   C
<u>immigrate into</u> the country. <u>No error.</u>
       D   E

28. The Governor asked the attorney <u>to head</u> the
                               A
committee because <u>he</u> <u>was convinced</u> <u>that</u> the
                 B   C   D
committee needed to start work immediately.

<u>No error.</u>
       E

29. <u>Both</u> my sisters <u>participate</u> in sports, but my <u>older</u>
       A   B   C
sister is the <u>better</u> athlete. <u>No error.</u>
            D   E

Directions: The following passage is an early draft of an essay. Some parts of the passage need to be rewritten.

Read the passage and select the best answers for the questions that follow. Some questions are about particular sentences or parts of sentences and ask you to improve sentence structure or word choice. Other questions ask you to consider organization and development. In choosing answers, follow the requirements of standard written English.

Questions 30–35 refer to the following passage.

[1]It has been proved beyond doubt that using seat belts in automobiles and wearing helmets while riding motorcycles can save lives. [2]The federal government has passed laws requiring the installation of seat belts in all new cars. [3]Still, there are people who argue that government has no right to interfere with individual comfort and freedom by mandating the installation and use of these safety devices. [4]In many states, laws prohibit motorcyclists from riding without helmets. [5]What these people fail to realize is that, although wearing a seat belt may be somewhat uncomfortable or confining, it is not as uncomfortable as broken bones nor as confining as a wheelchair or a coffin. [6]Motorcyclists who refuse to wear helmets may enjoy a degree of pleasure in feeling the free wind blow through their hair, but, if thrown in an accident, their heads can be as easily squashed as "free and natural" cantaloupes. [7]These safety devices may limit pleasure and freedom in small ways because they greatly increase the opportunity to live pleasant and free lives in more important ways.

30. What should be done with sentence four?

    (A) It should be placed before sentence one.
    (B) It should be attached to sentence three with and.
    (C) Nothing should be done with it.
    (D) It should be placed after sentence two.
    (E) It should be attached to sentence five with a semicolon.

31. In sentence three, mandating should be

    (A) omitted
    (B) left as it is
    (C) changed to prohibiting
    (D) placed before individual
    (E) changed to issuing directions that are in favor of

32. In sentence six, what change is needed?

    (A) These riders are should be inserted before thrown.
    (B) Cantaloupes should be changed to balloons.
    (C) They should be substituted for their heads.
    (D) Commas should be placed around who refuse to wear helmets.
    (E) Degree should be changed to measure.

33. Sentence seven would be improved by

    (A) turning it into two sentences, the first to end after small ways
    (B) putting a comma after devices
    (C) beginning the sentence with while
    (D) omitting in more important ways
    (E) changing because to but

34. Which would get the author's point across more effectively?

    (A) Inserting a sentence that would describe statistics about the danger of not wearing seat belts or helmets.
    (B) Describing the mechanics of how a seat belt works and how a helmet protects the head.
    (C) Describing the governmental agency that enforced the laws.
    (D) Pinpointing the states that enforce the helmet law.
    (E) Citing the safest cars and motorcycles.

35. To begin the author's paragraph,

    (A) sentence 2 should be placed first.
    (B) sentence 4 should be placed first.
    (C) sentence 6 should be placed first.
    (D) sentence 7 should be placed first, deleting the first word, "These," in that sentence.
    (E) sentence 1 should remain as the introductory sentence.

STOP

If you finish before time is called, you may check your work on this section only.
Do not turn to any other section in the test.

SECTION 3

Time: 10 Minutes—Turn to Section 3 (page 181) of your answer sheet to answer the questions in this section.
14 Questions

Directions: For each question in this section, select the best answer from among the choices given and fill in the corresponding circle on the answer sheet.

The following sentences test correctness and effectiveness of expression. Part of each sentence or the entire sentence is underlined; beneath each sentence are five ways of phrasing the underlined material. Choice A repeats the original phrasing; the other four choices are different. If you think the original phrasing produces a better sentence than any of the alternatives, select choice A; if not, select one of the other choices.

In making your selection, follow the requirements of standard written English; that is, pay attention to grammar, choice of words, sentence construction, and punctuation. Your selection should result in the most effective sentence—clear and precise, without awkwardness or ambiguity.

EXAMPLE:

Laura Ingalls Wilder published her first book and she was sixty-five years old then.

(A) and she was sixty-five years old then
(B) when she was sixty-five
(C) at age sixty-five years old
(D) upon the reaching of sixty-five years
(E) at the time when she was sixty-five

1. I find Henry James' prose style more difficult to read than James Joyce.

(A) I find Henry James' prose style more difficult to read than James Joyce.
(B) I find Henry Jame's prose style more difficult to read than James Joyce'.
(C) I find Henry James's prose style more difficult to read than James Joyce's.
(D) I find the prose style of Henry James more difficult to read than James Joyce.
(E) Henry James' prose style I find more difficult to read than I find James Joyce.

2. Neither Dr. Conant nor his followers knows what to do about the problem.

(A) Neither Dr. Conant nor his followers knows what to do about the problem.
(B) Neither Dr. Conant or his followers knows what to do about the problem.
(C) Neither Dr. Conant nor his followers know what to do about the problem.
(D) Neither Dr. Conant nor his followers know what to do as far as the problem goes.
(E) As to the problem, neither Dr. Conant nor his followers know what to do.

3. The students requested a meeting with the chancellor since they desired a greater voice in university policy.

(A) The students requested a meeting with the chancellor
(B) A meeting with the chancellor was requested by the students
(C) It occurred to the students to request a meeting with the chancellor
(D) The chancellor was the one with whom the students requested a meeting
(E) The students insisted upon a meeting with the chancellor

4. Three American scientists were jointly awarded the Nobel Prize in Medicine for their study of viruses which led to discoveries.

(A) for their study of viruses which led to discoveries
(B) for their discoveries concerning viruses
(C) as a prize for their discoveries about viruses
(D) the discovery into viruses being the reason
(E) for their virus discoveries

5. <u>You must convince me of promptness in returning the money</u> before I can agree to lend you $100.

(A) You must convince me of promptness in returning the money
(B) The loan of the money must be returned promptly
(C) You must understand that you will have to assure me of a prompt money return
(D) You will have to convince me that you will return the money promptly
(E) You will return the money promptly

6. Because Bob was an outstanding athlete in high school, <u>in addition to a fine scholastic record,</u> he was awarded a scholarship at Harvard.

(A) in addition to a fine scholastic record
(B) also a student of excellence
(C) and had amassed an excellent scholastic record
(D) his scholastic record was also outstanding
(E) as well as a superior student

7. Although pre-season odds against the Mets had been 100 to 1, <u>the Orioles were trounced by them in the World Series.</u>

(A) the Orioles were trounced by them in the World Series
(B) the World Series victors were the Mets who trounced the Orioles
(C) they won the World Series by trouncing the Orioles
(D) which is hard to believe since the Orioles were trounced in the World Series
(E) it was the Mets who trounced the Orioles in the World Series

8. Before you can make a fresh fruit salad, <u>you must buy oranges, bananas, pineapples and peaches are necessary.</u>

(A) you must buy oranges, bananas, pineapples and peaches are necessary
(B) you must buy oranges and bananas and pineapples and peaches
(C) you must buy oranges and bananas. And other fruit such as pineapples and peaches
(D) you must buy oranges and bananas and other fruit. Such as pineapples and peaches
(E) you must buy oranges, bananas, pineapples, and peaches

9. The physical education department of the school offers instruction <u>to learn how to swim, how to play tennis, and how to defend oneself.</u>

(A) to learn how to swim, how to play tennis, and how to defend oneself
(B) in swimming, playing tennis, and protecting oneself
(C) in regard to how to swim, how to play tennis, and how to protect oneself
(D) for the purpose of swimming, playing tennis, and protecting oneself
(E) in swimming, playing tennis, and to protect oneself

10. <u>He is not only chairman of the Ways and Means Committee, but also of the Finance Committee.</u>

(A) He is not only chairman of the Ways and Means Committee, but also of the Finance Committee.
(B) He is the chairman not only of the Ways and Means Committee, but also of the Finance Committee.
(C) He is the chairman of the Ways and Means Committee and the chairman of the Finance Committee.
(D) Not only is he the chairman of the Ways and Means Committee, but also of the Finance Committee.
(E) Both the Finance Committee and the Ways and Means Committee are committees in which he is the chairman.

11. First the student did research in the library, <u>and then his English composition was written.</u>

(A) and then his English composition was written
(B) and then the English composition was written by the student
(C) and following this he then wrote his English composition
(D) and then he wrote his English composition
(E) then he wrote his English composition

12. <u>Two candidates for the U.S. Senate, Buckley and him, made speeches to the group.</u>

(A) Two candidates for the U.S. Senate, Buckley and him, made speeches to the group.
(B) Two candidates for the U.S. Senate, Buckley and he, made speeches to the group.
(C) Buckley and him, two candidates for the U.S. Senate, made speeches to the group.
(D) Speeches to the group were made by Buckley and he, two candidates for the U.S. Senate.
(E) Buckley and he made speeches to the group.

GO ON TO THE NEXT PAGE

13. <u>A student of American history for many years,</u> Stephen Douglas and his economic policies were thoroughly familiar to him.

(A) A student of American history for many years
(B) After having been a student of American history for many years
(C) He was a student of American history for many years
(D) Being that he was student of American history for many years
(E) Since he was a student of American history for many years

14. Does anyone know <u>to who this book belongs?</u>

(A) to who this book belongs
(B) to whom this book belongs to
(C) to whom this book belongs
(D) who this book belongs to
(E) to whom this belongs

STOP

If you finish before time is called, you may check your work on this section only.
Do not turn to any other section in the test.

How Did You Do on
This Test?

Step 1. Go to the Answer Key on page 196.

Step 2. Calculate your "raw score" using the directions on page 197.

Step 3. Get your "scaled score" for the test by referring to the Raw Score/ Scaled Score Conversion Tables on pages 198–199.

*THERE'S ALWAYS ROOM FOR
IMPROVEMENT!*

Answer Key for SAT Writing Test 1

Section 1

_____

Essay score

Section 2			Section 3		
	Correct Answer			Correct Answer	
1	A		1	C	
2	A		2	C	
3	E		3	A	
4	B		4	B	
5	B		5	D	
6	E		6	E	
7	A		7	C	
8	C		8	E	
9	B		9	B	
10	D		10	B	
11	E		11	D	
12	D		12	B	
13	A		13	E	
14	B		14	C	
15	C				
16	E				
17	A				
18	C				
19	D				
20	A				
21	B				
22	D				
23	D				
24	B				
25	C				
26	A				
27	E				
28	B				
29	E				
30	D				
31	B				
32	A				
33	E				
34	A				
35	E				

Number correct (Section 3)
_____

Number incorrect (Section 3)
_____

_____

Number correct

_____

Number incorrect

Get Your Writing Score

How many multiple-choice writing questions did you get **right?**

Section 2: Questions 1–35   _____

Section 3: Questions 1–14   + _____

                  Total   = _____ **(A)**

How many multiple-choice questions did you get **wrong?**

Section 2: Questions 1–35   _____

Section 3: Questions 1–14   + _____

                  Total   = _____ **(B)**

                  × 0.25   = _____

            A – B   = _____

                  Writing Raw Score

Round writing raw score to the nearest whole number.

_____

Use the Score Conversion Table to find your writing multiple-choice scaled score.

_____

Estimate your essay score using the Essay Scoring Guide.

_____

Use the SAT Score Conversion Table for Writing Composite to find your writing scaled score. You will need your Writing Raw Score and your Essay Score to use this table.

_____

SAT Writing Score Conversion Table

Raw Score	Writing Multiple-Choice Scaled Score*	Raw Score	Writing Multiple-Choice Scaled Score*
		31	60
		30	58
		29	57
		28	56
		27	55
		26	54
		25	53
		24	52
		23	51
		22	50
		21	49
		20	48
		19	47
		18	46
		17	45
		16	44
		15	44
		14	43
49	80	13	42
48	80	12	41
47	80	11	40
46	79	10	39
45	78	9	38
44	76	8	38
43	74	7	37
42	73	6	36
41	71	5	35
40	70	4	34
39	69	3	32
38	67	2	31
37	66	1	30
36	65	0	28
35	64	−1	27
34	63	−2	25
33	62	−3	23
32	61	−4	20
		and below	

This table is for use only with the test in this book.

*The Writing Multiple-Choice score is reported on a 20–80 scale. Use the SAT Score Conversion Table for Writing Composite for the total writing scaled score.

SAT Score Conversion Table for Writing Composite

Writing Multiple-Choice Raw Score	Essay Raw Score						
	0	1	2	3	4	5	6
−12	200	200	200	210	240	270	300
−11	200	200	200	210	240	270	300
−10	200	200	200	210	240	270	300
−9	200	200	200	210	240	270	300
−8	200	200	200	210	240	270	300
−7	200	200	200	210	240	270	300
−6	200	200	200	210	240	270	300
−5	200	200	200	210	240	270	300
−4	200	200	200	230	270	300	330
−3	200	210	230	250	290	320	350
−2	200	230	250	280	310	340	370
−1	210	240	260	290	320	360	380
0	230	260	280	300	340	370	400
1	240	270	290	320	350	380	410
2	250	280	300	330	360	390	420
3	260	290	310	340	370	400	430
4	270	300	320	350	380	410	440
5	280	310	330	360	390	420	450
6	290	320	340	360	400	430	460
7	290	330	340	370	410	440	470
8	300	330	350	380	410	450	470
9	310	340	360	390	420	450	480
10	320	350	370	390	430	460	490
11	320	360	370	400	440	470	500
12	330	360	380	410	440	470	500
13	340	370	390	420	450	480	510
14	350	380	390	420	460	490	520
15	350	380	400	430	460	500	530
16	360	390	410	440	470	500	530
17	370	400	420	440	480	510	540
18	380	410	420	450	490	520	550
19	380	410	430	460	490	530	560
20	390	420	440	470	500	530	560
21	400	430	450	480	510	540	570
22	410	440	460	480	520	550	580
23	420	450	470	490	530	560	590
24	420	460	470	500	540	570	600
25	430	460	480	510	540	580	610

Writing Multiple-Choice Raw Score	Essay Raw Score						
	0	1	2	3	4	5	6
26	440	470	490	520	550	590	610
27	450	480	500	530	560	590	620
28	460	490	510	540	570	600	630
29	470	500	520	550	580	610	640
30	480	510	530	560	590	620	650
31	490	520	540	560	600	630	660
32	500	530	550	570	610	640	670
33	510	540	550	580	620	650	680
34	510	550	560	590	630	660	690
35	520	560	570	600	640	670	700
36	530	560	580	610	650	680	710
37	540	570	590	620	660	690	720
38	550	580	600	630	670	700	730
39	560	600	610	640	680	710	740
40	580	610	620	650	690	720	750
41	590	620	640	660	700	730	760
42	600	630	650	680	710	740	770
43	610	640	660	690	720	750	780
44	620	660	670	700	740	770	800
45	640	670	690	720	750	780	800
46	650	690	700	730	770	800	800
47	670	700	720	750	780	800	800
48	680	720	730	760	800	800	800
49	680	720	730	760	800	800	800

Chart for Self-Appraisal
Based on the Practice Test
You Have Just Taken

The Self-Appraisal Chart below tells you quickly where your SAT strengths and weaknesses lie. Check or circle the appropriate range in accordance with the number of your correct answers for each area of the Practice Test you have just taken.

	Writing *(Multiple-Choice)*
EXCELLENT	42–49
GOOD	37–41
FAIR	31–36
POOR	20–30
VERY POOR	0–19

SAT WRITING SCORE PERCENTILE CONVERSION TABLE

Writing

SAT scaled verbal score	Percentile rank
800	99.7+
790	99.5
740–780	99
700–730	97
670–690	95
640–660	91
610–630	85
580–600	77
550–570	68
510–540	57
480–500	46
440–470	32
410–430	21
380–400	13
340–370	6
300–330	2
230–290	1
200–220	0–0.5

Section 1—Essay

The following are guidelines for scoring the essay.

The SAT Scoring Guide

Score of 6	Score of 5	Score of 4
An essay in this category is *outstanding*, demonstrating *clear and consistent mastery*, although it may have a few minor errors. A typical essay	An essay in this category is *effective*, demonstrating *reasonably consistent mastery*, although it will have occasional errors or lapses in quality. A typical essay	An essay in this category is *competent*, demonstrating *adequate mastery*, although it will have lapses in quality. A typical essay
• effectively and insightfully develops a point of view on the issue and demonstrates outstanding critical thinking, using clearly appropriate examples, reasons, and other evidence to support its position	• effectively develops a point of view on the issue and demonstrates strong critical thinking, generally using appropriate examples, reasons, and other evidence to support its position	• develops a point of view on the issue and demonstrates competent critical thinking, using adequate examples, reasons, and other evidence to support its position
• is well organized and clearly focused, demonstrating clear coherence and smooth progression of ideas	• is well organized and focused, demonstrating coherence and progression of ideas	• is generally organized and focused, demonstrating some coherence and progression of ideas
• exhibits skillful use of language, using a varied, accurate, and apt vocabulary	• exhibits facility in the use of language, using appropriate vocabulary	• exhibits adequate but inconsistent facility in the use of language, using generally appropriate vocabulary
• demonstrates meaningful variety in sentence structure	• demonstrates variety in sentence structure	• demonstrates some variety in sentence structure
• is free of most errors in grammar, usage, and mechanics	• is generally free of most errors in grammar, usage, and mechanics	• has some errors in grammar, usage, and mechanics

Score of 3	Score of 2	Score of 1
An essay in this category is *inadequate*, but demonstrates *developing mastery*, and is marked by ONE OR MORE of the following weaknesses:	An essay in this category is *seriously limited*, demonstrating *little mastery*, and is flawed by ONE OR MORE of the following weaknesses:	An essay in this category is *fundamentally lacking*, demonstrating *very little* or *no mastery*, and is severely flawed by ONE OR MORE of the following weaknesses:
• develops a point of view on the issue, demonstrating some critical thinking, but may do so inconsistently or use inadequate examples, reasons, or other evidence to support its position	• develops a point of view on the issue that is vague or seriously limited, demonstrating weak critical thinking, providing inappropriate or insufficient examples, reasons, or other evidence to support its position	• develops no viable point of view on the issue, or provides little or no evidence to support its position
• is limited in its organization or focus, or may demonstrate some lapses in coherence or progression of ideas	• is poorly organized and/or focused, or demonstrates serious problems with coherence or progression of ideas	• is disorganized or unfocused, resulting in a disjointed or incoherent essay
• displays developing facility in the use of language, but sometimes uses weak vocabulary or inappropriate word choice	• displays very little facility in the use of language, using very limited vocabulary or incorrect word choice	• displays fundamental errors in vocabulary
• lacks variety or demonstrates problems in sentence structure	• demonstrates frequent problems in sentence structure	• demonstrates severe flaws in sentence structure
• contains an accumulation of errors in grammar, usage, and mechanics	• contains errors in grammar, usage, and mechanics so serious that meaning is somewhat obscured	• contains pervasive errors in grammar, usage, or mechanics that persistently interfere with meaning

Essays not written on the essay assignment will receive a score of zero.

Explanatory Answers for Practice Test 1

Section 2: Writing

> For further practice and information, please refer to Grammar and Usage Refresher starting on page 11.

1. **(A)** Choice A is correct. Choice B is incorrect because "on account" may not be used as a subordinate conjunction. Choice C is incorrect because it gives the meaning that the judge is doing the charging. Choice D is incorrect because the possessive noun ("defendant") modifying the gerund ("charging") must take the form "defendant's." Choice E creates a run-on sentence.

2. **(A)** Choice A is correct. Choices B, C, and D are incorrect because they change the meaning of the original sentence. Choice E creates a run-on sentence.

3. **(E)** Choices A and B are incorrect because they give the idea that the plans are trying to avoid the hot sun. Choice C is awkward. Choice D is a run-on sentence. Choice E is correct.

4. **(B)** Choice A is too wordy. Choice B is correct. Choice C is incorrect because it changes the tense of the original sentence—"Whatever (may) be her thoughts" is in the present tense. Choice D does not retain the meaning of the original sentence. Choice E makes no sense.

5. **(B)** Choices A and E are incorrect because the subject word "use" requires a singular verb ("makes"). Choice B is correct. Choices C and D are awkward.

6. **(E)** "Irregardless" (Choice A) is incorrect. "Regardless about" (Choice B) is unidiomatic. Choices C and D change the meaning of the original sentence. Moreover, Choice D makes the sentence ungrammatical. Choice E is correct.

7. **(A)** Choice A is correct. Choices B, C, and E change the meaning of the original sentence. Choice D is too wordy.

8. **(C)** The infinitive "to effect" means "to bring about"—this is not the meaning intended in the original sentence. Therefore, Choices A, B, and D are incorrect. Choice C is correct. Choice E changes the meaning of the original sentence.

9. **(B)** In the original sentence, "who" should replace "whom" as the subject of the subordinate clause ("who were policemen"). "I believe" is simply a parenthetical expression. Therefore, Choice A is incorrect and Choice B is correct. Choice C creates a run-on sentence. Choice D improperly changes the sentence from a complex type to a compound type. Choice E does not retain the meaning of the original sentence.

10. **(D)** Choices A and B suffer from improper ellipsis. Choice C changes the meaning of the original sentence. Choice D is correct. Choice E is too wordy.

11. **(E)** Sequence of tenses in a past contrary-to-fact condition requires the "had waited" form in the "if" clause. Therefore Choices A, B, C, and D are incorrect and Choice E is correct.

12. **(D)** "...but a security guard, a fireman, and *me*." The preposition *but* is understood before *me*. Since *me* is the object of the preposition *but*, it has an objective form (*me*)—not a nominative form (*I*).

13. **(A)** "Having drunk...the lemonade..." The past participle of *drink* is *having drunk*.

14. **(B)** "...to *whoever*...could present her..." The subject of the dependent clause must have a nominative case form (*whoever*)—not an objective case form (*whomever*).

15. **(C)** "...they had brought *not nearly* the number..." Do not use the expression *nowhere near* for *not nearly.*

16. **(E)** All underlined parts are correct.

17. **(A)** "*Because of* his not studying..." Do not begin a sentence with the words *due to. Due* is an adjective. As an adjective, it must have a noun to modify.

18. **(C)** "...to buy the *kind of* car..." Do not use the article *a* or *an* after *kind of, type of, sort of,* etc.

19. **(D)** "...compare their poems *with those of Robert Frost.*" We have an improper ellipsis in the original sentence. The additional words (*those of*) are necessary to complete the meaning of the sentence.

20. **(A)** "I appreciate *your* offering..." The subject of a gerund is in the possessive case. We, therefore, say *your offering*—not *you offering.*

21. **(B)** "...the *slower* of the two..." Since we are here comparing two runners, we must use the comparative degree (*slower*)—not the superlative degree (*slowest*).

22. **(D)** "...is usually easier than passing the driving test." This sentence requires parallelism: *Passing the driving test*" should parallel "*Passing* the written test..."

23. **(D)** "...each hoping that *he* would win..." A pronoun should be in the same number as the noun or pronoun to which it refers. In the sentence, *he* refers to *each,* which is a singular pronoun.

24. **(B)** "Her answer...was *altogether* incorrect..." *Altogether* means *entirely, wholly. All together* means *as a group.*

25. **(C)** "...they acted as if they never *had met* before..." We must use the past perfect tense (*had met*) to indicate an action taking place before another past action (*acted*).

26. **(A)** "The realtor felt *bad*...." After the copulative verb (*felt*), the word referring to the subject should be a predicate adjective (*bad*)—not an adverb (*badly*).

27. **(E)** All underlined parts are correct.

28. **(B)** The pronoun *he* has an indefinite antecedent. We cannot tell whether *he* refers to the Governor or the attorney. Accordingly, we must be specific by using either *the Governor* or *the attorney.*

29. **(E)** All underlined parts are correct.

30. **(D)** Choice A is incorrect because sentence one is needed to open the paragraph in order to establish the fact that safety devices have been proven to save lives. If this information does not precede every other idea in the paragraph, the logical reasons for the laws and for obeying them are not clear. Therefore, sentence four should not be placed before sentence one. Choices B and C are incorrect in that sentence four is in an illogical position in the paragraph and should be moved rather than attached to sentence three (Choice B) or left in its present position (Choice C). Choice D is correct: The logical position for the idea about laws governing the use of motorcycle helmets is directly following the idea about laws governing the installation of seat belts. (The two ideas are so closely related that they might appropriately be joined in a complex sentence.) Additionally, in the present position of sentence four, "these safety devices" seems to apply only to "seat belts" in sentence two, whereas the clear intent of the paragraph as a whole is that "safety devices" refers to both seat belts and helmets. Choice E is incorrect because the present position of sentence four is not logical and creates the inaccurate reference to only one safety device.

31. **(B)** Choice A is incorrect since omitting "mandating" creates the illogical sense that government interferes with individuals by using safety devices. Government might possibly be said to interfere with individuals by installing seat belts, but it cannot interfere with individuals by using seat belts, an idea that is awkward in any case since "government" does not constitute an entity capable of using a seat belt. Choice B is correct because "mandating" means "issuing an authoritative command or instruction," a sense that agrees with the idea of passing a law. Choice C is incorrect in that "prohibiting" or "forbidding" the use of safety devices results in a meaning that runs counter to the whole sense of the paragraph. Choice D is incorrect in that nonsense would result from placing "mandating" before "individual." The government would then be said to interfere with the issuing of commands making individual comfort and freedom obligatory. Choice E is incorrect in that such a wordy substitute is never preferable to one correct word; moreover, the phrase is inaccurate in that the "directions" (or laws) do not express a preference ("in favor of") but an order.

32. **(A)** Choice A is correct: The insertion of "these riders are" is necessary to correct the existing situation in which the modifier "if thrown in an accident" incorrectly attaches itself to "their heads." Choice B is

incorrect not only because the dangling modifier is not corrected but also because a cantaloupe, with its hard rind and juicy interior, is a better figure of speech for a human head than a flexible, partially transparent balloon filled with gas or air. Choice C is incorrect because replacing "their heads" with "they" would create a situation in which "if thrown in an accident" would modify a pronoun which might refer either to motorcyclists or to helmets. The rest of the sentence referring to cantaloupes would make a poor comparison if applied to the bodies of the motorcyclists and would convey no pertinent meaning if applied to helmets. Choice D is incorrect because "who refuse to wear helmets" is a restrictive clause defining particular motorcyclists and should not be made into a nonrestrictive clause by placing commas around it. Choice E is incorrect in that the dangling modifier would not be corrected and nothing would be gained in sense by creating the awkwardly repetitive sounds of "measure of pleasure."

33. **(E)** Choice A is incorrect: Turning sentence seven into two sentences with the first ending after "small ways" would leave the second sentence as a dependent clause fragment. Choice B is incorrect because the subject and its verb should not be separated with a comma. Choice C is incorrect: Beginning the sentence with "while" would be a good choice if "because" were removed; but Choice C does not

specify this omission, and "because" is not an appropriate conjunction. Choice D is incorrect: While the phrase "in more important ways" could be omitted (even though it adds balance to the sentence in paralleling "in small ways"), the major problem in the sentence would be passed over in making only this deletion. Choice E is correct: The word "because" should be changed to "but." The second idea in the sentence is not "a reason for" or "the result of" the first idea, relationships indicated by "because." The two ideas in the sentence are contrasting (that devices may "limit" but also "greatly increase" comfort and freedom) and should be connected with a conjunction showing this contrast.

34. **(A)** Statistical backup would qualify the author's position and show the dangers more specifically and in a more documented fashion. Choices B, C, D are weak, and choice E is irrelevant.

35. **(E)** Since the paragraph is in favor of wearing seat belts and helmets, the author must have a strong first introductory statement for why seat belts and helmets are warranted. Sentence 1 serves that purpose and should be kept as the first sentence.

Explanatory Answers for Practice Test 1 (continued)

Section 3: Writing

For further practice and information, please refer to Grammar and Usage Refresher starting on page 11.

1. **(C)** We are concerned here with the apostrophe use with a singular name ending in -s. We are also concerned with improper ellipsis. In Choice A, "James'" is correct but we must either say "to read than *the prose style* of James Joyce" or "to read than James Joyce's." In Choice B, "Jame's" is incorrect—his name is not "Jame." Choice C is correct. Choices D and E are incorrect for the same reason that Choice A is incorrect—improper ellipsis.

2. **(C)** Choice A is incorrect because in a "neither…nor" construction, the number of the verb is determined by the "nor" subject noun ("followers"). Since "followers" is plural, the verb must be plural ("know"). Choices B, D, and E are incorrect for the same reason. Moreover, Choice B is incorrect for another reason: the correlative form is "neither…nor"—not "neither…or." Choice C is correct.

3. **(A)** Choice A is correct. Choice B's passive verb ("was requested") interferes with the flow of the sentence. "It occurred" in Choice C is unnecessary. Choice D is too wordy for what has to be expressed. Choice E changes the meaning of the original sentence—the students did not "insist."

4. **(B)** Choice A is indirect. Choice B is correct. In Choice C, "as a prize" repeats unnecessarily the "Nobel Prize." Choice D is much too awkward. Choice E is incorrect—the scientists did not discover viruses.

5. **(D)** The important thing is not "promptness"; accordingly, Choice A is wrong. Choice B is incorrect because it is not the "loan" that must be returned. In Choice C, "You must understand" is unnecessary. Choice D is correct. Choice E changes the meaning of the original sentence.

6. **(E)** Choice A, as a phrase, hangs without clearly modifying anything else in the sentence. Choice B would be correct if it were preceded and followed by a dash in order to set the choice off from what goes before and after. Choice C is wrong because one does not "amass a scholastic record." Choice D is a complete sentence within a sentence, thus creating a run-on sentence. Choice E is correct.

7. **(C)** In Choice A, the use of the passive verb ("were trounced") reduces the effectiveness of expression. Choice B is indirect. Choice C is correct. In Choice D, "which is hard to believe" is unnecessary. Choice E is indirect.

8. **(E)** In Choice A, "are necessary" not only is not necessary, but also makes the sentence ungrammatical with the additional complete predicate ("are necessary"). There are too many "ands" in Choice B. Some grammarians call this an "Andy" sentence. In Choice C, "And other fruit…peaches" is an incomplete sentence—also called a sentence fragment. Choice D also suffers from sentence fragmentation: "Such as pineapples and peaches." Choice E is correct.

9. **(B)** In Choice A, it is unidiomatic to say "instruction to learn." Choice B is correct. Choice C is too wordy. Choice D is not as direct as Choice B. Choice E suffers from lack of parallelism.

10. **(B)** Choice A is incorrect because the words "not only…but also" should be placed immediately before the parallel terms, which are "of the Ways and Means Committee" and "of the Finance Committee." Choice B is correct. Choice C is too wordy. Choice D is incorrect because it does not place the words "not only…but also" directly before the parallel terms. Choice E is awkward.

11. **(D)** Choices A and B are incorrect because they both contain an unnecessary shift from active to passive voice, resulting in awkwardness. Choice C is too wordy. Choice D is correct. Choice E is a complete sentence making the original a run-on sentence.

12. **(B)** Choice A is incorrect because "Buckley" and "him" are in apposition with "candidates," the subject of the sentence. Since the subject is nominative, the appositive must also be nominative; hence "he" should be used instead of "him." Choice B is correct. Choice C uses "him" incorrectly for "he." The use of the passive voice ("were made") makes Choice D unnecessarily indirect. Choice E omits "two candidates for the U.S. Senate" which is necessary to the meaning of the sentence.

13. **(E)** Choices A and B are incorrect because they are both misplaced as modifiers—it is not clear who is the student. Choice C is a complete sentence making the original sentence a run-on sentence. Choice D is incorrect because "being that" is poor English. Choice E is correct.

14. **(C)** Choice A is not correct because the word "who" is incorrectly used; as the object of the preposition, the word "whom" is used. In Choice B, the second "to" is redundant. Choice C is correct. Choice D uses the word "who" instead of "whom." Choice E does not include a reference to the book, which is in the original sentence.

What You Must Do Now to Raise Your SAT Writing Score

1. a) Follow the directions on page 195 to determine your scaled score for the SAT Test you've just taken. These results will give you a good idea about whether or not you ought to study hard in order to achieve a certain score on the actual SAT.

   b) Using your Test correct answer count as a basis, indicate for yourself your areas of strength and weakness as revealed by the "Self-Appraisal Chart" on page 201.

2. Eliminate your weaknesses in each of the SAT test areas (as revealed in the "Self-Appraisal Chart") by taking the following Giant Step toward SAT success:

Giant Step

Take a look at Part 3—The SAT Writing Test, which describes the various item types in the Writing Section and sample questions with answers and explanations. Read "A Brief Review of English Grammar," Part 1. Also make use of the Grammar Refresher, Part 2.

If you do the job *right* and follow the steps listed above, you are likely to raise your SAT score on the writing parts of the test 150 points—maybe 200 points—and even more.

I am the master of my fate;
I am the captain of my soul.

—From the poem "Invictus"
by William Ernest Henley

SAT WRITING TEST 2

SECTION 1

Time: 25 Minutes—Turn to page 216 of your answer sheet to write your ESSAY.

The purpose of the essay is to have you show how well you can express and develop your ideas. You should develop your point of view, logically and clearly present your ideas, and use language accurately.

You should write your essay on the lines provided on your answer sheet. You should not write on any other paper. You will have enough space if you write on every line and if you keep your handwriting to a reasonable size. Make sure that your handwriting is legible to other readers.

You will have 25 minutes to write an essay on the assignment below. *Do not write on any other topic. If you do so, you will receive a score of 0.*

Think carefully about the issue presented in the following quotation and the assignment below.

> "One of the main purposes of education is to get students excited about the 'process' behind problem solving instead of rushing into an answer and just concentrating on the final result. Often students can extract something from a problem that leads to the answer. Students can relax and think more clearly when they concentrate on the game or the wonderful process, if you will, of thinking."
> —Adapted from G. Gruber, "A Superlative Guide to the Hows and Wise," Omni Magazine

Assignment: Do you agree with the above quote? In many cases, is the problem solver concerned just about getting an answer, and not about concentrating on the "process" to get the answer? Do you agree that by not having faith in the process, he or she often does not arrive at the solution? In answering these questions, describe, based on your own experience, why you agree or disagree. What rewards are lost or gained when you just concentrate on an answer without being aware of or interested in the process of arriving at the answer?

DO NOT WRITE YOUR ESSAY IN YOUR TEST BOOK. You will receive credit only for what you write on your answer sheet.

BEGIN WRITING YOUR ESSAY ON PAGE 216 OF THE ANSWER SHEET.

If you finish before time is called, you may check your work on this section only.
Do not turn to any other section in the test.

Answer Sheet for Practice Test 2

SECTION 1

Begin your essay on this page. If you need more space, continue on the next page. Do not write outside of the essay box.

Continue on the next page if necessary.

Continuation of ESSAY Section 1 from previous page. Write below only if you need more space.

Start with number 1 for each new section. If a section has fewer questions than answer spaces, leave the extra answer spaces blank. Be sure to erase any errors or stray marks completely.

SECTION

2

1 Ⓐ Ⓑ Ⓒ Ⓓ Ⓔ	11 Ⓐ Ⓑ Ⓒ Ⓓ Ⓔ	21 Ⓐ Ⓑ Ⓒ Ⓓ Ⓔ	31 Ⓐ Ⓑ Ⓒ Ⓓ Ⓔ
2 Ⓐ Ⓑ Ⓒ Ⓓ Ⓔ	12 Ⓐ Ⓑ Ⓒ Ⓓ Ⓔ	22 Ⓐ Ⓑ Ⓒ Ⓓ Ⓔ	32 Ⓐ Ⓑ Ⓒ Ⓓ Ⓔ
3 Ⓐ Ⓑ Ⓒ Ⓓ Ⓔ	13 Ⓐ Ⓑ Ⓒ Ⓓ Ⓔ	23 Ⓐ Ⓑ Ⓒ Ⓓ Ⓔ	33 Ⓐ Ⓑ Ⓒ Ⓓ Ⓔ
4 Ⓐ Ⓑ Ⓒ Ⓓ Ⓔ	14 Ⓐ Ⓑ Ⓒ Ⓓ Ⓔ	24 Ⓐ Ⓑ Ⓒ Ⓓ Ⓔ	34 Ⓐ Ⓑ Ⓒ Ⓓ Ⓔ
5 Ⓐ Ⓑ Ⓒ Ⓓ Ⓔ	15 Ⓐ Ⓑ Ⓒ Ⓓ Ⓔ	25 Ⓐ Ⓑ Ⓒ Ⓓ Ⓔ	35 Ⓐ Ⓑ Ⓒ Ⓓ Ⓔ
6 Ⓐ Ⓑ Ⓒ Ⓓ Ⓔ	16 Ⓐ Ⓑ Ⓒ Ⓓ Ⓔ	26 Ⓐ Ⓑ Ⓒ Ⓓ Ⓔ	36 Ⓐ Ⓑ Ⓒ Ⓓ Ⓔ
7 Ⓐ Ⓑ Ⓒ Ⓓ Ⓔ	17 Ⓐ Ⓑ Ⓒ Ⓓ Ⓔ	27 Ⓐ Ⓑ Ⓒ Ⓓ Ⓔ	37 Ⓐ Ⓑ Ⓒ Ⓓ Ⓔ
8 Ⓐ Ⓑ Ⓒ Ⓓ Ⓔ	18 Ⓐ Ⓑ Ⓒ Ⓓ Ⓔ	28 Ⓐ Ⓑ Ⓒ Ⓓ Ⓔ	38 Ⓐ Ⓑ Ⓒ Ⓓ Ⓔ
9 Ⓐ Ⓑ Ⓒ Ⓓ Ⓔ	19 Ⓐ Ⓑ Ⓒ Ⓓ Ⓔ	29 Ⓐ Ⓑ Ⓒ Ⓓ Ⓔ	39 Ⓐ Ⓑ Ⓒ Ⓓ Ⓔ
10 Ⓐ Ⓑ Ⓒ Ⓓ Ⓔ	20 Ⓐ Ⓑ Ⓒ Ⓓ Ⓔ	30 Ⓐ Ⓑ Ⓒ Ⓓ Ⓔ	40 Ⓐ Ⓑ Ⓒ Ⓓ Ⓔ

SECTION

3

1 Ⓐ Ⓑ Ⓒ Ⓓ Ⓔ	11 Ⓐ Ⓑ Ⓒ Ⓓ Ⓔ	21 Ⓐ Ⓑ Ⓒ Ⓓ Ⓔ	31 Ⓐ Ⓑ Ⓒ Ⓓ Ⓔ
2 Ⓐ Ⓑ Ⓒ Ⓓ Ⓔ	12 Ⓐ Ⓑ Ⓒ Ⓓ Ⓔ	22 Ⓐ Ⓑ Ⓒ Ⓓ Ⓔ	32 Ⓐ Ⓑ Ⓒ Ⓓ Ⓔ
3 Ⓐ Ⓑ Ⓒ Ⓓ Ⓔ	13 Ⓐ Ⓑ Ⓒ Ⓓ Ⓔ	23 Ⓐ Ⓑ Ⓒ Ⓓ Ⓔ	33 Ⓐ Ⓑ Ⓒ Ⓓ Ⓔ
4 Ⓐ Ⓑ Ⓒ Ⓓ Ⓔ	14 Ⓐ Ⓑ Ⓒ Ⓓ Ⓔ	24 Ⓐ Ⓑ Ⓒ Ⓓ Ⓔ	34 Ⓐ Ⓑ Ⓒ Ⓓ Ⓔ
5 Ⓐ Ⓑ Ⓒ Ⓓ Ⓔ	15 Ⓐ Ⓑ Ⓒ Ⓓ Ⓔ	25 Ⓐ Ⓑ Ⓒ Ⓓ Ⓔ	35 Ⓐ Ⓑ Ⓒ Ⓓ Ⓔ
6 Ⓐ Ⓑ Ⓒ Ⓓ Ⓔ	16 Ⓐ Ⓑ Ⓒ Ⓓ Ⓔ	26 Ⓐ Ⓑ Ⓒ Ⓓ Ⓔ	36 Ⓐ Ⓑ Ⓒ Ⓓ Ⓔ
7 Ⓐ Ⓑ Ⓒ Ⓓ Ⓔ	17 Ⓐ Ⓑ Ⓒ Ⓓ Ⓔ	27 Ⓐ Ⓑ Ⓒ Ⓓ Ⓔ	37 Ⓐ Ⓑ Ⓒ Ⓓ Ⓔ
8 Ⓐ Ⓑ Ⓒ Ⓓ Ⓔ	18 Ⓐ Ⓑ Ⓒ Ⓓ Ⓔ	28 Ⓐ Ⓑ Ⓒ Ⓓ Ⓔ	38 Ⓐ Ⓑ Ⓒ Ⓓ Ⓔ
9 Ⓐ Ⓑ Ⓒ Ⓓ Ⓔ	19 Ⓐ Ⓑ Ⓒ Ⓓ Ⓔ	29 Ⓐ Ⓑ Ⓒ Ⓓ Ⓔ	39 Ⓐ Ⓑ Ⓒ Ⓓ Ⓔ
10 Ⓐ Ⓑ Ⓒ Ⓓ Ⓔ	20 Ⓐ Ⓑ Ⓒ Ⓓ Ⓔ	30 Ⓐ Ⓑ Ⓒ Ⓓ Ⓔ	40 Ⓐ Ⓑ Ⓒ Ⓓ Ⓔ

SECTION 2

Time: 25 Minutes—Turn to Section 2 (page 218) of your answer sheet to answer the questions in this section. 35 Questions

Directions: For each question in this section, select the best answer from among the choices given and fill in the corresponding circle on the answer sheet.

The following sentences test correctness and effectiveness of expression. Part of each sentence or the entire sentence is underlined; beneath each sentence are five ways of phrasing the underlined material. Choice A repeats the original phrasing; the other four choices are different. If you think the original phrasing produces a better sentence than any of the alternatives, select choice A; if not, select one of the other choices.

In making your selection, follow the requirements of standard written English; that is, pay attention to grammar, choice of words, sentence construction, and punctuation. Your selection should result in the most effective sentence—clear and precise, without awkwardness or ambiguity.

EXAMPLE:

Laura Ingalls Wilder published her first book and she was sixty-five years old then.

(A) and she was sixty-five years old then
(B) when she was sixty-five
(C) at age sixty-five years old
(D) upon the reaching of sixty-five years
(E) at the time when she was sixty-five

1. Joe couldn't wait for his return to his home after being in the army for two years.

(A) Joe couldn't wait for his return to his home
(B) There was a strong desire on Joe's part to return home
(C) Joe was eager to return home
(D) Joe wanted home badly
(E) Joe arranged to return home

2. Trash, filth, and muck are clogging the streets of the city and that's not all, the sidewalks are full of garbage.

(A) that's not all, the sidewalks are full of garbage
(B) another thing: garbage is all over the sidewalks
(C) the garbage cans haven't been emptied for days
(D) in addition, garbage is lying all over the side walks
(E) what's more, the sidewalks have garbage that is lying all over them

3. Tired and discouraged by the problems of the day, Myra decided to have a good dinner, and then lie down for an hour, and then go dancing.

(A) Myra decided to have a good dinner, and then lie down for an hour, and then go dancing.
(B) Myra decided to have a good dinner, lying down for an hour, and then dancing.
(C) Myra decided to have a good dinner, lie down for an hour, and then dancing.
(D) Myra decided to have a good dinner, lay down for an hour, and then dance.
(E) Myra decided to have a good dinner, lie down for an hour, and then go dancing.

4. I am not certain in respect to which courses to take.

(A) in respect to which courses
(B) about which courses
(C) which courses
(D) as to the choice of which courses
(E) for which courses I am

5. The people of the besieged village had no doubt that the end was drawing near.

(A) that the end was drawing near
(B) about the nearness of the end
(C) it was clear that the end was near
(D) concerning the end's being near
(E) that all would die

6. There isn't a single man among us <u>who is skilled in the art of administering first-aid</u>.

   (A) who is skilled in the art of administering first aid
   (B) who knows how to administer first aid
   (C) who knows the administration of first aid
   (D) who is a first aid man
   (E) who administers first aid

7. This is the hole <u>that was squeezed through by the mouse</u>.

   (A) that was squeezed through by the mouse
   (B) that the mouse was seen to squeeze through
   (C) the mouse squeezed through it
   (D) that the mouse squeezed through
   (E) like what the mouse squeezed through

8. <u>She soundly feel asleep</u> after having finished the novel.

   (A) She soundly feel asleep
   (B) She decided to sleep
   (C) She went on to her sleep
   (D) She fell to sleep
   (E) She fell fast asleep

9. This is one restaurant I won't patronize because <u>I was served a fried egg by the waitress that was rotten</u>.

   (A) I was served a fried egg by the waitress that was rotten
   (B) I was served by the waitress a fried egg that was rotten
   (C) a fried egg was served to me by the waitress that was rotten
   (D) the waitress served me a fried egg that was rotten
   (E) a rotten fried egg was served to me by the waitress

10. Watching the familiar story unfold on the screen, he was glad <u>that he read the book with such painstaking attention to detail</u>.

    (A) that he read the book with such painstaking attention to detail
    (B) that he had read the book with such painstaking attention to detail
    (C) that he read the book with such attention to particulars
    (D) that he read the book with such intense effort
    (E) that he paid so much attention to the plot of the book

11. If anyone requested tea instead of coffee, <u>it was a simple matter to serve it to them</u> from the teapot at the rear of the table.

    (A) it was a simple matter to serve it to them
    (B) it was easy to serve them
    (C) it was a simple matter to serve them
    (D) it was a simple matter to serve it to him
    (E) he could serve himself

GO ON TO THE NEXT PAGE

The following sentences test your ability to recognize grammar and usage errors. Each sentence contains either a single error or no error at all. No sentence contains more than one error. The error, if there is one, is underlined and lettered. If the sentence contains an error, select the one underlined part that must be changed to make the sentence correct. If the sentence is correct, select choice E. In choosing answers, follow the requirements of standard written English.

EXAMPLE:

The other delegates and him immediately
   A   B   C

accepted the resolution drafted by
                           D

the neutral states. No error.
                 E

12. Since we first started high school, there has been
    A   B
great competition for grades between him and I .
                         C   D
No error.
  E

13. Many people in the suburbs scarcely know about
                      A   B
the transportation problems that city dwellers
                         C
experience every day. No error.
        D   E

14. The subject of the evening editorial was us
                              A
instructors who have refused to cross the picket
        B   C
lines of the striking food service workers.
           D
No error.
  E

15. After the contestants had completed their speeches,
               A
I knew that the prize would go to he whom
                          B   C
the audience had given a standing ovation.
                 D
No error.
  E

16. Falsely accused of a triple-murder and imprisoned
                   A   B
for 19 years, Ruben (Hurricane) Carter, a former
boxer, was freed when a federal judge declared
        C
him guiltless. No error.
 D   E

17. Your math instructor would have been happy to
                            A
give you a makeup examination if you would have
                           B
gone to him and explained that your parents were
             C
hospitalized. No error.
  D   E

18. The child asking a difficult question was perhaps
    A   B
more shocking to the speaker than to the child's
                  C   D
parents. No error.
     E

19. Now that the pressure of selling the house and
   A   B
packing our belongings is over, we can look forward
              C   D
to moving to our new home in California.
No error.
  E

20. My grandmother leads a more active life than
             A   B
many other retirees who are younger than her.
             C   D
No error.
  E

21. I appreciate your offering to change my flat tire,
          A   B
but I would rather have you drive me to my meeting
         C
so that I will be on time. No error.
 D   E

22. The novelists who readers choose as their
         A   B   C
favorites are not always the most skilled writers.
                    D
No error.
  E

GO ON TO THE NEXT PAGE

23. The problem of <u>how to deal</u> with all the
                         A
mosquitoes <u>disturb</u> many <u>residents</u> of the tropics.
              B   C   D
<u>No error.</u>
    E

24. The <u>family's</u> only son <u>could of</u> <u>gone</u> to college, but
        A   B   C
he decided to join the army after he graduated

<u>from</u> high school. <u>No error.</u>
    D   E

25. <u>Yesterday</u> at the race track many <u>persons</u> were
        A   B
<u>fearful of</u> betting on the horse <u>who</u> had fallen in the
    C   D
last race. <u>No error.</u>
                E

26. If someone wants to buy <u>all</u> the antiques <u>that</u> I have
                             A   B
for the rummage sale, <u>then</u> <u>they</u> should make me
                        C   D
a reasonable offer. <u>No error.</u>
                        E

27. The man <u>who</u> Mexican authorities believe <u>to be</u>
            A   B
the country's number 1 drug <u>trafficker</u> <u>has been</u>
                              C   D
<u>arrested</u> in a Pacific resort area. <u>No error.</u>
    D   E

28. <u>While</u> her mother was inside the house <u>talking</u> on
    A   B
the phone, the child fell <u>off of</u> the <u>unscreened</u>
                            C   D
porch. <u>No error.</u>
            E

29. The racehorse ran <u>swifter</u> in <u>today's</u> race than he
                        A   B
<u>ran</u> in his practice sessions <u>last week</u>. <u>No error.</u>
    C   D   E

GO ON TO THE NEXT PAGE

Directions: The following passage is an early draft of an essay. Some parts of the passage need to be rewritten.

Read the passage and select the best answers for the questions that follow. Some questions are about particular sentences or parts of sentences and ask you to improve sentence structure or word choice. Other questions ask you to consider organization and development. In choosing answers, follow the requirements of standard written English.

Questions 30–35 refer to the following passage.

¹Lampe-Pigeon is the charming name for a tall kerosene lamp, over nine and one-half inches in height, created more than 100 years ago for use in the wine caves of France. ²Its diminutive size makes it suitable for being used on a mantel, as a centerpiece in lieu of candles, or even bracketed as a wall sconce. ³The brass lamp, which contains within it a glass globe, is still being handmade by the same company, though one is more likely to see it in a French home these days than in a cave. ⁴And, of course, it would be a handy source of light in the event of a power failure. ⁵Other antique-type lamps have been manufactured and they do not have the elegance or simplicity of the Lampe-Pigeon. ⁶Many people prefer more modern lamps especially those of the halogen variety.

30. What should be done with sentence 3?

(A) It should end after the word company.
(B) It should remain as it is.
(C) It should be placed after sentence 4.
(D) It should follow sentence 1.
(E) It should introduce the passage.

31. Sentence 1 would be more logical if it read, Lampe-Pigeon is the charming name for

(A) a tall kerosene lamp, measuring nine and one-half inches, created…
(B) a kerosene lamp, although nine and one-half inches tall, created…
(C) a nine-and-one-half-inch-tall kerosene lamp, created…
(D) a tall nine-and-one-half inch kerosene lamp, created…
(E) a kerosene lamp, of a height of nine and one half inches, created…

32. The phrase for being used in sentence 2 should be

(A) changed to for use.
(B) left as it is.
(C) changed to for one to use it.
(D) changed to to being used.
(E) changed to as a piece used on a mantel.

33. Sentence 3 would read more smoothly were it to begin

(A) The glass globed brass lamp…
(B) The brass lamp with a glass globe…
(C) The glass globe, found in the brass lamp…
(D) as it does now.
(E) The brass lamp, inside of which is a glass globe…

34. What should be done with sentence 6?

(A) It should be left as it is.
(B) It should be deleted from the paragraph.
(C) It should be placed before sentence 5.
(D) It should be placed before sentence 4.
(E) It should be placed before sentence 3.

35. In sentence 5,

(A) "manufactured" should be changed to "produced."
(B) "Lampe-Pigeon" should be changed to "lamp in question."
(C) "elegance and simplicity" should be changed to "modernization."
(D) "and" should be changed to "but."
(E) The sentence should remain as it is.

STOP
If you finish before time is called, you may check your work on this section only.
Do not turn to any other section in the test.

SECTION 3

Time: 10 Minutes—Turn to Section 3 (page 218) of your answer sheet to answer the questions in this section.
  14 Questions

Directions: For each question in this section, select the best answer from among the choices given and fill in the corresponding circle on the answer sheet.

The following sentences test correctness and effectiveness of expression. Part of each sentence or the entire sentence is underlined; beneath each sentence are five ways of phrasing the underlined material. Choice A repeats the original phrasing; the other four choices are different. If you think the original phrasing produces a better sentence than any of the alternatives, select choice A; if not, select one of the other choices.

In making your selection, follow the requirements of standard written English; that is, pay attention to grammar, choice of words, sentence construction, and punctuation. Your selection should result in the most effective sentence—clear and precise, without awkwardness or ambiguity.

EXAMPLE:

Laura Ingalls Wilder published her first book and she was sixty-five years old then.

(A) and she was sixty-five years old then
(B) when she was sixty-five
(C) at age sixty-five years old
(D) upon the reaching of sixty-five years
(E) at the time when she was sixty-five

1. He bought <u>some bread, butter, cheese and decided</u> not to eat them until the evening.

    (A) some bread, butter, cheese and decided
    (B) some bread, butter, cheese and then decided
    (C) a little bread, butter, cheese and decided
    (D) some bread, butter, cheese, deciding
    (E) some bread, butter, and cheese and decided

2. The things the children liked best were <u>swimming in the river and to watch the horses being groomed by the trainer</u>.

    (A) swimming in the river and to watch the horses being groomed by the trainer
    (B) swimming in the river and to watch the trainer grooming the horses
    (C) that they liked to swim in the river and watch the horses being groomed by the trainer
    (D) swimming in the river and watching the horses being groomed by the trainer
    (E) to swim in the river and watching the horses being groomed by the trainer

3. If an individual wishes to specialize in electrical engineering, <u>they should take courses in trignometry and calculus</u>.

    (A) they should take courses in trigonometry and calculus
    (B) trigonometry and calculus is what he should take courses in
    (C) trigonometry and calculus are what they should take courses in
    (D) he or she should take courses in trigonometry and calculus
    (E) take courses in trigonometry and calculus

4. If the dog will not <u>eat its food, put it through</u> the meat grinder once more.

    (A) eat its food, put it through
    (B) eat it's food, put it through
    (C) eat its food, you should put it through
    (D) eat food, put it through
    (E) eat its food, put the food through

5. The bank agreed to lend <u>Garcia the money, which made</u> him very happy.

    (A) Garcia the money, which made
    (B) Garcia the money, a decision which made
    (C) Garcia the money; this made
    (D) Garcia the money, this making
    (E) the money to Garcia and found

6. Miami's daytime attire is <u>less formal than New York</u>.

   (A) less formal than New York
   (B) less formal then that in New York
   (C) less formal than that in New York
   (D) less formal than in New York
   (E) less formal than the daytime attire we see in New York

7. <u>As the fisherman explained that he wanted to hire a guide and row</u> upstream in order to catch game fish.

   (A) As the fisherman explained that he wanted to hire a guide and row
   (B) The reason was as the fisherman explained that he wanted to hire a guide and row
   (C) As the fisherman explained that he wanted to hire a guide and to row
   (D) The fisherman explained that he wanted to hire a guide and row
   (E) The fisherman explaining that he wanted to hire a guide and row

8. The speaker was praised <u>for his organization, choice of subject, and because he was brief</u>.

   (A) for his organization, choice of subject, and because he was brief
   (B) for his organization, his choice of subject and the speech having brevity
   (C) on account of his organization and his choice of subject and the brevity of his speech
   (D) for the organization of his speech, for his choice of subject, and because he was brief
   (E) for his organization, his choice of subject, and his brevity

9. <u>The fact that Charles did not receive a college scholarship</u> disappointed his parents.

   (A) The fact that Charles did not receive a college scholarship
   (B) Because Charles did not receive a college scholarship was the reason he
   (C) Being that Charles did not receive a college scholarship
   (D) Charles not receiving a college scholarship
   (E) Charles did not receive a college scholarship

10. The porch of a famous home collapsed during a party last week, <u>which injured 23 people</u>.

    (A) which injured 23 people
    (B) causing 23 people to be injured
    (C) injuring 23 people
    (D) damaging 23 people
    (E) resulting in 23 people being injured

11. Jack's favorite summer supper includes barbecued chicken, grilled corn on the cob, sliced tomatoes, <u>and he likes green salad</u>.

    (A) and he likes green salad
    (B) in addition to green salad
    (C) adding green salad
    (D) including green salad
    (E) and green salad

12. I want the <u>best price</u> I can get for my car.

    (A) best price
    (B) most highest price
    (C) price which is the best
    (D) most best price
    (E) premium price

13. The injured man was taken to the hospital, <u>where he was treated for facial lacerations and released</u>.

    (A) where he was treated for facial lacerations and released
    (B) where he was treated and released for facial lacerations
    (C) where his facial lacerations were treated and he was released from the hospital
    (D) where his treatment was for facial lacerations and he was released from the hospital
    (E) where he received facial lacerations treatment and was released

14. The wife of the new leader is tough, single-minded, and <u>tries to be independent</u>.

    (A) tries to be independent
    (B) acting independent
    (C) independent
    (D) an independent person
    (E) an independent

STOP

If you finish before time is called, you may check your work on this section only.
Do not turn to any other section in the test.

How Did You Do on This Test?

Step 1.   Go to the Answer Key on page 228.

Step 2.   Calculate your "raw score" using the directions on page 229.

Step 3.   Get your "scaled score" for the test by referring to the Raw Score/ Scaled Score Conversion Tables on pages 230–231.

THERE'S ALWAYS ROOM FOR IMPROVEMENT!

Answer Key for SAT Writing Test 2

Section 1

_____

Essay score

Section 2

	Correct Answer
1	C
2	D
3	E
4	B
5	A
6	B
7	D
8	E
9	D
10	B
11	D
12	D
13	E
14	A
15	B
16	E
17	B
18	A
19	E
20	D
21	E
22	A
23	C
24	B
25	D
26	D
27	A
28	C
29	A
30	D
31	C
32	A
33	B
34	B
35	D

_____

Number correct

_____

Number incorrect

Section 3

	Correct Answer
1	E
2	D
3	D
4	E
5	B
6	C
7	D
8	E
9	A
10	C
11	E
12	A
13	A
14	C

_____

Number correct

_____

Number incorrect

Get Your Writing Score

How many multiple-choice writing questions did you get **right?**

Section 2: Questions 1–35   _____

Section 3: Questions 1–14   +   _____

Total   =   _____ **(A)**

How many multiple-choice questions did you get **wrong?**

Section 2: Questions 1–35   _____

Section 3: Questions 1–14   +   _____

Total   =   _____ **(B)**

$\times\ 0.25$ =   _____

A – B   =   _____

Writing Raw Score

Round writing raw score to the nearest whole number.

_____

Use the Score Conversion Table to find your writing multiple-choice scaled score.

_____

Estimate your essay score using the Essay Scoring Guide.

_____

Use the SAT Score Conversion Table for Writing Composite to find your writing scaled score. You will need your Writing Raw Score and your Essay Score to use this table.

_____

SAT Writing Score Conversion Table

Raw Score	Writing Multiple-Choice Scaled Score*	Raw Score	Writing Multiple-Choice Scaled Score*
		31	60
		30	58
		29	57
		28	56
		27	55
		26	54
		25	53
		24	52
		23	51
		22	50
		21	49
		20	48
		19	47
		18	46
		17	45
		16	44
		15	44
		14	43
49	80	13	42
48	80	12	41
47	80	11	40
46	79	10	39
45	78	9	38
44	76	8	38
43	74	7	37
42	73	6	36
41	71	5	35
40	70	4	34
39	69	3	32
38	67	2	31
37	66	1	30
36	65	0	28
35	64	−1	27
34	63	−2	25
33	62	−3	23
32	61	−4	20
		and below	

This table is for use only with the test in this book.

*The Writing multiple-choice score is reported on a 20–80 scale. Use the SAT Score Conversion Table for Writing Composite for the total writing scaled score.

SAT Score Conversion Table for Writing Composite

Writing Multiple-Choice Raw Score	Essay Raw Score						
	0	1	2	3	4	5	6
−12	200	200	200	210	240	270	300
−11	200	200	200	210	240	270	300
−10	200	200	200	210	240	270	300
−9	200	200	200	210	240	270	300
−8	200	200	200	210	240	270	300
−7	200	200	200	210	240	270	300
−6	200	200	200	210	240	270	300
−5	200	200	200	210	240	270	300
−4	200	200	200	230	270	300	330
−3	200	210	230	250	290	320	350
−2	200	230	250	280	310	340	370
−1	210	240	260	290	320	360	380
0	230	260	280	300	340	370	400
1	240	270	290	320	350	380	410
2	250	280	300	330	360	390	420
3	260	290	310	340	370	400	430
4	270	300	320	350	380	410	440
5	280	310	330	360	390	420	450
6	290	320	340	360	400	430	460
7	290	330	340	370	410	440	470
8	300	330	350	380	410	450	470
9	310	340	360	390	420	450	480
10	320	350	370	390	430	460	490
11	320	360	370	400	440	470	500
12	330	360	380	410	440	470	500
13	340	370	390	420	450	480	510
14	350	380	390	420	460	490	520
15	350	380	400	430	460	500	530
16	360	390	410	440	470	500	530
17	370	400	420	440	480	510	540
18	380	410	420	450	490	520	550
19	380	410	430	460	490	530	560
20	390	420	440	470	500	530	560
21	400	430	450	480	510	540	570
22	410	440	460	480	520	550	580
23	420	450	470	490	530	560	590
24	420	460	470	500	540	570	600
25	430	460	480	510	540	580	610

Writing Multiple-Choice Raw Score	Essay Raw Score						
	0	1	2	3	4	5	6
26	440	470	490	520	550	590	610
27	450	480	500	530	560	590	620
28	460	490	510	540	570	600	630
29	470	500	520	550	580	610	640
30	480	510	530	560	590	620	650
31	490	520	540	560	600	630	660
32	500	530	550	570	610	640	670
33	510	540	550	580	620	650	680
34	510	550	560	590	630	660	690
35	520	560	570	600	640	670	700
36	530	560	580	610	650	680	710
37	540	570	590	620	660	690	720
38	550	580	600	630	670	700	730
39	560	600	610	640	680	710	740
40	580	610	620	650	690	720	750
41	590	620	640	660	700	730	760
42	600	630	650	680	710	740	770
43	610	640	660	690	720	750	780
44	620	660	670	700	740	770	800
45	640	670	690	720	750	780	800
46	650	690	700	730	770	800	800
47	670	700	720	750	780	800	800
48	680	720	730	760	800	800	800
49	680	720	730	760	800	800	800

Chart for Self-Appraisal Based on the Practice Test You Have Just Taken

The Self-Appraisal Chart below tells you quickly where your SAT strengths and weaknesses lie. Check or circle the appropriate range in accordance with the number of your correct answers for each area of the Practice Test you have just taken.

	Writing (Multiple-Choice)
EXCELLENT	42–49
GOOD	37–41
FAIR	31–36
POOR	20–30
VERY POOR	0–19

SAT WRITING SCORE PERCENTILE CONVERSION TABLE

Writing

SAT scaled verbal score	Percentile rank
800	99.7+
790	99.5
740–780	99
700–730	97
670–690	95
640–660	91
610–630	85
580–600	77
550–570	68
510–540	57
480–500	46
440–470	32
410–430	21
380–400	13
340–370	6
300–330	2
230–290	1
200–220	0–0.5

Section 1—Essay

The following are guidelines for scoring the essay.

The SAT Scoring Guide

Score of 6	**Score of 5**	**Score of 4**
An essay in this category is *outstanding,* demonstrating *clear and consistent mastery,* although it may have a few minor errors. A typical essay	An essay in this category is *effective,* demonstrating *reasonably consistent mastery,* although it will have occasional errors or lapses in quality. A typical essay	An essay in this category is *competent,* demonstrating *adequate mastery,* although it will have lapses in quality. A typical essay
• effectively and insightfully develops a point of view on the issue and demonstrates outstanding critical thinking, using clearly appropriate examples, reasons, and other evidence to support its position	• effectively develops a point of view on the issue and demonstrates strong critical thinking, generally using appropriate examples, reasons, and other evidence to support its position	• develops a point of view on the issue and demonstrates competent critical thinking, using adequate examples, reasons, and other evidence to support its position
• is well organized and clearly focused, demonstrating clear coherence and smooth progression of ideas	• is well organized and focused, demonstrating coherence and progression of ideas	• is generally organized and focused, demonstrating some coherence and progression of ideas
• exhibits skillful use of language, using a varied, accurate, and apt vocabulary	• exhibits facility in the use of language, using appropriate vocabulary	• exhibits adequate but inconsistent facility in the use of language, using generally appropriate vocabulary
• demonstrates meaningful variety in sentence structure	• demonstrates variety in sentence structure	• demonstrates some variety in sentence structure
• is free of most errors in grammar, usage, and mechanics	• is generally free of most errors in grammar, usage, and mechanics	• has some errors in grammar, usage, and mechanics

Score of 3	**Score of 2**	**Score of 1**
An essay in this category is *inadequate,* but demonstrates *developing mastery,* and is marked by ONE OR MORE of the following weaknesses:	An essay in this category is *seriously limited,* demonstrating *little mastery,* and is flawed by ONE OR MORE of the following weaknesses:	An essay in this category is *fundamentally lacking,* demonstrating *very little* or *no mastery,* and is severely flawed by ONE OR MORE of the following weaknesses:
• develops a point of view on the issue, demonstrating some critical thinking, but may do so inconsistently or use inadequate examples, reasons, or other evidence to support its position	• develops a point of view on the issue that is vague or seriously limited, demonstrating weak critical thinking, providing inappropriate or insufficient examples, reasons, or other evidence to support its position	• develops no viable point of view on the issue, or provides little or no evidence to support its position
• is limited in its organization or focus, or may demonstrate some lapses in coherence or progression of ideas	• is poorly organized and/or focused, or demonstrates serious problems with coherence or progression of ideas	• is disorganized or unfocused, resulting in a disjointed or incoherent essay
• displays developing facility in the use of language, but sometimes uses weak vocabulary or inappropriate word choice	• displays very little facility in the use of language, using very limited vocabulary or incorrect word choice	• displays fundamental errors in vocabulary
• lacks variety or demonstrates problems in sentence structure	• demonstrates frequent problems in sentence structure	• demonstrates severe flaws in sentence structure
• contains an accumulation of errors in grammar, usage, and mechanics	• contains errors in grammar, usage, and mechanics so serious that meaning is somewhat obscured	• contains pervasive errors in grammar, usage, or mechanics that persistently interfere with meaning

Essays not written on the essay assignment will receive a score of zero.

Explanatory Answers for Practice Test 2

Section 2: Writing

> For further practice and information, please refer to Grammar and Usage Refresher starting on page 11.

1. **(C)** Choice A is awkward and wordy. Choice B is indirect. Choice C is correct. Choice D is unacceptable idiomatically even though the meaning intended is there. Choice E changes the meaning of the original sentence.

2. **(D)** Choice A has incorrect punctuation. A dash (not a comma) is required after "that's not all." In Choice B, the expression "another thing" is too general. Choice C changes the meaning of the original sentence. Choice D is correct. Choice E is too indirectly expressed.

3. **(E)** Choice A suffers from too many "ands." Choice B and C are incorrect because they lack parallel construction. In Choice D, the correct form of the infinitive meaning "to rest" is "(to) lie"—not "(to) lay." Choice E is correct.

4. **(B)** Choice A is awkward. Choice B is correct. Choice C is ungrammatical—"courses" cannot act as a direct object after the copulative construction "am not certain." Choice D is too wordy. Choice E does not make sense.

5. **(A)** Choice A is correct. Choice B is too indirectly stated. Choice C is verbose—since the people "had no doubt," there is no need to use the expression "it was clear." Choice D is indirect and awkward. Choice E changes the meaning of the original sentence.

6. **(B)** Choice A is too wordy. Choice B is correct. Choice C is indirectly stated. Choices D and E change the meaning of the original sentence.

7. **(D)** Choice A is indirectly stated. Choice B deviates from the original statement. Choice C makes the whole sentence run-on. Choice D is correct. Choice E changes the meaning of the original sentence.

8. **(E)** Choice A is awkward. Choice B has a meaning which differs from that of the original sentence. Choices C and D are unidiomatic. Choice E is correct.

9. **(D)** The clause "that was rotten" is misplaced in Choices A, B, and C. Choice D is correct. Choice E is incorrect because the passive use of the verb is not as effective as the active use, in this context.

10. **(B)** Choice A uses wrong tense sequence. Since the reading of the book took place before the watching of the picture, the reading should be expressed in the past perfect tense, which shows action prior to the simple past tense. Choice B corrects the error with the use of the past perfect tense, "had read," instead of the past tense, "read." Choices C, D, and E do not correct the mistake, and Choice E in addition changes the meaning.

11. **(D)** Choice A is wrong because the word *them*, being plural, cannot properly take the singular antecedent, *anyone*. Choices B and C do not correct this error. Choice D corrects it by substituting "him" for "them." Choice E, while correcting the error, changes the meaning of the sentence.

12. **(D)** "...between *him* and *me*." The object of the preposition *between* must be an objective case form (*me*—not *I*).

13. **(E)** All underlined parts are correct.

14. **(A)** "The subject...was *we*..." The predicate nominative form is *we*—not *us*.

15. **(B)** "...the prize would go to him..." The object of the preposition *to* must be an objective case form (*him*—not he).

16. **(E)** All underlined parts are correct.

17. **(B)** "...if you *had gone to him*..." In the "if clause" of a past contrary-to-fact condition, one must use the past perfect subjunctive form *had gone*—not the future perfect subjunctive form *would have gone*.

18. **(A)** "The *child's* asking…" The subject of a gerund is in the possessive case. We, therefore, say *child's asking*—not *child asking*.

19. **(E)** All underlined parts are correct.

20. **(D)** "…who are younger than *she.*" The nominative case (*she*—not *her*) must be used after the conjunction *than* when the pronoun is the subject of an elliptical clause ("than she is").

21. **(E)** All underlined parts are correct.

22. **(A)** "The novelists *whom* readers choose…" The direct object of the verb (*choose*) must be the objective case form (*whom*—not *who*).

23. **(C)** "The problem…disturbs…" The subject (*problem*) is singular. Therefore the verb (*disturbs*) must be singular.

24. **(B)** "…son *could have* gone…" The phrase *could of* is always considered substandard. Do not use *of* for *have*.

25. **(D)** "…the horse *which* had fallen…" The pronoun *which* should be used to refer to animals and things; *who* should be used to refer only to people.

26. **(D)** "…then *he* should make…" A pronoun must agree with its antecedent (*someone*) in number. Since *someone* is singular, the pronoun must be singular (*he*—not *they*).

27. **(A)** "The man *whom* Mexican authorities believe to be…" The subject of an infinitive must be in the objective case. The pronoun *whom* in the objective case—not *who* in the nominative case—is the subject of the verbal infinitive "to be."

28. **(C)** "…the child fell *off* the unscreened porch." The correct preposition is simply "off"—not "off of"—to introduce a noun or pronoun.

29. **(A)** "…ran *more swiftly*…" We must use an adverb—not an adjective—to modify a verb. Therefore, we use the adverbial comparative construction *more swiftly* instead of the comparative adjective *swifter* to modify the verb *ran*.

30. **(D)** Choice A is incorrect because ending the sentence after *company* would destroy the charming contrasting idea which follows. Choice B is incorrect because sentence 3 clearly interrupts the flow of thought between sentences 2 and 4. Choice C is incorrect because sentence 3 relates closely in structure and content to sentence 1, especially in the reference to the caves of France, and should follow sentence 1. Choice D is correct. Choice E is incorrect because the explanation for Lampe-Pigeon which now introduces the passage is the best opening sentence. Sentence 3 clearly needs prior information to explain its references to the lamp and to the caves of France.

31. **(C)** Choices A and D are incorrect because they create a contradictory impression by equating "tall" with "nine and one-half inches," even though Choice D is preferable because it is more concise. Choice B is incorrect because it conveys an unwarranted apologetic note for the height of the lamp by using the conjunction *although*. Choice C is correct because it concisely and clearly describes the height and type of lamp being described. Choice E is incorrect because it is wordy and therefore awkward.

32. **(A)** Choice A is correct because the simple prepositional phrase is preferable to the more awkward gerund form of the incorrect Choice B. Choice C is incorrect because it is too wordy and awkward. Choice D, in addition to being the above-mentioned more awkward gerund form, is incorrect also because of the inappropriate use of the preposition *to* after the adjective *suitable*. Choice E is incorrect because it is overly long and also would create an inappropriate repetition with the word *centerpiece*, which is used in the next phrase.

33. **(B)** Choice A is incorrect because "glass globed" is an awkward descriptive phrase. Choice B is correct because it is more concise than the repetitive clause *which contains within it a glass globe*. Choice C is incorrect and completely changes the focus of the sentence from the lamp to the globe. Choice D is incorrect because it is wordy and repetitive. Choice C is incorrect because it is too verbose.

34. **(B)** Sentence 6 contradicts and is not consistent with the paragraph, and it should be deleted. It would also make no sense to include that sentence in any other part of the paragraph.

35. **(D)** Since the author of the paragraph wants to show the beauty of the Lampe-Pigeon, he would contrast that lamp with the modern lamps and use the word *but*, not *and*. For choice A, "manufactured" is appropriate, and it is not necessary to change the word to "produced." For Choice B, "Lampe-Pigeon" sounds better than "lamp in question." After all, this is not a legal document! For Choice C, "modernization" would contradict the antiquity of the lamp.

Explanatory Answers for Practice Test 2 (continued)

Section 3: Writing

For further practice and information, please refer to Grammar and Usage Refresher starting on page 11.

1. **(E)** Choice A contains a "false series," meaning that the word *and* connects the three words in the series—bread, butter, cheese—with a wholly different clause, instead of with a similar fourth word. The series, therefore, needs its own "and" to complete it. Only Choice E furnishes this additional "and."

2. **(D)** Choice A violates the principle of parallel structure. If the first thing the children liked was "swimming" (a gerund), then the second thing they liked should be not "to watch" (an infinitive), but "watching" (the gerund). Choice B does not improve the sentence. Choice C repeats the beginning of the sentence with the repetitious words "that they liked." Choice D is correct. Choice E simply reverses the gerund and the infinitive without correcting the error.

3. **(D)** Choice A is incorrect because the pronoun must be singular (*he*—not *they*) since the antecedent (*individual*) is singular. Choice C is incorrect for the same reason. Moreover, this choice is roundabout. Choice B is incorrect because it is roundabout. Choice D is correct for the reason that Choice A is incorrect. Choice C is incorrect because its subject is "you" (understood). A third person subject is required to coincide with the third person of the antecedent *individual*.

4. **(E)** Choices A, B, C, and D are incorrect because these choices do not make it clear whether the dog or the food ought to be put through the meat grinder. Moreover, "it's" in Choice B is wrong. Choice E is correct because it makes clear that the food—not the dog—is to be put through the meat grinder.

5. **(B)** Choices A, C, and D are incorrect because the word *money* is incorrectly the antecedent of "which" in these three choices. Choice B is correct because "a decision" correctly refers to the whole idea—"The bank agreed to lend Garcia the money." Choice E is incorrect because it does not retain the complete meaning of the original sentence.

6. **(C)** Choices A and D are incorrect because the expression *that in* is required to complete the comparison. Choice C is correct because it includes the required expression *that in*. Choice B is incorrect because "then" is incorrect here for "than." Choice E is incorrect because it changes the meaning of the original sentence.

7. **(D)** Choices A, C, and E are incorrect because they do not fulfill the requirement of contributing to the composition of a complete sentence. Choice D is correct because it does complete that requirement. Choice B is incorrect because it is awkward.

8. **(E)** Choices A, B, and D are incorrect because they lack balance of grammatical structure. Choice C is incorrect because the "and...and" construction is frowned upon by stylists. Choice E is correct because the grammatical structure is balanced. This choice consists of three well-formed prepositional phrases.

9. **(A)** Choice A is correct. The words which make up the choice act as the subject of the sentence. Choice B is incorrect because it is awkward. Choice C is incorrect because one should never begin a sentence with "Being that." Choice D is incorrect as it stands. If "Charles" were changed to the possessive "Charles'" or "Charles's," the choice would be correct. Choice E is incorrect because it,

in itself, is a complete sentence, which, as it stands, cannot act as the grammatical subject of the verb *disappointed.*

10. **(C)** Choice A is incorrect because the pronoun *which* has an indefinite antecedent. Choices B and E are incorrect because they are too wordy. Choice C is correct. Choice D is incorrect because *damaging* is an inappropriate word choice.

11. **(E)** In this sentence we are looking for correct parallel structure in the last of a series of nouns. Choices A, B, C, and D are incorrect because they destroy the noun balance. Choice E is correct.

12. **(A)** Choice A is correct. Choices B and D are incorrect because the word *most* is unnecessary

and incorrect here. Choice C is incorrect because it is wordy. Choice E is incorrect because *premium* is not the correct word for the meaning intended.

13. **(A)** Choice A is correct. Choice B is incorrect because the phrase *for facial lacerations* is misplaced. Choices C and D are incorrect because they are wordy. Choice C also contains the pronoun *it*, which has an indefinite antecedent. Choice E is incorrect because of the awkward use of *facial lacerations* as an adjective modifying treatment.

14. **(C)** In this sentence we must have an adjective to balance with *tough* and *single-minded.* Choices A, B, D, and E are incorrect because they do not maintain the required parallel structure. Choice C is correct.

What You Must Do Now to Raise Your SAT Writing Score

1. a) Follow the directions on page 227 to determine your scaled score for the SAT Test you've just taken. These results will give you a good idea about whether or not you ought to study hard in order to achieve a certain score on the actual SAT.

   b) Using your Test correct answer count as a basis, indicate for yourself your areas of strength and weakness as revealed by the "Self-Appraisal Chart" on page 233.

2. Eliminate your weaknesses in each of the SAT test areas (as revealed in the "Self-Appraisal Chart") by taking the following Giant Step toward SAT success.

Giant Step

Take a look at Part 3, "The SAT Writing Test," which describes the various item types in the Writing Section and sample questions with answers and explanations. Read "A Brief Review of English Grammar," Part 1. Also make use of the Grammar and Usage Refresher, Part 2.

Remember, if you do the job *right* and follow the steps listed above, you are likely to raise your SAT score on the Writing parts of the test 150 points—maybe 200 points—and even more.

I am the master of my fate;
I am the captain of my soul.

—From the poem "Invictus"
by William Ernest Henley

Essentials from
Dr. Gary Gruber

and the creators of My Max Score

"Gruber can ring the bell on any number
of standardized exams."
—*Chicago Tribune*

$19.99 U.S./ $23.99 CAN/ £14.99
978-1-4022-4307-3

$19.99 U.S./ £14.99
978-1-4022-5331-7

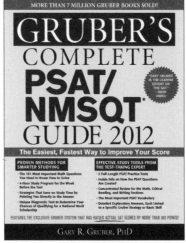

$16.99 U.S./ $19.99 CAN/ £11.99
978-1-4022-4308-0

$13.99 U.S./ $9.99
978-1-4022-5334-8

"Gruber's methods make the questions
seem amazingly simple to solve."
—*Library Journal*

"Gary Gruber is the leading expert on the SAT."
—*Houston Chronicle*

$14.99 U.S./ £9.99
978-1-4022-5340-9

$14.99 U.S./ £9.99
978-1-4022-5337-9

$12.99 U.S./ £6.99
978-1-4022-6072-8

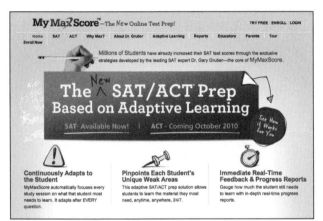